FORBIDDEN BROADWAY

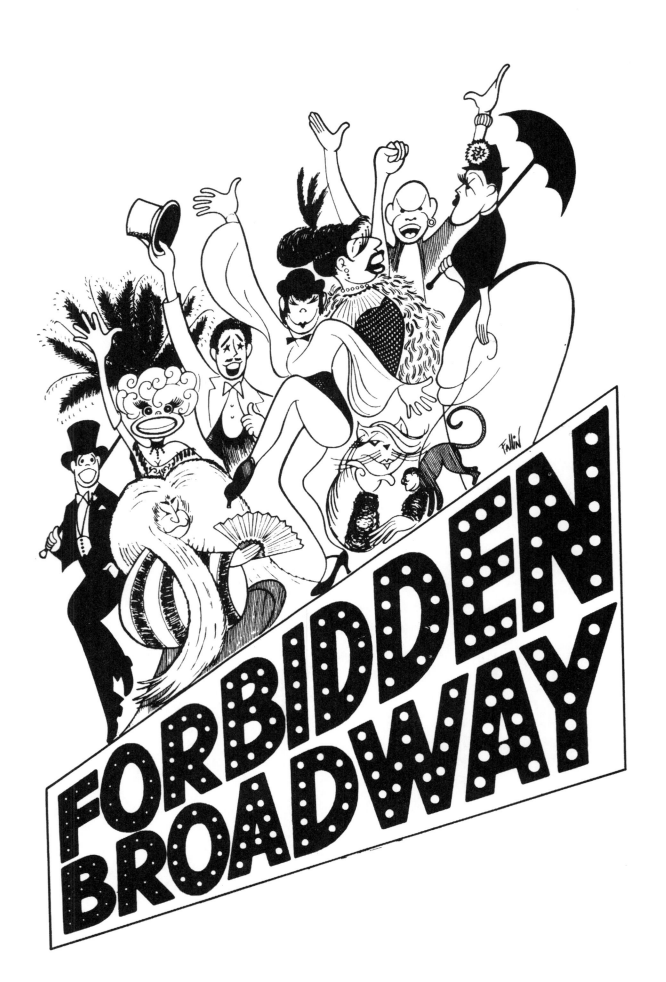

FORBIDDEN BROADWAY

BEHIND THE MYLAR CURTAIN

Gerard Alessandrini

with Michael Portantiere

APPLAUSE
THEATRE & CINEMA BOOKS

AN IMPRINT OF HAL LEONARD CORPORATION

NEW YORK

Published in 2009 by Applause Theatre & Cinema Books
An Imprint of Hal Leonard Corporation
7777 West Bluemound Road
Milwaukee, WI 53213

Trade Book Division Editorial Offices
19 West 21st Street
New York, NY 10010

Printed in the United States of America

Book design by Mark Lerner

Illustrations by Ken Fallin

For information about booking *Forbidden Broadway*, contact Playkill II, Inc., at 212-840-5564 or jfreedson@forbiddenbroadway.com.

For information about licensing *Forbidden Broadway*, contact Theatrical Rights Worldwide at 866-378-9758.

Photographs from *Forbidden Broadway* productions 1982–1988 are used with the permission of Henry Grossman, and photographs from *Forbidden Broadway* productions 1988–2009 are used with the permission of Carol Rosegg. All other photographs are from the personal collection of Gerard Alessandrini.

Library of Congress Cataloging-in-Publication Data
Alessandrini, Gerard.
  Forbidden Broadway : behind the mylar curtain / by Gerard Alessandrini with Michael Portantiere.
      p. cm.
  Includes index.
  ISBN 978-1-55783-743-1 (hardcover)
  1. Revues—History and criticism. 2. Parody in music. 3. Alessandrini, Gerard. I. Portantiere, Michael. II. Title.
  ML2054.A44 2009
  792.6'42—dc22
                         2009019386

www.applausepub.com

To my family, who taught me that no matter how brilliant a show is,
you can always find something in it to criticize

CONTENTS

Forbidden Broadway in a Cardboard Box

On a late spring afternoon in 1967, I was riding my bike up a hill on Richdale Road in Needham, Mass., when I saw a strange sight: Gerard Alessandrini was in his driveway, talking into a cardboard appliance box. Curious, I pulled over. I was twelve that year, Gerard was thirteen. We knew each other from school, we lived on the same block and took the bus together every day. Everybody knew Gerard was an eccentric kid, but why the heck was he talking into that big box?

Moving closer, I heard him mimicking Robert Preston hosting the 1967 Tony Awards. Inside the box was his friend Joey, applauding and cheering wildly. Gerard was recording the whole bizarre performance on a Grundig cassette recorder. Still not getting it, I asked him, "Why the box?" His answer—something about trying to electronically rechannel the sound for "360 Stereo"—eluded me. But that afternoon, hanging out with Gerard and Joey, I got hooked. I was entering a showbiz Neverland, all in Gerard's head, a place where a cardboard box in a driveway could be the Shubert Theatre on Broadway.

It was like joining a secret club, and the clubhouse was Gerard's basement. Any kid with an imagination can create fun in a furnace room; Gerard's obsessions, even then, were on a higher level. First, there was his record collection: every Broadway cast album, movie soundtrack, and opera record. On the walls, he had painted by hand perfect replicas of his favorite show album covers. There were movie posters and souvenir programs. I called it the Gerard Alessandrini Broadway Musical/Movie Museum. Music was always playing on the stereo, filling the room with that big, brassy Broadway sound. It was all so over the top! Walking down the stairs to Gerard's basement, you'd feel like you were descending the grand staircase at the Harmonia Gardens.

During high school, Gerard was always writing song lyrics and plays. In freshman year, he wrote a comedy called *Thanks a Million,* an irreverent farce featuring Jackie O. as a kleptomaniac. In sophomore year, he wrote his first original musical with a starring role for me; it was called *Peter Get Your Slide Rule* (with apologies to Irving

Gerard Alessandrini as Curly in *Oklahoma!* at Xaverian Brothers High School in Westwood, Massachusetts.

Berlin). Gerard was cutting his teeth writing lyrics, constantly coming up with new, often blue, parody songs. He'd write them anywhere, often scribbling in the back of a textbook.

One day, our geometry teacher caught Gerard in the act. To make an example of him, he held up the lyrics for the class to see and said in a disgusted voice, "Mr. Alessandrini, you will never make a living doing this!" I remember feeling so embarrassed for my friend, but it didn't faze Gerard. He headed off to English class and penned a Gypsy Rose Lee striptease number, "Put Your Best Breast Forward (And Let It All Hang Out!)."

It's a good thing Miss Murphy, our English teacher, never caught him writing that one. She actually encouraged Gerard by raving about a pre-Broadway performance of *Company,* a new musical she'd just seen. From then on, Gerard never missed a new Sondheim musical. He even cornered the composer after a performance, questioning him about the hook of a lyric. (These days, Mr. Sondheim returns the favor, giving Gerard notes on every new edition of *Forbidden Broadway.*)

Of course, Gerard was first to audition for the school musical. For reasons still unclear, he chose to sing "So Long, Dearie" from *Hello, Dolly!* His song styling was probably more Streisand than Channing, but the distinction was lost on everyone except him. The director asked if he could sing something with a little more weight. Gerard replied, "You mean, more like Ezio Pinza?" And then he sang "Some Enchanted Evening" in a rich, deep baritone. Jaws and pencils dropped.

Gerard was immediately cast as Curly in *Oklahoma!* His performance was a smash, even though he literally broke a leg on opening night (during the "Farmer and the Cowman" fight scene) and completed the rest of the run on crutches. After that, he was a star at school—and until he graduated, no one else ever auditioned for the male lead in the school musicals. That role was always reserved for Gerard. You'd think people would have resented him, but no one did. He had found his place. He went from being an oddball and an outcast to being the star of the show, a big man on campus. In an all-boys school filled with jocks, Gerard found respect, and he did it on his own terms. He repeated that success in college, and after he graduated, he moved to New York. All of his classmates from his school days were pretty sure Gerard was going to make it.

I moved to New York that same year, and our friendship began a new chapter. Gerard kept performing and writing, and before long, he had a trunk full of parody lyrics. Some were quite blue. He became the hit of our annual New Year's Eve parties, singing his dirty ditties. All the titles are unprintable. One song, to the tune of "Razzle-Dazzle" from *Chicago*, included the line "How can they see with urine in their eyes?" (This was almost a quarter of a century before *Urinetown*.)

Peter Brash and Gerard Alessandrini in *The Fantasticks* at Xaverian.

In those days, there were many piano bars around town with an open-mike policy that gave new talent a free showcase. Gerard got the idea that singing his parody lyrics—the G-rated ones!—might get some attention, so he put together a show for himself and fellow performer Nora Mae Lyng. Since my partner and I happened to have a piano in our shoebox apartment, that's where Gerard and Nora rehearsed their act, with Pete Blue at the piano.

When they had enough songs ready, they decided to try them out in front of an audience, so we invited some friends over for a party and a show at our place on June 28, 1981. It was a backers' audition without backers. (None of us had any money.) We moved the dining table, set up rows of chairs and the sofa facing a makeshift stage, and dimmed the lights. The show began with Gerard singing, "There's a Great White Way where the white is gray, and the great is only okay . . ."

By the time the show was over, the dozen or so invited guests were on their feet cheering. We didn't want the night to end, so we all paraded over to Palsson's Supper Club on West 72nd Street. It was late, the mike was open, and Gerard and Nora took to the stage, reprising their earlier blockbuster performance. The club's manager sat up at the bar.

There was something in the air that night, a certain feeling of stars aligning. The manager booked the act, and the cast of two was expanded to four. Numbers were added, including that amazing opening, with Gerard and Nora as waiters rushing the

As a performer, Gerard peaked at age nineteen. Here he is in a Christopher Ryder House revue circa 1979.

stage. This was the era when punk rock performers would get "rushed" by fans. Gerard was never influenced by punk, but that same spirit of anarchy infused *Forbidden Broadway.* My friend threw his own Molotov cocktail onto a stage of an Upper West Side supper club, and the New York theatre establishment took notice. Before long, the show was the hottest ticket in town.

My one regret about *Forbidden Broadway* is that I never kept track of how many times I've seen the show. By now, I'm sure it must be in the hundreds. And every time when the show is over, I hear the sound Gerard captured years ago in that cardboard appliance box in his driveway: the sound of wild cheering and applause. His audience is cheering to this day.

—*Peter Brash*

Peter Brash has been a writer of daytime dramas for twenty-eight years. He won a Daytime Emmy Award for his work on The Guiding Light *and two Writers' Guild Awards for Outstanding Script/Daytime Serial for* Days of Our Lives *(in 1999) and* As the World Turns *(in 2009).*

"Don't Cry for Me, Barbra Streisand"

The year was 1984. The place: tech rehearsal for a Staten Island community theatre production of *Evita*. At one point, we were focusing the lights that would come up on the woman playing Eva Perón for her Big Moment. Suddenly, one of the stagehands walked to center stage, extended his arms above his head, and began to sing full-out, "Don't cry for me, Barbra Streisand!" The entire company dissolved in laughter.

I had certainly been aware of *Forbidden Broadway* beforehand, but this spontaneous moment of mirth was my first indication that the show might turn into a long-running phenomenon. If one of Gerard Alessandrini's hilarious parody lyrics had already been burned into the brain of that young stagehand, who was involved in our show mainly for social reasons and wasn't that much into theatre, I could only imagine how popular *FB* was becoming among hard-core show queens of all ages, genders, and sexual orientations.

My guess is that parody lyrics have existed since time immemorial. For all we know, some ancient Athenian wag set his own irreverent words to choral odes from the plays of Aeschylus and Euripides. There was probably a decrease in this sort of snarky entertainment during the dour Dark Ages; but it's a safe bet that in the Renaissance, some fellows wrote their own bawdy lyrics to the tunes of various madrigals and lute songs.

With the rise of film, television, and recording technology over the past hundred years or so, the song parody became a popular art form. Remember the Marx Brothers' takeoff on the Habanera from *Carmen*? In the '60s, Allan Sherman had a huge hit with "Hello Muddah, Hello Faddah," set to music from *La Gioconda*. (Technically speaking, that wasn't a parody lyric, since the original tune had no lyrics; but it's the same basic principle.) More recently, "Weird Al" Yankovic made a career with his rejiggered versions of such pop songs as "Beat It" ("Eat It") and "Another One Bites the Dust"

("Another One Rides the Bus"). And I don't know about you, but one of my favorite Christmastime treats is radio airplay of Bob Rivers's spoof of "Winter Wonderland," titled "Walking 'Round in Women's Underwear."

Gerard traffics in this same zany mode of expression, and he does so with great skill and talent. He can take a complex Sondheim lyric like "Putting It Together" and come up with an equally complex but hilarious parody. On the other hand, Gerard knows how to keep it simple when necessary, and he has often stated that some of his best parody lyrics are those in which he makes only slight changes to the originals. For example, he took the line "At the end of the day, you're another day older" from *Les Misérables* and changed only two words to come up with "At the end of the play, you're another year older." (A lesser, more literal lyricist might have used "show" instead of "play," since musicals aren't often called plays. But Gerard realized his parody would be ten times funnier if it not only scanned perfectly with the original but also rhymed with it. Well, hey, God is in the details.)

Forbidden Broadway is Gerard's baby, so it seemed only natural that the story of the show should be told in his own words, as it is in the following pages. But literally hundreds of behind-the-scenes individuals have contributed to *FB*'s success over the past three decades. Then there are the scores upon scores of super-talented singing actors who've cavorted in *FB* through the years. I use the word "cavorted" because that's what it looks like to the audience, but as is pointed out several times in this book, playing *Forbidden Broadway* is no day at the beach. Simply to list the names of everyone who's appeared in the show would require more space than we have here, but many of these people are acknowledged in the book's chapters, and several have provided *Forbidden* reminiscences.

A note about the lyrics included in this book: We have chosen samples from each edition of the show, but they represent only about 20 percent of Gerard's total output. As of this writing, Gerard is taking a hiatus from *Forbidden Broadway* in order to work on other projects. But when and if he chooses to return to the field of musical theatre parody, we're sure to get another tremendous rush of his own special brand of comic genius.

— *Michael Portantiere*

Acknowledgments

Throughout the near thirty-year history of *Forbidden Broadway*, literally hundreds of people have contributed to the show's success. I would like to take this opportunity to thank them all, while giving a special nod to the following individuals for their efforts above and beyond the call of duty: Pete Blue, the brilliant musician who helped me put the show together way back in 1982; Sella Palsson, who gave *Forbidden Broadway* its first home; Fred Barton, ace musical director/pianist; Phill George, who co-directed several editions of the show, contributing many brilliant and hysterically funny ideas for numbers as well as contributing dialogue for some of the more recent editions; John Freedson, our tireless producer; Alvin Colt, our iconic costume designer; Carol Sherry, who designed the wigs for the show from 1998 through 2008, and Teresa Vuoso, who designed the wigs for our earlier editions; Jerry James and Jim Griffith, our terrific stage managers; Hugh Fordin of DRG Records, who produced our cast albums; Mark Sendroff, entertainment lawyer extraordinaire; Becky Flora, our first publicist, who helped to establish *Forbidden Broadway* in New York; and press agent Glenna Freedman, who for over twenty-two years has kept the show running and exhibited finesse in her dealings with all of the personalities involved.

FORBIDDEN BROADWAY

Genesis: "I Wonder What the King Is Drinking Tonight?"

Like so many other young hopefuls, I came to New York to be an actor on Broadway, but I could never get an audition. I remember that they wouldn't even see me for *Merrily We Roll Along*, though I was exactly the right age. As it happened, *Forbidden Broadway* premiered around the same time as *Merrily*, and I ultimately used a parody of their artwork—the three silhouettes on the roof—for our show. But I'm getting ahead of my story. . . .

Since I wasn't being seen for anything, I channeled my energy into writing. The first theatre parody lyric I wrote was a spoof of Richard Burton in *Camelot*. He was doing the show at the New York State Theatre at Lincoln Center in 1981, and I was working as a waiter and a maitre d' at Avery Fisher Hall across the plaza. As soon as the run started, I would hear people gossiping about Burton: "He went up on his lines tonight." "He looked unsteady onstage."

My friend Peter Brash was also a waiter at Avery Fisher. He told me that he was chosen to be Burton's personal waiter at the opening night party for *Camelot*. The producers gave Peter specific instructions not to serve him alcohol, but Burton took him aside that night and said, in that voice of his: "My wife *really* loves white wine, so I want you to keep her glass full at all times."

About two nights later, they brought the curtain down on Burton in the middle of his first number, "I Wonder What the King Is Doing Tonight?," reportedly because he had some kind of bad reaction to medication. The next morning, the *New York Post* headline—in red!—was "It's Curtains for Burton." I thought, "How embarrassing and funny at the same time." So I took that song and wrote a parody lyric:

I WONDER WHAT THE KING IS DRINKING TONIGHT?

WHAT MERRIMENT ARE HIS GAUNTLETS CLINKING TONIGHT?

THE CANDLES IN HIS EYES HAVE NEVER BURNED AS BRIGHT.

I WONDER WHAT THE KING IS SLURPING TONIGHT?

At the time, I was trying to write real musicals; I was in Lehman Engel's BMI workshop. When I showed the Burton lyric to friends, they all thought it was hilarious, so I was encouraged to write parodies of other shows and performers.

My takeoff on "Don't Cry for Me, Argentina" came about after I saw Patti LuPone sing the song on the Grammys. She was literally weeping while she was singing; I was watching with some friends, and I jokingly said, "She's not crying because she's into the drama of the song, it's because Barbra Streisand bought the film rights for *Evita*." Everybody laughed, and that spurred me on to write a parody lyric:

DON'T CRY FOR ME, BARBRA STREISAND;
THE TRUTH IS, I NEVER LIKED YOU.
YOU'LL DO THE MOVIE, BUT WHAT A BUMMER
WHEN YOU SING EVA LIKE DONNA SUMMER.

Then I wrote a Lauren Bacall/*Woman of the Year* lyric, inspired by her performance on the Tonys. Again, I was watching with friends. When Bacall sang, "I'm one of the girls who's one of the boys," somebody—I think it was Peter Brash—said, "I think she's one of the girls who's really a boy." That was all I needed to get me going.

While I was working at Lincoln Center as a maitre d', I had lots of time to jot down lyrics. I would be at the host stand, and sometimes it would get very busy, but mostly I'd stand there for hours with nothing to do. So I'd write parody lyrics on these big paper placemats. I wrote out the Burton, Bacall, and Patti LuPone in *Evita* spoofs. On my breaks, I would call friends and sing the lyrics into their phone machines. (People had phone machines in those days.)

During the summer, the host stand was moved outside to the plaza, near the fountain. One day, the wind blew my whole set of lyrics off the stand, and I thought they were gone forever. But my manager, Bob Arnold, came up to me the next day, grinning from ear to ear. He was holding a bunch of crinkled papers, and he said, "Somebody found these floating in the fountain last night. I read them and I thought they *must* be yours." The papers had gotten wet, of course, and the ink had run a bit, but

Gerard Alessandrini in the Reagan years.

Gerard's cover art for his original *Forbidden Broadway* folder.

you could still read the lyrics. Thank heaven Bob rescued them and had a good sense of humor, or there might never have been a *Forbidden Broadway.*

At the time, I was also studying musical theatre at The New School with Aaron Frankel, who has been a great mentor and friend to me. All of us would bring in songs from book musicals we were working on and present them to the class. There would usually be some time left at the end of each session when we would entertain each other, so I thought, "Let me see how they like these parody lyrics." Everybody loved them, and Aaron said, "You should put those songs into an act and do it at a nightclub somewhere."

I took his advice to heart, but I didn't want to perform the songs alone, since many of them were about Broadway divas and I really wasn't into drag. So I enlisted the help of a talented singer-actress-comic genius I knew. She was as unique as her name, Nora Mae Lyng, and I had always wanted to write a show for her.

I had already come up with the *Forbidden Broadway* concept; I kept the lyrics in a folder that had that title on the cover, along with my own cheesy, hand-drawn version of what the logo art would look like. It featured a grinning and winking *Amadeus* hovering over a *42nd Street* chorine, plus the face of Richard Burton, a *Timbuktu* chorus boy, and Mrs. Lovett grabbing the crotch of Sweeny Todd. It was a mess, but the point of view was all there. (To this day, whenever I do a new edition or show, I sketch out the poster art first. That helps me set the tone.)

Another friend of mine who was also wonderfully supportive and encouraging at the time was Pete Blue, whom I had met in Aaron's workshop. Pete and I tried writing a few songs together, and we joined the BMI workshop as a team. During his off hours from his job as conductor and pianist for the original Broadway production of *The Best Little Whorehouse in Texas,* Pete was generous enough to help me put together *Forbidden Broadway* as a club act.

By the summer of 1981, Nora, Pete, and I were ready to go. The first presentation of *Forbidden Broadway* was in June 1981, in Peter Brash's living room. Nora and I sang about fifteen songs, with Pete at the piano. We used "costumes" from our closets, evening wear and hats. The audience consisted of Peter; his partner, Jim Lynnes; my friend Laura Henry; and Nora's husband, George Kmeck. They were rolling on the floor with laughter, and I thought, "Maybe this really *is* a good idea for a show."

Someone at Peter's said, "You know, they have open mike at Palsson's tonight." So we picked ourselves up, walked over to Palsson's in our evening wear, and asked if we could do our material. One of the men in Aaron's New School workshop was there that night, and he knew Sella Palsson, the owner, pretty well. He told her, "You should let them get up and do these songs. They're very funny."

Nora, Pete, and I performed for about forty minutes, and it went so well that the Palsson's people asked if we'd like to be booked there for a full evening or two that summer. I thought it was a great idea, but I couldn't agree to do it when they wanted

"WOW! WHAT A CHICK!"

MORE MOVIES FOLLOWED, AND NOBODY GUESSED
THAT I WAS A GIRL ONLY WHEN I WAS DRESSED.
NOBODY KNOWS THE EQUIPMENT I'VE GOT;
I SING LIKE A BOY BECAUSE A LADY I'M NOT.

AND WHEN I CAME EAST TO STAR IN
    A SHOW,
MY FRIEND JULIE ANDREWS SAID,
    "YOU SING TOO LOW."
BUT KANDER AND EBB HAD A
    BALLAD OR TWO
ORIGINALLY WRITTEN FOR LEN
    CARIOU.

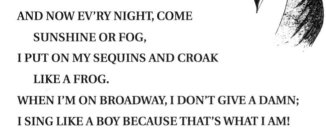

AND NOW EV'RY NIGHT, COME
    SUNSHINE OR FOG,
I PUT ON MY SEQUINS AND CROAK
    LIKE A FROG.
WHEN I'M ON BROADWAY, I DON'T GIVE A DAMN;
I SING LIKE A BOY BECAUSE THAT'S WHAT I AM!

AND WHEN I PASS ON TO ETERNITY,
THEY'LL SAY, "WHAT A LOOKER AND A LADY WAS
    SHE."
AND ONLY MY MOTHER, THE DOCTOR, AND ME
WILL KNOW I SANG LIKE A BOY,
OH, I SANG LIKE A BOY,
SANG LIKE A BOY BECAUSE I WAS A HE!

FORBIDDEN MEMORIES: **Nora Mae Lyng**

I met Gerry in Florida, when we were doing this dreadful, non-Equity production of *The Unsinkable Molly Brown* at a Wild West theme park. The producer-slash-director was formerly with the Ice Capades, and his wife played Molly Brown. One night, when my husband, Gerry, and I were driving back to the hotel, our car was rear-ended by

some guy whom we later found out was a drug kingpin. Our van rolled down a hill. My husband's neck was injured, my hip was injured, and Gerry broke his shoulder, so he left the show.

The next time I saw him, we were both working as waiters at Lincoln Center. I had started something called "The Wednesday Get-the-Guts-Up-to-Sing Club" for the waiters, so we could keep ourselves in vocal shape for auditions. We hit every piano bar in town. Gerry came to me one day and said, "Would you mind singing some of my parody lyrics?" When I read them, I flipped out. He and I made the rounds of the piano bar circuit, and some of the numbers really went over. This was before we did the first run-through of *Forbidden Broadway* at Peter Brash's apartment.

At Palsson's, the show was a celebrity magnet, almost from day one. I'll never forget the night Ann Miller came backstage afterwards in a floor-length white mink coat; she pushed right past us in the dressing room to fix the Ann Miller wig we were using in the show. Also, from time to time, Joan Bennett used to call me for tickets for her and her husband. One night, she asked me for an extra ticket for "a girlfriend I'd like you to meet." It was Myrna Loy.

I always say that *Forbidden Broadway* became a hit because John Lennon was shot. I should explain. The day after he was shot in front of the Dakota, Rex Reed gave an interview where he said something like, "It's very difficult to live in this building when you have crazy

Nora Mae Lyng.

fans hanging around, hoping to see Leonard Bernstein, Lauren Bacall, and the other celebrities who live here." The day after that, Bacall gave an interview and said, "It's very difficult to live in this building when you have assholes like Rex Reed telling the world where you live." They hated each other, and their feud escalated over the next few months.

Rex heard about the really mean Bacall parody in our show, so he came to see it, and he told all his celebrity friends about it. This was just when the *Night of 100 Stars* was happening at Radio City Music Hall. All of these stars were in town, they all wanted to be seen, and they all came to our show. Rex wrote an amazing valentine to *Forbidden Broadway* that appeared in the *Daily News,* and that review really put us on the map.

I knew from the beginning that *Forbidden Broadway* was very special. I turned down other jobs to do it, because it was such an amazing showcase. Thanks to Gerry, I found out that I had a four-octave range. I was not a trained singer—I was an actress who sang—but he would hand me material ranging from the Bacall number to operetta parodies,

Nora as Eva.

and it really worked my voice. I developed disciplines I didn't know I had.

I loved being in the audience for the twenty-fifth-anniversary performance. The show was just as tight as it always was, and the cast was wonderful. There's something about *Forbidden Broadway* that brings out the monster in everyone who does it. That performance was so electric, it felt like it was about five minutes long. It was really frustrating for me to be in the house instead of onstage!

Nora's favorite celebrity night at *FB*: Myrna Loy brought Joan Bennett, and they both met up with Phyllis Diller!

New York's Biggest Little Hit

Probably the biggest blessing the universe bestowed on me when we first did *Forbidden Broadway* at Palsson's was my utter naïveté. I didn't have a clue that shows were actually produced and investors put up cash. I had been watching too many Mickey Rooney–Judy Garland MGM musicals, and I was sure that if you wanted to do a hit show, you just did it! Never mind rights, contracts, unions, theatre politics, or the feelings of Patti LuPone. So when one of the booking managers at Palsson's asked that I expand our cast by adding his best girlfriend and his boyfriend, my first thought was, "How sweet! He wants our show to be a family affair."

My second thought was that I wasn't sure how to write for these new actors, because I didn't know them. I did know the very talented Bill Carmichael from working at LOOM [Light Opera of Manhattan], and I wanted to use him in *Forbidden Broadway*. So I made a deal with the booker that we would cast his girlfriend if we could cast Bill.

As green as I might have been in some ways, I understood *Forbidden Broadway*'s peculiar type of satire. Even though I was far too young to have ever seen Julius Monk's "Upstairs at the Downstairs" revues, I was fascinated with that era of New York nightlife. I tried to give *Forbidden Broadway* a 1950s look by having the cast appear during the title number in tuxedos and simple black *Breakfast at Tiffany's* gowns. (In case you're wondering, the men wore the tuxes and the girls wore the gowns.)

The song-blackout-song format was not only a bow to Julius Monk but also to *commedia d'ell arte,* in which segments would start and end in a tableau. (Our most famous tableau was a smoking Annie suddenly appearing in a spotlight with her hands raised like Eva Peron. For 30 years, that image brought gales of uproarious laughter.) Also, some of the characters we used in our show were not-too-distant relations of the *commedia* archetypes.

As for spoofing Broadway itself, that was not really anything new. In the nineteenth and early twentieth centuries, there were parody shows that actually played on Broadway. And just a season or two prior to the debut of our show, there was the hit revue

Bill Carmichael (as Jim Dale), Chloe Webb (as Annie), Gerard Alessandrini (as Yul Brynner), and Nora Mae Lyng (as Linda Ronstadt) in *Forbidden Broadway.*

Scrambled Feet. The major difference between earlier satirical escapades and our show is that *FB* is completely made up of specific spoofs of current Broadway shows, utilizing the actual music with new lyrics inserted.

Also, I believe we were the first show that was entirely self-referential, with lyrics like "This is the end of Act I! Intermission!"). I remember a conversation, years later, in which Stephen Sondheim and I were discussing the self-referential elements of *Spamalot* and *Dirty Rotten Scoundrels*. Mr. Sondheim called them "Meta-musicals." When I asked him what that meant, he looked shocked and said, "Don't you know what a meta-musical is? You invented it! I'm just surprised it took so many years for them to start copying you."

We started with five performances a week at Palsson's, and then we kept adding on. At one point, we were doing nine a week. That was hard. We tried a "brunch" show for a while, and once we played to a lone couple who just happened to stop by for a romantic breakfast. They ran out when Nora belted her high E, and we literally finished the show to an empty house. Well, I guess we needed the dress rehearsal. But the late shows, at midnight(!) on Thursdays, Fridays, and Saturdays, were filling up with show people.

Harold Prince was there one night, and I heard he came because he was angry that we had spoofed the *Merrily We Roll Along* logo. I had even taken an ad in *Back Stage* that featured my hand-drawn parody of the logo. Looking back, I think, "What gall!" But Prince loved the show. He was very complimentary afterwards, and he came back a few weeks later with Stephen Sondheim!

We had taken a few publicity photos, but we didn't have a press agent, so the show wasn't getting coverage. Then, in late December, Bob Ansel—one of the owners of Palsson's—got Rex Reed to come. Rex had been having a public feud with Lauren Bacall over something at the Dakota, where they both lived, so he wanted to see our Bacall number. I remember watching his reaction during the number; he was laughing so hard that he was crying. We thought maybe he'd write something good about the show.

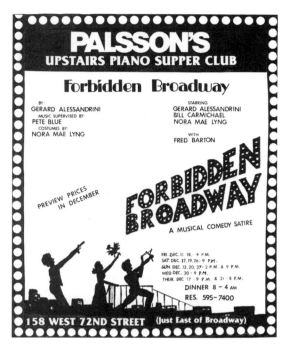

Gerard's hand-drawn flyer for *FB* at Palsson's.

New Year's came and went, and there was no review from Rex Reed in the *Daily News*—but we had a full house for every performance, and all these celebrities started to show up. First it was Prince and Sondheim, then it was Cher, then Ann Miller, then Mary Martin, Carol Channing, and George Burns.

Every night, there would be limousines in front of Palsson's. People like Christopher Reeve, Carrie Fisher, Paul Simon, and Jonathan Demme came to see the show.

The great Ethel Merman at *Forbidden Broadway*.

Our biggest thrill was when Ethel Merman arrived with a whole entourage of theatre luminaries. She stayed around afterwards, and we had a great time talking with her. She asked the four of us, "So, what shows have you kids done on Broadway?" We looked at each other, and Nora said, "None, Miss Merman. That's the point!" There was an awkward silence. Merman didn't really get it.

One night, this very nice man from CBS was in the audience. He came up to me and said, "Do you know why all these stars are coming to your show?" I said, "No!" He said, "Rex Reed loved the show and he's written a full-page, rave review. But before it runs, he's been calling all his favorite celebrities and telling them to go see *Forbidden Broadway*—because after his review hits the paper, nobody will be able to get a ticket for a year."

When that review finally appeared, it opened up the floodgates, and all of the other papers ran reviews. The *Times* really embraced the show; they not only printed a rave by Mel Gussow, but there was a follow-up review on Sunday, and then I was featured on the front page of the Friday Arts & Leisure section. Later, Frank Rich wrote about *Forbidden Broadway,* and he didn't love the show the first time he saw it. In his season round-up piece, he wrote, "It's a merry entertainment but also an uneven one." I was disappointed, but he was probably correct; the show did improve the more I worked on it over the years.

My euphoria over the response from audiences, celebrities, and critics was tempered by the realities of showbiz. Besides not knowing how to write special material for the new girl, I recall feeling that she wasn't very grateful about being in the show. She used to constantly complain that I had given Nora and myself all the good material; she actually told me, "I don't want to be in The Nora and Gerard Show." It got so bad that one afternoon she came in and removed all the costumes and props in order to stop us from going on. The rest of us arrived at Palsson's and saw that everything was missing. Nora said, "What the hell, we'll do the show anyway!"

So we re-divided all of the numbers between Nora, Bill, and me. The only thing we couldn't figure out how to do was the Merman-Martin duet. Nora said, "That's easy. I'll still do Merman, and Gerard, you can be Fernando Llamas!" But when the new girl heard that we were going on without her, she ran back to Palsson's with the costumes and props. She did the whole performance in tears. Needless to say, the audience was baffled as to exactly what kind of show they were seeing.

In those days, the costumes weren't as elaborate as they were later. We'd start out dressed as waiters, in tuxes and basic black. Nora had an Annie costume. In my closet, I had found a gorgeous *Kismet* costume that my aunt, Zia Nina (who once worked for Adrian), had designed, and I used that for Yul Brynner in the *King and I* number. Nora made aprons for the *Fiddler* number, and she had two '50s dresses that we used for Merman and Martin.

After the incident of the stolen costumes, Sella Palsson advised me to hire another woman as a standby so we could still do the show if someone was out. One of my best friends, Chloe Webb, had just come to New York to be in *Once a Catholic,* but she was replaced during rehearsals. I knew she was an exceptional talent, so I asked her if she'd like to stand by in *Forbidden Broadway,* and she agreed. Even during rehearsals, everyone could tell that she was a hundred times better than the other girl. Sella said, "I think you need to make a cast change. This is a business, and sometimes you have to replace people to keep things running smoothly." So the other girl was out, and Chloe was in.

The real Carol Channing with Gerard and his mother, Florinda.

When Carol Channing had come to see the show, she had told me afterwards that she loved it but felt a little hurt because she wasn't included. So I wrote a Channing number for Chloe, "Dolly Is a Girl's Best Friend." Believe it or not, Charles Lowe—Channing's husband and a great fan of *Forbidden Broadway*—had called me up very early one morning and made suggestions about spoofing Carol, going so far as to suggest how we should do the hair and makeup. He said it would bring the house down, and for many years, it did.

Carol is one celebrity who really embraced *Forbidden Broadway* early on. I assume that's not only due to her legendary sense of humor and her status as one of the greatest satirical chanteuses of the twentieth century, but also because she has a musical-revue background. Most famously she starred in Gower Champion's revue *Lend an Ear* long before *Gentlemen Prefer Blondes* and *Hello, Dolly!*

Whenever I speak with Carol, she likes to remind me that it was she who first brought Mary Martin and then Ethel Merman to see our show. The night she came with Merman, my mother, Florinda, was also in attendance. Carol told me that, right after the show, my mother ran up to her and Merman to apologize profusely for what I, her son, had written. She said, "Please pay no attention to anything my son says in the show. He really loves you and is a great fan of you both, so please forgive him." According to Carol, every time my "sweet little Italian mother" encountered her from then on, she would apologize again and bless her. Carol was both amused and touched by this, and she and my mother have long since become good friends.

Bill Carmichael, Gerard Alessandrini, and Chloe Webb (as Carol Channing).

Carol quickly became part of the *FB* family. In fact, she's featured on one of our cast albums, *Forbidden Broadway: Volume 3*. I wrote a specialty number for her, "Imitation Is the Sincerest Form of Flattery," wherein she teaches the cast how to do a Carol Channing imitation. At the start of her career, Carol had been known for her imitations of Carmen Miranda and Marlene Dietrich, so I also wrote mini spoofs of those icons for her to do on the recording. She has continued to be a supporter of our show through the years, returning frequently to see us and almost always bringing another big star along with her.

The show suddenly seemed more complete with Chloe Webb on board and with the Channing number in place. That's when Equity came in. Nora and I were both in the union, but we assumed that since we were performing in a nightclub, it wasn't an issue. At that time, the King Cole Room at the St. Regis Hotel had songwriter revues with

Chloe Webb, Bill Carmichael, Nora Mae Lyng, and Gerard Alessandrini.

some major stars. Equity really wanted to work up a contract for those shows, and I think they turned their attention on us to strong-arm the St. Regis. The funny thing is that, when we had first started doing *Forbidden Broadway* at Palsson's, I had gone to Equity and asked for help to make sure I was doing everything right, but they basically said, "We can't be bothered with something minor like this."

Four months later, they changed their tune. They came to us and said, "This is an Equity show and you need to post a $10,000 bond." At that point, I was living on about $200 a week. I didn't know how to make money from the show, and there was no way I could come up with $10,000. But the

Palsson's booking manager was trying to gain ownership of *Forbidden Broadway*, so he posted the bond. Equity recognized him as the producer and sent us a contract. A registered letter told us we had to sign it or we'd get a cease and desist notice.

Nora and I read the contract in shock. Then the "bad seed" gene that we share came out. We looked at each other and laughed maniacally. Nora said, "Let's send this back unsigned!" I said, "No! Let's send a nasty note or a dirty lyric!" Nora, always ready to one-up me, said, "No! Let's smear the contract with liver pâté from the kitchen. By the time it gets to Equity, it will stink to high heaven." So we smeared the smelly pâté all over the papers, as thick as we could, and mailed them back to the union unsigned. Later that night, Sella came up to us accusingly and asked, "Did the two of you eat all of our liver pâté?" When we confessed to her what we had done, she expressed concern about the way things were going.

Sella and I started talking about how the money from ticket sales was being distributed, and in comparing notes, we realized that the booking manager was taking more than we knew. He was paying the cast in cash after the show, one dollar per ticket. He'd take $65 and go, "One for Bill, one for Nora, one for Gerard." I'd leave very excited with about $18 in cash, thinking it was a good night's salary. It wasn't till later that I discovered how much the show was actually making.

Sella took me to a lawyer named Jay Julian, a sharp showbiz veteran who set us straight. The booking manager got his own lawyer and sued me for control of the show, but fortunately I had established copyright, and he couldn't infringe on that. So we agreed on a settlement in order to get him to go away. Then Sella and Jay set up a production company for us called

Sella Palsson.

"Playkill." Sella managed the show from that point on, and she did a wonderful, honest job of it. She was incredibly supportive and loving to all involved, and we became great friends. She was also very tolerant of my "angry young man" outbursts, which provided her with plenty of offstage melodrama and, I'm sure, comedy.

Early on, we also received a lot of wonderful guidance from Becky Flora, our original press agent. Liz Hermann, a keen person with a fantastic sense of humor, became our general manager for the early years. Sella, Becky, and Liz all helped build *Forbidden Broadway* into the "institution" it became.

We eventually did post our own Equity bond, but it wasn't till August that we finally signed the union contract. It was a new cabaret contract designed specifically for *Forbidden Broadway*. People told me that we should move the show, but I thought,

"Where? If we do it at a bigger theatre, maybe it will run a year. If we stay at Palsson's, it could run a lot longer, and I can update the material whenever I want."

I honestly think *Forbidden Broadway* was successful largely because it was the right show at the right time. The early '80s were the end of what I think of as the golden era of Broadway; the industry was running out of gas, and the city had gotten very seedy during the '70s. It was a time when you could make jokes about the fact that a lot of the new shows were creaky, there were starting to be lots of revivals, and the greatest musical theatre leading lady on the boards was Lauren Bacall. Before that, I think Broadway was too much of a sacred cow for anyone to have gotten away with a show like ours. And five years later, there was almost no Broadway left, so there was very little to make fun of. We came along just when we were needed.

Carol Channing: "Dolly Is a Girl's Best Friend"

BOYS

CALL ON CAROL!

SHE'S THE ONE PRODUCERS RECOMMEND

WHEN THEY'RE PRODUCING *DOLLY*!

EITHER BROADWAY OR SUMMER STOCK,

SHE'LL PLAY DOLLY LEVI FROM SEVEN TILL TWELVE
    O'CLOCK.

CALL ON CAROL!

SHE'LL DO *HELLO, DOLLY!* ANYTIME.

GERARD

Tell us, Miss Channing, what's in all this for you?

CAROL

Well, it's a living, Mr. Carmichael and Mr. Alessandrini. Some people sing, some people dance, some people act . . . I do *Hello, Dolly!*

I'VE PLAYED *LORELEI* AND I'VE DONE *MODERN
    MILLIE*
    BUT DOLLY IS A GIRL'S BEST FRIEND.

AND ONCE I DID SHAW, BUT I LOOKED AWF'LLY
    SILLY

AS A MILIONAIRE WITH WOOLWORTH WIGS
    INSTEAD OF HAIR.

ROLES ARE FEW AND FAR BETWEEN,
    AND TALK SHOWS I DON'T RECOMMEND.

BUT WHY SHOULD I GRIEVE, I

CAN PLAY DOLLY LEVI!

DOLLY IS A GIRL'S BEST FRIEND.

I'VE HOSTED AWARDS AND I'VE SOLD KITTY LITTER,

BUT DOLLY IS A GIRL'S BEST FRIEND.

I'VE DONE SEVERAL FLOPS, BUT YOU CAN'T CALL
    ME BITTER,

THOUGH MY WHOLE CAREER IS MESSY AS MY
    LIPSTICK SMEAR.

LOVE BOAT'S NICE, I'VE DONE THAT TWICE,

BUT THERE'S ONE SHOW I'LL DO TO THE END . . .

I'LL DIE OR GO BONKERS, OR END UP IN YONKERS,

DOLLY IS A GIRL'S BEST FRIEND.

SO WHO NEEDS SONDHEIM?

DOLLY IS A GIRL'S BEST FRIEND!

[*GERARD and* BILL *enter dressed as waiters with long white aprons.*]

GERARD and BILL

OH NO, CAROL

OH NO, NO, CAROL

DON'T YOU DARE DO *HELLO, DOLLY!* ONCE AGAIN.

FOR AS YOU KNOW, CAROL

THIS WHOLE SHOW, CAROL

HAS BEEN DRUMMED INTO OUR BRAINS

SINCE WE WERE ONLY TEN.

YES, ONCE WAS SWELL, CAROL;

TWICE IS HELL, CAROL.

YOU'VE BEEN DOING THIS SAME ROLE SINCE GOD
    KNOWS WHEN,

SO . . .

CAROL

DON'T BE ANNOYED, FELLAS,

I'M KEEPING YOU EMPLOYED, FELLAS

GERARD and BILL

PROMISE YOU'LL NEVER DO THIS SHOW . . .

CAROL

EITHER IT'S THIS OR *LORELEI*

GERARD and BILL

PROMISE YOU'LL NEVER DO THIS SHOW

ALL THREE

AGAIN!

[*They lift* CAROL *high in the air and strike a pose. Suddenly, they let her go and she falls as the lights black out.*]

Rex Harrison: "I've Grown Accustomed"

REX HARRISON

Good evening, ladies and gentlemen. Now that I have finished *My Fair Lady,* I should like to do something Shakespearean for you. "To be or not to be, that is the question any ordinary man asks. . ." Oh, no, let's try something simpler: "If I could talk to the animals, learn their languages, maybe teach the English how to speak. . ." Perhaps something historical: "Cleopatra, my love, all of Rome is yours if you'll only say 'The Rain in Spain'" . . . No, no, no, no! Damn, damn, damn, damn!

I'VE GROWN ACCUSTOMED TO THIS SHOW,

FOR IT'S THE ONLY ROLE I KNOW.

I'VE GROWN ACCUSTOMED TO THE HAT

THAT HIDES MY BALDING HEAD.

I'LL PLAY THIS ROLE UNTIL I'M DEAD.

I'VE GROWN ACCUSTOMED TO THE WAY

I'VE GROWN ACCUSTOMED TO THE PAY.

ALTHOUGH I USED TO BE AN ACTOR WITH A RANGY
    REPERTOIRE,

I'VE GOT TO PAY THE LOAN OFF ON MY FANCY
    FOREIGN CAR.

SO ONCE MORE BEFORE I GO,

YOU'LL SIMPLY HAVE TO GROW

ACCUSTOMED TO THIS SHOW.

"Merman and Martin"

ETHEL

CURTAIN UP!

LIGHT THE CYCS!

AND YOU BETTER TURN OFF
ALL THE MIKES!

CROSS YOUR LEGS,
HOLD YOUR EARS,
CAUSE NO ONE LEAVES THIS ROOM
UNTIL I'M THROUGH.

HONEY, EVERYTHING'S COMIN' UP MERMAN
FOR ME AND FOR . . . ME!

Swell. And now I'd like to introduce one of America's
oldest theatrical institutions, Miss Mary Martin.

MARY

THOUGH MY HAIR IS A BRIGHT CANARY YELLOW
I FORGET EVERY SONG I EVER SING
SO THEY CALL ME A COCKEYED VOCALIST
BUT I'M REALLY A SILLY DING-A-LING.

I HAVE HEARD CRITICS RANT AND RAVE AND
    BELLOW
THAT I SING HALF A TONE BELOW THE NOTE,
SO I QUACK LIKE A DUCK WHEN THE NOTE GETS
    STUCK
'CAUSE I CAN'T GET IT OUT OF MY THROAT!
NOT THIS THROAT.

ETHEL

Swell. What a career she had. Now, how'd you like to
hear me do a duet? Wouldn't that be great?

MARY

LET'S SING AN OLD-FASHIONED BALLAD,
SUNG IN THE GOOD OLD-FASHIONED STYLE.
FIRST WE'LL REVIVE SIGMUND ROMBERG,
THEN RICHARD RODGERS FOR A LITTLE WHILE.

I'LL SING THE VERSE, THEN THE CHORUS,
THEN YOU JOIN IN ON THE REFRAIN.

OH, LET'S SING AN OLD-FASHIONED BALLAD,
THE KIND THAT GERSHWIN WROTE
WHILE TRAVELING ON A TRAIN.

ETHEL

[*Snaps the rhythm and pushes* MARY *out of the way
with her hip.*]

LET'S DO A NUMBER THAT'S MODERN
AND BOUNCY WITH RAZZMATAZZ!
WITH CLEVER STAGING LIKE BOB FOSSE'S
DANCIN' OR *ALL THAT JAZZ,*
LET'S DO A NUMBER FROM *A CHORUS LINE*
OR *PIPPIN* OR *THE WIZ,*
ANOTHER "GOD, I HOPE I GET IT"
WITH THE TEMPO OF THE DANCIN' BIZ.

LET'S DO A NUMBER 'BOUT GOOD TIMES,
WITH FUN RHYMES AND CLEVER WORDS.
THE KIND OF NUMBER THAT YOU WANT
IS DATED AND FOR THE BIRDS.
LET'S DO A NUMBER LIKE TOMMY TUNE DOES,
EVERYTHING LOUD AND TALL.
IF I CAN'T DO THAT KIND OF A NUMBER,
THEN I DON'T WANT TO DO ONE AT ALL!

[*To* MARY.]

Are you ready? Let's bounce!

[*They sing both their parts in counterpoint. At the
conclusion, they shout, "Let's not." They do a runaround
bow and exit.* ETHEL *looks back at the audience.*]

ETHEL

Swell!

Ann Miller: "I'm Entertainment"

ANN

I'M THE GAL WTH THE TAPS ON HER SHOES,
I'M THE DAME IN THE RED, WHITE, AND BLUES,
I'M THE GIRL WHO LIGHTS UP LIKE A FUSE:
I'M ENTERTAINMENT!

I SING WHILE MY LEGS PIROUETTE,
AND MY FEET MOVE AS FAST AS A JET,
AND MY HAIR IS AS BIG AS A SET:
I'M ENTERTAINMENT!

WHEN I WAS A GIRL BACK AT OL' MGM,
THEY OFFERED ME ROLES SORTA LIKE AUNTIE EM.
I GUESS I REALLY SHOWED THEM
WHEN I KILLED L. B. MAYER
BY HITTING HIM WITH MY HA-IR.

[*Dance break.* ANN *dances to the sound of hundreds of prerecorded, tapping feet.*]

I'M ENTERTAINMENT!
AND NOW I'M A STAR ON MY OWN.
EV'RY NIGHT, I'M A SHOW ALL ALONE,
THOUGH MY SMILE IS CONSTRUCTED OF STONE.
WHY SHOULD I LIE
WHEN I SAY THAT I
AM ENTERTAINMENT!

Yul Brynner: "Do I Shave?"

YUL

WHEN I PLAY THE KING,
THE CROWDS CHEER VERY WELL,
ET CETERA ET CETERA ET CETERA, AND SO,
SO MANY MEN AND GIRLS
FOLLOW ME AND TELL

HOW GREAT AM I,
BUT THEY LIE.
I KNOW WHAT THEY WANT TO KNOW:

DO I SHAVE?
DO I SPLASH AQUA VELVA ON MY HEAD?
DO I SHAVE,
OR JUST PAINT HARD ENAMEL ON INSTEAD?

DEBORAH KERR
ASKED THE SAME QUESTION
WHEN WE WERE IN BED.
I SAID, "HOW DO YOU WANT IT?"
SHE SAID, "YUL, YOU MUSN'T FLAUNT IT.
BEING BALD MAKES THE CRITICS RAVE,
BUT YOUR HEAD IS SO SHINY
I KEEP THINKING THAT'S YOUR HINEY!"
DO I SHAVE?
DO I SHAVE?
DO I SHAVE?

Yah!!! All right now, all Siamese children must learn song of King, if you want to grow up to be brave, strong Oscar-winning King like me. Now, do you know melody? Answer is "yes." DO YOU KNOW MELODY???

[AUDIENCE: *YES!!!*]

Good-good-good-good-good!!! Because is very simple . . .

[*An* ACTOR, *still offstage, holds out large sign with lyrics.*]

But wait! I no teach you song. I get you special scientific English teacher—Mrs. Anna —to teach you song. Mrs. Anna, where are you?

[*He pulls an unsuspecting* "ANNA" *from the audience.*]

Mrs. Anna, you've come back! Mrs. Anna, come over here where light is better—for me. Now, what is your name?

[*She answers.*]

Next question: Do you remember golden rule you promised long ago in Siam? No? Well, I remind you. Golden rule is head must always be lower than King! Always lower . . .

[*He begins to crouch, forcing* "ANNA" *down. The lights black out.*]

Good, good. Oh no, Anna, that's too good!
No, no, lights up quickly, please. Mrs. Anna! All right now, you take this.

[*He hands her a pointer.*]

Stand here and point to the sign so we know where your hands are. Now, all Siamese children sing song of King. Mrs. Anna point at words, we sing!

YUL, AUDIENCE, and ANNA

DO I SHAVE?
DO I SPLASH AQUA VELVA ON MY HEAD?
DO I SHAVE,
OR JUST PAINT HARD ENAMEL ON INSTEAD?
DEBORAH KERR
ASKED THE SAME QUESTION
WHEN WE WERE IN BED.
I SAID, "HOW DO YOU WANT IT?"
SHE SAID, "YUL, YOU MUSN'T FLAUNT IT.
BEING BALD MAKES THE CRITICS RAVE,
BUT YOUR HEAD IS SO SHINY
I KEEP THINKING THAT'S YOUR HINEY!"
DO I SHAVE?
DO I SHAVE?
DO I SHAVE?

YUL

Wonderful! Good-bye, Mrs. Anna, you were wonderful!

[*He kisses her hand and* "ANNA" *goes back to her seat.*]

Children, say good-bye to Mrs. Anna! Good-bye!

[*He motions for silence.*]

And what is the moral of this song?

DO I SHAVE?
DO I SHAVE?
DO I SHAVE?

[*He flings his arms straight up in the air.*]

YAH!!!

[FOOTNOTE: One night a woman came up to me after the show. It was the same woman I had only minutes before pulled up from the audience and humiliated in this Yul Brynner spoof. She said to me, "I'm so glad you picked me to play Anna, because my father wrote that song." I laughed haughtily and said, "Oh no, you must be mistaken, Richard Rodgers wrote that song." She looked at me completely deadpan and said, "That's right." I must have turned several shades of colors as I realized the women I had made crawl on the floor was none other than Mary Rodgers, daughter of Richard. When she saw my chagrin, she laughed heartily. We were even!]

"I Enjoy Being a Cat"

ACTOR

[*Enters dressed half in tux and half as a cat.*]

REMEMBER WHEN ACTORS PLAYED HUMANS?

NOW, TO BRING HOME A PAYCHECK,
I DRESS UP IN FUR.
SO I GLUE ON MY WHISKERS, TAIL, AND ANIMAL
   HAIR,
AND I GRIN IT AND I BEAR IT
WITH A PURR.

WHEN I WEAR MY BRAND-NEW COLLAR
AND MY FUR IS ALL SMOOTH AND PAT,
I LOVE TO HEAR THE PUBLIC HOLLER.
I ENJOY BEING A CAT!
I'D RATHER DO SERIOUS DRAMAS,
BUT AS LONG AS MY PAYCHECK'S FAT,
THIS SHOW IS THE CAT'S PAJAMAS.
I ENJOY BEING A CAT!

THOUGH FOLKS SAY THE SHOW IS LONG AND
   BORING
AND WE DANCE LIKE NEUROTIC CHIMPANZEES,
AS LONG AS THE CRITICS ARE ADORING,
I'M WILLING TO WEAR A COSTUME FULL OF FLEAS.

I'M STRICTLY A METHOD MORRIS
AND A PUSS-IN-BOOTS ACROBAT.
AND I LOVE PURRING IN THE CHORUS,
BEING CUTE, CUDDLY AND COY,
'CAUSE I ENJOY BEING A CAT.

REMEMBER
WHEN NO ONE WOULD CAST ME?
NOW I'VE GOT ME A CO-OP
AND I'M RAKIN' IT IN.
NEXT SEASON, I'M STARRING IN LLOYD WEBBER'S
   NEW SHOW;
I'LL BE PLAYING RIN TIN TIN!

"Ambition" (*Fiddler on the Roof*)

[GERARD *enters dressed as a waiter, with bow tie and side towel. He also wears a Russian cap and he speaks a lot like Tevye in* Fiddler on the Roof.]

GERARD

An actor in New York. Sounds crazy, no? But in our little village of Manhattan, there are over 50,000 actors all trying their best not to end up in Baltimore. It isn't easy. You may ask, why do we stay here if it is competitive? We stay because everyone else is here. And what keeps us from ending up in Baltimore? That I can tell you in one word: Ambition!

AMBITION, AMBITION.

[NORA, BILL, *and* CHLOE *enter, dressed as the townspeople from* Fiddler.]

ALL

AMBITION!
AMBITION, AMBITION. AMBITION!

[GERARD *and* BILL *dance. They collide.* BILL *goes back into line.*]

GERARD

Goyim! You may ask: How did these ambitions get started? I'll tell you. I don't know. But this much I do remember . . .

WHEN I WAS TEN I SAW A SHOW ON TV,
SAW A SHOW ON TV STARRING GARRY MOORE.
I WROTE HIM AND ASKED TO PUT ME ON HIS SHOW
BUT HE SAID, "GO ASK DINAH SHORE."
REJECTION, REJECTION.

ALL

AMBITION!

REJECTION. REJECTION.
AMBITION!

NORA

WHEN I WAS AN INGENUE AD NAUSEAM
MY VOICE WAS LIKE A LITTLE LAMB.
NOBODY WOULD HIRE ME OR GAVE A DAMN
UNTIL I LEARNED TO USE MY DIAPHRAGM.
PROJECTION, PROJECTION.

ALL

AMBITION!
PROJECTION, PROJECTION.
AMBITION!

BILL

AT TEN, I WAS A PRETTY BOY,
AT SEVENTEEN, A DREAM.
I NEVER HAD A PIMPLE,
SO I DO COMMERCIALS.
COMPLEXION, COMPLEXION.

ALL

AMBITION!
COMPLEXION, COMPLEXION.
AMBITION!

CHLOE

AND WHEN I WAS A CHILD
NOBODY LOOKED MY WAY
UNTIL I GOT THE LEAD
IN MY HIGH SCHOOL SENIOR PLAY.
ATTENTION, ATTENTION.

ALL

AMBITION!
ATTENTION, ATTENTION.
AMBITION!

[*They repeat verses as a round.*]

GERARD

Ambition, ambition. Without our ambitions, our lives would be as crazy as . . . as . . . as an actor in New York!

ALL

FOLLOW EV'RY RAINBOW TILL YOU FIND YOUR
    DREAM!

[*They turn and aim slings, arrows, and pistols at the* Forbidden Broadway *marquee. The marquee glows. Tableau.*]

FORBIDDEN MEMORIES: **Dee Hoty**

My best contribution to *Forbidden Broadway,* I am told, was my rendition of Lauren Bacall. I had never done any kind of impersonations before my audition for Gerard, and I was asked to work up Julie Andrews singing "Wouldn't It Be Loverly?" and something else—a Merman number, I think.

When I got the job, I went to see a late show that Saturday night at Palsson's. The audience was screaming with laughter, and I wondered how I was ever lucky enough to get into a show as good as this obviously was. It was great to join *Forbidden Broadway* early on, when Gerard was still in it; I replaced Nora Mae Lyng, and the other two people in the cast were Chloe Webb and Bill Carmichael.

I never worked as hard as I did in that show, but I also never had so much fun or was in such great physical shape (the black dress!) or vocal shape. I felt like I could sing anything. We all shared one dressing room— make that "closet"—and we all helped each other make the quick changes, laughing and cursing all the way. There were no dressers but us, and in those days, the costumes came by way of someone's good will or Goodwill.

Dee Hoty.

My worst experience was forgetting the words to the new *Cats* parody; I was overwhelmed by so many other additions to the show, and I guess I just snapped. The next day, Gerard gave the number to Bill. I was relieved, if embarrassed.

Anyway, back to Bacall. She was on Broadway in *Woman of the Year*. I hadn't seen the show and had no idea how to "do" her, but when I discovered the "head back, eyes half open" stance, she was mine! How I miss those days. *Forbidden Broadway* was the best on-the-job training I ever had, and I will never forget it.

P.S.: In the "You Know You've Made It When . . ." department, the best compliment I've ever been paid was that Gerard mentioned me by name—quite nicely, thank you—in the lyrics for his Stritch parody. Everyone in town called to tell me about it. How cool is that?!

Screamgirls and Gypsies: 1983–85

When *Forbidden Broadway* started, we were just kids, and we did the show because it was fun. But, suddenly, everyone in New York was coming to see it. I think some of the initial charm has been lost over the years; now, we need seasoned performers to do all the imitations effectively. But in the beginning, it must have been very delightful to see twenty-four-year-olds making like Merman and Martin and Yul Brynner.

We did the first edition of *Forbidden Broadway* right around the time when *Dreamgirls* was opening, but we didn't spoof that show because we were already set with numbers from *The Pirates of Penzance, Woman of the Year,* and *Evita.* Those were the big-ticket items that everyone had seen. I began to realize that you have to wait about six months after a show opens and give everyone a chance to see it—or, at least, read and hear about it—before you can make fun of it, so we didn't get around to *Dreamgirls* until almost a year later.

By that time, Jennifer Holliday was all the rage; she had won the Tony, although *Nine* had won over *Dreamgirls* for Best Musical. They were both wonderful shows, but *Dreamgirls* was spectacular and a mainstream triumph. There was a feeling that *Nine* had sort of stolen the Tony. I remember being in a taxi headed to an interview. We pulled up alongside a bus that had a huge poster on the side. It screamed "See *Dreamgirls!*" I thought to myself, "We should call it 'Screamgirls.'" So I wrote a parody titled "And I Am Telling You I'm Not Singing."

Chloe Webb was still in the show, and the *Dreamgirls* number turned out to be her particular masterpiece. She really pulled out all the stops. We invented this huge pink costume that was about eight times the size of Jennifer Holliday. As I remember, we didn't really hesitate to have a white person play a black person. We were all in our twenties and somewhat naïve. Also, I had known Chloe since college, and she was never very concerned about being politically correct. We may have become more sensitive about that sort of thing later on. But Jennifer Holliday's performance in *Dreamgirls* transcended race; she immediately became a theatrical icon, like Merman or Liza.

Chloe Webb as "Jennifer Holler-day" in "Screamgirls."

Gerard Alessandrini at work, writing *Forbidden Broadway.*

Altogether, I think we added three numbers to the show: 'Screamgirls,' a *Cats* number ("I Enjoy Being a Cat"), and a parody of "Be Italian" from *Nine,* called "Be a Catholic." Once word got around that there was new material in *Forbidden Broadway*, lots of people came back to see it again. And from then on, we pretty much followed that pattern.

I really enjoyed updating the show, and I think the cast had a good time trying out new material. We would change the order of the numbers and switch off; I originally did the Rex Harrison number, then Bill Carmichael took it over, and so on. But it wasn't until later that I decided to start doing whole new editions with catchy titles.

In the spring of 1983, we thought we would see how the show would play in other cities. So Bill, Chloe, Fred, Dee Hoty (replacing Nora, who was expecting her second child), and I went off to do it in L.A. Jason Alexander joined the New York company, as did Ann Morrison. Both had recently co-starred in *Merrily We Roll Along*—the show that had inspired our original logo design. It became clear that super-talented actors such as Jason and Ann could keep the show going like gangbusters.

In L.A., we did the show at The Comedy Store, but it was only moderately successful. That really wasn't the best venue for us, because we had to work around the club's schedule. I remember that we couldn't do a show on Saturdays at 8:00 because Jim Carrey had that spot. When we played in L.A. in later years, it was in actual theaters, and the show was a huge hit. There is a theatrical community there, even though it's much smaller than in New

1983: Ann Morrison, Jason Alexander, and Marilyn Pasekoff sing "Be a Catholic."

York. And by the time we came back to L.A., we had the imprimatur of being a hit in New York, so that helped us bring in an audience.

I remember that Vincente Minnelli, Robert Stack, and their wives came to see the show twice. I wish I'd had the chance to talk with them more. When Minnelli came, I thought, "Thank God we don't have a Liza number." But after he left, I started to think, "Maybe we *should* have a Liza number." As soon as we got back to New York, I wrote "Liza One-Note," and we put it in the show. Vincente Minnelli never came back to see *Forbidden Broadway* again.

By the fall of '83, I was back in New York, and we had a fabulous new cast that included Marilyn Pasekoff, Jan Neuberger, and the supremely gifted Patrick Quinn in all his glory. Patrick was one of the quintessential *Forbidden Broadway* leading men; he had all the experience and expertise of delivering a big baritone performance but he

Left: The cast of *Forbidden Broadway '84* (clockwise from left): Marilyn Pasekoff, Patrick Quinn, Jan Neuberger, and Doug Voet. Right: Patrick Quinn, as Richard Burton in *Camelot,* happily displays his $1.95 cardboard crown.

knew how to heighten everything just enough to make it look absurd. He also oozed a sense of, "I know *everything* about theater *and* I know who's sleeping with whom!" Especially for Patrick, I wrote a parody of Alfred Drake, a legendary stage star who had recently appeared in the movie *Trading Places* with Eddie Murphy.

I wrote the Drake parody lyrics to Fred/Petruchio's songs from *Kiss Me, Kate*. Patrick knew those songs well; I believe he had performed the role himself once. In our show, the first time he did the number, he entered in a tight lavender doublet, looking ridiculous. He knowingly smiled . . . and then proceeded to sing the entire song with all of the original Cole Porter lyrics. His eyes glazed over, and I could see the sweat dripping from his red face. With great bravado and impeccable diction, Patrick sang "Where Is the Life That Late I Led?" to a very confused audience. He finished with a big flourish, and with his doublet soaking wet. The audience sat there silently, but I was doubled over in laughter.

Since there was so much activity on Broadway, we made a lot of changes to the show and decided to present a new edition, titled *Forbidden Broadway 1984*. I finally wrote that Liza Minnelli number, "Liza One-Note," and I loved setting my own lyrics to George Gershwin's music for our spoof of *My One and Only*.

Even though I was back in New York, I stopped performing in the show myself so I could concentrate more on writing and directing. Besides, how could I compete with the likes of Jason Alexander and Patrick Quinn? I started to pay more attention to honing the show and routining the numbers. It became clear how important it was to place each number properly in the running order, according to whether it was broad or wordy or ballad-y, so everything would work in context. This remained true for the entire run; we would go into rehearsal with fifteen new numbers, and it would take weeks to find the right order.

One of my favorite numbers that I added to the show at this time was "Chita/ Rita." I had been searching for a good idea for a spoof of Chita Rivera, whom I consider to be one of the greatest stars

Jan Neuberger and Davis Gaines, flying high as Twiggy and Tommy Tune in our version of *My One and Only*.

in Broadway history. I spent hours listening to her cast albums, and while *West Side Story* was playing one night, I began to remember her club act, which I had seen several years before. Then I thought, "Wait a minute, that was Rita Moreno's act. No, it was Chita. No, it was Rita. Chita! Rita!" To this day, I'm not sure *whose* act it was. But as my thoughts bounced back and forth between their names, the song "America" was playing on the stereo, and all the words fit perfectly.

When I handed the parody to the girls in the show, they went wild with enthusiasm, and Fred Barton said, "This is exactly what the doctor ordered." The girls' joy was short-lived when they tried to memorize some of the wordiest lyrics I'd ever written. I had even put words to Bernstein's dance music. (I thought, "That'll show you, Steve Sondheim!" I was young.) There wasn't a moment of rest in the number, but everybody's hard work paid off.

Sue Terry as Chita and Roxie Lucas as Rita. Oh no, sorry; that's Sue as Rita and Roxie as Chita. Or maybe it's the other way around . . .

When *Forbidden Broadway* originally opened, it wasn't very polished. You might even say it was sophomoric. The show was a hit because it was so outrageous; nobody had seen anything like it, and we performed it with unabashed commitment. But by 1984, the show started to have an arc to it. We had so much fun at Palsson's in those days. It seemed as if every Broadway star came to see us, along with other major celebrities, and they would hang out afterwards and talk with us—people like Jeremy Irons, Maggie Smith, Mary Tyler Moore.

I don't know how much of this was due to the success of our show and how much to the fact that the Upper West Side was becoming more trendy, but Palsson's became a real celebrity spot. Liz Taylor came in one night after *The Little Foxes*, wearing a full-length white ermine cape with a dragon embroidered on the back of it. Cher would show up after *Come Back to the Five and Dime, Jimmy Dean, Jimmy Dean*—and she'd still be in costume. You could go to Palsson's after our show and see Al Pacino, Robert De Niro, Robin Williams, Raul Julia. I remember that Sella Palsson was a little overwhelmed to have mega-celebrities like that in the club. It was a small place, and the staff just wasn't used to it.

You might say that we missed some opportunities. Madeline Kahn dropped by Palsson's one afternoon; she found me backstage painting some props, and she hinted that she'd like to do the show, but I didn't pick up on it. There was some talk of our moving the show to Broadway, to the Helen Hayes. But because we didn't cash in and do a Broadway run, an HBO special, or anything like that, I think that allowed us to keep going Off-Broadway for years.

In those days especially, *Forbidden Broadway* wasn't about making a lot of money and winning awards. We were just a bunch of young people affectionately thumbing our noses at Broadway and trying to cause as much trouble as we could. And we did.

"Jennifer Holler-day in 'Screamgirls'"

JENNIFER

AND I AM TELLING YOU . . .

[*The lights come up on* JENNIFER *as Effie White with her back to the audience, wearing a very thickly padded, pink satin pant suit and a black wig. She slowly turns around to face the audience.*]

. . . I'M NOT SINGIN'!

COMPARED TO MY RASPY TRILLS,

LOUIS ARMSTRONG IS BEVERLY SILLS.

YES, I'M A SCREAMGIRL

YES, I'M A SCREAMGIRL

SO WHO NEEDS THE RIGHT NOTE?

I JUST WANNA BE HEARD

AND YOU AND YOU AND YOU,

YOU'RE GONNA HEAR ME!

WHEN MICHAEL BENNETT SAID
"PLEASE DON'T SHOUT,"
I SAID, "I DO WHAT I WANTS TO
OR I'S WALKIN OUT!"
NOBODY CARES WHAT LYRICS I SING,
AS LONG AS I MAKE THEIR INNER EAR RING.

[MAN *enters as Ben Harney/Curtis Taylor, Jr. She sees him and goes over to tenderly sing in his ear, but then she blasts him on the "I'm."*]

AND I AM TELLING YOU
I'M NOT SINGIN'

[*The force of her note lifts him straight up in the air and smashes him against the proscenium. He slides to the floor and crawls offstage.*]

A GIMMICK'S WHAT MAKES YOU GREAT,
THAT'S WHY I HYPER-HYPER-VENTILATE.

NO-NO-NO-NO NECK,
SO I INHALE LIKE AN OLD VACUUM CLEANER.
I'M A BIG STAR
I'M A HUGE STAR
I'LL NEVER BE SMALL
I'M HUGE, I'M HUGE, I'M HUGE,
I'M HUGE AS A TOWNHOUSE.
MY THIGHS HAVE GONE CONDO,
YES THEY HAVE!

SCREAMGIRL, SCREAMGIRL!

[MAN *enters as a stagehand, with a hand truck. He waits for her to finish.*]

SCREAMGIRL, SCREAMGIRL!
YOU'RE GONNA
HEEEEEEAAAAAAAR . . .

[*With great effort, the* MAN *hoists* JENNIFER *onto the truck and rolls her offstage.*]

MEEEEEEEEEEEE!!!!!!!!!

"The Impossible Song"

DON QUIXOTE

TO SING THE IMPOSSIBLE SONG,
TO CLEAR MY UNCLEARABLE THROAT,
TO BEAR MY UNBEARABLE WARBLE,
WHEN I REACH THE UNREACHABLE NOTE . . .

THIS IS MY QUEST,
TO FINISH THIS SONG,
NO MATTER HOW GRUELING,
NO MATTER HOW LONG,

TO FIGHT WITH THE WORDS
AND TO STAMMER AND PAUSE;
THOUGH IT LOOKS LIKE I'M GOING THROUGH
    HELL,
IT'S JUST MALE MENOPAUSE.

AND I KNOW
IF I ONLY GET THROUGH
TILL THE CURTAIN DESCENDS,
I CAN DO
WHAT A MAN HAS TO DO
    WHEN HE'S WEARING DEPENDS . . .

AND THE WORLD WILL BE WORSE OFF FOR THIS:
THAT ONE MAN, SO INCREADIBLY WRONG,
STILL STROVE WITH HIS LAST OUNCE OF
    CHUTZPAH
TO SING THE IMPOSSIBLE SONG!

"Alfred Drake"

ALFRED

[*He enters flamboyantly, dressed as Petruchio in* Kiss Me Kate, *with Van Dyke beard. He jumps on the piano, lies on his side, and sings.*]

AS I REACH THE AGE OF MY RETIREMENT,
MY CAREER IS ON HIATUS AWHILE.
I HAVE EV'RY LEADING MAN REQUIREMENT,
BUT BARITONES ARE SADLY OUT OF STYLE.
NOW WHEN I SING "POOR JUDD," HOW BLUE AM I?
'CAUSE EVERYONE KEEPS WONDERING, "WHO AM I?"

ALFRED DRAKE, ALFRED DRAKE.
WHO REMEMBERS ALFRED DRAKE?
BUT I'M HE, NO MISTAKE,
I'M THE DASHING ALFRED DRAKE.

HAVE YOU SEEN *TRADING PLACES*?
IN THE BACKGROUND, I PLAY A JUDGE.
EDDIE MURPHY'S A DOLL,
BUT MY PART WAS SO SMALL
THAT I FELT LIKE A WALNUT IN FUDGE.

ALFRED DRAKE, ALFRED DRAKE,
NOT JOHN RAITT OR BOB GOULET;
NEXT TO ME, THEY'RE OPAQUE,
AND THEY'RE TENORS ANYWAY.

OKLAHOMA!, KEAN, AND *KISMET*
WERE SUCESSFUL ON THE WHOLE.
KISS ME KATE'S GREAT,
YES IT IS, YET
HOWARD KEEL STOLE
MY BIG FILM ROLE!

ALFRED DRAKE, ALL FOR NAUGHT;
NEVER WAS A MOVIE STAR,
AND THAT'S WHY YOU FORGOT
ALFRED DRAKE WAS WUNDERBAR!

"Chita and Rita"

CHITA

[*Enters dressed in purple, like Anita in* West Side Story.]

MISS MORENO, HER RUDE GYRATIONS
ARE ALL LOUSY IMITATIONS.
THOUGH WE BOTH DID *WEST SIDE STORY,*
HERS WAS LIKE CHICKEN CACCIATORE.
SHE GOT ALL THE GLORY,
BUT DON'T LET THAT CAT IN;
I'M THE FIERY LATIN.
I WAS THE WORLD'S FIRST ANITA.
DON'T MIX US UP,
I AM CHITA!

CHITA RIVERA IS NOT RITA
RITA MORENO IS NOT CHITA
CHITA IS CHITA AND NOT RITA
I WOULD PREFER YOU FORGOT RITA!

THIS LITTLE DITTY REMINDS YOU
WHO IS THE WHAT AND THE WHO'S WHO:
SHE GETS THE MOVIES AND BRAVOS,
I GET THE NIGHTCLUBS AND BOMB SHOWS!

MY NAME IS CHITA AND NOT RITA
RITA IS RITA AND NOT CHITA
LIZA LIKES CHITA BUT NOT RITA
I WOULDN'T MIND IF THEY SHOT RITA!

I'M THE ONE WHO STARRED ON BROADWAY
FROM THE '50S AND THE '60S TO THE CURRENT DAY,
  PEOPLE.
AND I INVENTED THE "AYE, AYE"
WHILE RITA WAS LISPING IN *KING AND I.*

I HAVE DONE *BYE BYE BIRDIE, CHICAGO, BAJOUR,*
AND I NEVER MISS A MATINEE, PEOPLE.
AND WHEN CHORUS BOYS SCREAM AND YELL, "AYE,
  AYE, AYE,"
HOW I LOVE ALL OF THE GAY PEOPLE!

MY NAME IS CHITA AND NOT RITA
RITA IS RITA AND NOT CHITA
LIZA HATES RITA, BUT NOT CHITA.
WHY WON'T THE UNION BOYCOTT RITA?

[RITA *enters, dressed exactly the same.*]

RITA

Hello, Chita.

CHITA

Rita, what are you doing here?

RITA

I'll be doing the movie version of *Kiss of the Spider Woman.* I'll probably win another Oscar. You can present it.

CHITA

I'd sooner die.

RITA

You probably will. I just came by to clarify one t'ing:

MY NAME IS RITA AND NOT CHITA
THOUGH I LOOK LIKE YOU A LOT, CHITA
WHEN PEOPLE SMOKE TOO MUCH POT, CHITA
THEY THINK YOU'RE ME AND I'M NOT RITA.

I AM A BERSATILE A'TRESS . . .

CHITA

LONG AS YOU STAY ON THE MATTRESS.
I CAN PLAY ANY ROLE I CHOOSE . . .

RITA

GYPSIES, ITALIANS, AND BLACK JEWS.

[CHIT*A sings "Ai!" at the beginning of each of the next lines.*]

(AI!) WHEN I GO OUT ON A DATE, CHITA
(AI!) PEOPLE SAY THERE GOES THE GREAT RITA
(AI!) BUT WHEN THEY SEE YOU THEY STATE, CHITA,
LOOKS LIKE YOU PUT ON SOME WEIGHT, CHITA.

[*They dance and fight.*]

BOTH

SO IF YOU WANT TO KEEP WHO'S WHO STRAIGHT,
HERE'S HOW TO SETTLE THE GREAT DEBATE:
I AM THE ONE YOU SHOULD EMULATE,
SHE IS THE ONE WHO SHOULD MIGRATE!

THERE'S RITA AND CHITA AND LIZA
AND LISA AND LIZA AND CHITA
AND PIA ZADORA AND LISA
AND MIA AND LIZA AND CHITA
MIA, LIZA, RITA, CHITA
RIO RITA, LIZA, PIA, PITA
DEBBIE ALLEN . . . AND ME!

"Liza One-Note"

LIZA

MAMA TAUGHT ME TO SING ONE NOTE
AND THE NOTE I SING IS THIS:
AAAAAAAAAAAAAAAAAAAAAAAAAAAH!!!!!!!

I'M LIZA ONE-NOTE,
GOT NO VIBRATO
AND CAN'T SING LEGATO AT ALL . . .

I'M LIZA ONE-NOTE,
SQUEEZING MY HIGH NOTES
AND SNEAKING RIGHT BY NOTES TAKES GALL
TO BOUNCE ROUND THE STAGE LIKE A BALL.

I'M A LITTLE BRASS
AND A LOT OF DRUMS.
MAY BE KIND OF CRASS;
STILL, THE PUBLIC COMES.

I'M LIZA ONE-NOTE,
DADDY MINNELLI
AND UNCLE GENE KELLY SAID, "KID!
SQUEEZE OUT YOUR ONE NOTE.
YOU'LL BE A STAR
AND THEY'LL KNOW YOU AS FAR AS MADRID!"
AND MAMA MADE SURE THAT I DID.

NOW I HAVE HER VOICE,
AS YOU MIGHT SUPPOSE,
    BUT IF I'D THE CHOICE,
I'D HAVE FIXED MY NOSE.

I DRESS IN RED SEQUIN,
BLUE SEQUIN,
GREEN SEQUIN,
BEIGE SEQUIN,
    AND SOMETIMES IN HALSTON CHIFFFON!

AAAAAAAAAAAAAAHHHHHHH!!!!!!!!

I'M LIZA ONE-NOTE,
WHEN I START SINGING
YOUR EARS WILL BE RINGING IN PAIN!
THAT'S WHY ALL MY FANS SNORT COCAINE.

[*She speaks while fidgeting all around the stage.*]

Oh, God! I love showbiz! The lights! The audience! The curtain! The piano player . . . whoever he is. But, no, really . . . he's terrific, he's just terrific. And speaking of terrific: I feel terrific! How do you feel? Good. You know, I recently played Carnegie Hall just like my Mama, Judy Garland, did thirty years ago . . . but better! Ahh! Ahh! Ahh! Hello, I love you! Thank you so much for coming. Touch me. Would you like to? Go ahead . . . it's all right. Go on.

[*She reaches out to an audience member, then pulls away sharply.*]

That's enough. Can I be serious for a minute? Okay. You know, now that we're here together like this, I just want you to know how truly terrific it feels so sing one note the way I do. So when I get to the part of the song where I sing AAAAAAAHHHHHH!!!! Do you know the part I mean? Oh you do, you do! I love you! Both of you. Well, we're going to sing it together, and it's really terrific because—Oh! Oh! Ahh! Ahh! I have an idea! We will have . . . a practice! We'll have a practice! Now when I count to three, we'll all sing together. Ready? One . . . two . . . three . . . AAAAAAAAHHHHHHH!!!!!

[*She is humiliated that no one joins in.*]

Darlings! It was this close, but you see, in order for this to work, all my darlings have to sing with me! You see, all my darlings have to sing together [*She giggles nervously.*] at . . . the . . . same . . . time!

[*She giggles even more nervously, then suddenly turns threatening.*]

Look, if you won't do it for me, do it for Mama. Okay, ready? One . . . two . . . three . . .

AAAAAAAAAAHHHHHHH!!!! Oh, that's
terrific. We'll sing 'em all, we'll stay all night!
AAAAAAAAAAHHHHHHH!!!!!

MY SINGING WILL GIVE YOU A PAIN.
I'M LIZA ONE-NOTE,
MY SINGING WILL DRIVE YOU
  INSAAAAAAAAAANE!!!!

FORBIDDEN MEMORIES: **Roxie Lucas**

In the 1980s, Broadway was in a bit of a slump. For aspiring performers like me, *Forbidden Broadway* was the perfect playground in which to sing, dance, and poke fun. The show was a hit, and lots of big stars came to see it. We were thrilled to get the chance to meet so many legends of theatre and film.

Roxie Lucas.

One of the oddest experiences I had was meeting composer Richard Adler. He had gotten wind that we were using the tune of "Hernando's Hideaway" from *The Pajama Game,* one of the two shows he co-wrote with the late Jerry Ross. Although music rights were always cleared for our show, he felt that he had final approval on our parody. A press kit was sent to him, and an invitation to the show was extended. He declined and insisted that we come to his home and do the number for him personally.

The parody was of *Tango Argentino.* I was dressed in a black strapless gown with slicked-back hair, and I sang and danced the tango with my partner, Mark Martino. At the climax of the number, I spun offstage and was replaced by a dummy dressed exactly like me; it was one of those life-size blowup dolls from a porno shop, with an O-shape for a mouth. Mark flung the doll around, pounded it on the piano, and generally abused it before throwing it offstage. That's when I staggered back on. This was extreme physical comedy, and we were a bit apprehensive about doing the number in someone's apartment.

On the appointed day, we all met at the theatre to get into costume and pick up my twin. Hailing a cab on West

72nd Street when we were dressed like that, with a matching blow-up doll in our group, was perhaps the silliest situation I've ever been in. But at Mr. Adler's apartment on the East Side, the mood was serious. A grand piano dominated the living room, with two leather-bound scores on top: *The Pajama Game* and *Damn Yankees*. Mr. Adler pulled up a chair and we began. As he listened to the lyrics, he began to smile, and by the end, he was laughing and grinning broadly. He loved it, and he invited us to stay all afternoon. We had gotten his blessing.

Years later, when I was appearing in a revival of *Damn Yankees* on Broadway, Mr. Adler came in as a consultant. I asked him if he remembered me, and with a twinkle in his eye he said, "How could I forget?!"

Ya Got Trouble in New York City: 1986–87

In 1986–87, we were still playing at Palsson's, and it became apparent that there was less and less on Broadway to make fun of. There just weren't many new musicals, due in part to the AIDS crisis in the industry. For a while, we started our show by saying, "And now, *Forbidden Broadway* spoofs the hits of the 1985-86 season." The lights would come up on an empty stage, and then go down again.

In 1985, *Quilters* had gotten a Tony nomination for Best Musical, and *Big River* won the award. That's not an inferior show; it's a very nice musical of *Huckleberry Finn*, but it never really caught the public's imagination. This was also true of *Edwin Drood*, but that show was great fodder for us. We were able to spoof the idea of the audience voting for who the murderer was by having our audience vote on which star we would murder. Almost every night, they wanted to see our version of Linda Ronstadt in *La Bohème* as she sang to the tune of "Musetta's Waltz":

L.A. BOHÈME!
WATCH ME MAKE DOMINGO'S TOUPÉE CURL
WHEN I MAKE MIMI A VALLEY GIRL.
L.A. BOHÈME!
AND AS FOR ALL MY ROCK FANS,
NOW THAT I'M A DIVA,
WHO NEEDS THEM?

JOE PAPP PRODUCED IT ALL, AND IT WAS ALL FOR ME.
HE IS A DARLING—REALLY, ISN' HE?
HE DIDN'T EVEN MIND WHEN I TOOK FOUR NIGHTS OFF
ON A SIX-DAY WORK WEEK.

I TOOK PUCCINI, AND THEN I SIMPLIFIED IT
TILL IT SOUNDED LIKE WALT DISNEY.
NO CHORUS DISTRACTING,
NO HIGH NOTES, NO ACTING.

L.A. BOHÈME!
WEAR YOUR SPEEDOS AND YOUR FOSTER GRANTS;
MY RODOLFO'S WEARING SPANDEX PANTS.
AND SO WHAT? WE CLOSED?
I THINK THAT'S FINE.
NOW I'LL DO *MADAME BUTTERFLY* IN SAN FRANCISCO
WITH KEVIN KLINE!

To give you an idea of how inactive Broadway was at the time, we had to look to a revival of *The Music Man* that Dick Van Dyke did at City Center. So I wrote a number called "Ya Got Trouble in New York City," about the lack of exciting entertainment on Broadway.

More and more theatre was being imported from London to fill in the void. The Royal Shakespeare Company bought over several excellent productions that were the

talk of the town. This gave me a wonderful opportunity to steal some more songs from *My Fair Lady*. We turned "The Ascot Gavotte" on its ear by dancing "The RSC Gavotte." I've always found it a joy to parody Lerner and Loewe songs, because the lyrics are so sharp and witty, and Alan Jay Lerner clearly lays out where the punch-lines should be. As for Frederick Loewe's music, it's heady and infectious to say the least, and it even sounds headier with silly parody lyrics.

Our cast performed the gavotte absolutely deadpan, and ten times snobbier than any Anglophile. I enjoyed that number—especially the night when Mr. Lerner himself attended the show and laughed and laughed. About six weeks later, I heard that he had died from cancer, and I realized what a great compliment he had paid us: *Forbidden Broadway* must have been one of the last shows he chose to attend.

Although it was a very quiet time on Broadway, the Upper West Side was gentrifying, and our show was doing very well. When we did a new edition, we'd get a huge amount of attention from the press, partly because there was almost nothing else going on. We couldn't really spoof shows like *Quilters* or *Starmites*, because they didn't run long enough for people to get to know the music.

Ron Bohmer as "The Music Man" in 1986.

Left: Gerard at a rehearsal in the mid-'80s. "These boots are made for walkin' over people's careers!"
Right: Craig Wells, Nora Mae Lyng, and John Vandertholen do the "RSC Gavotte."

Artistically, Broadway was hanging on by two threads: Jerry Herman and Stephen Sondheim, giants from the golden age who were still turning out musical theatre gems. *La Cage aux Folles* and *Sunday in the Park with George* had opened in the same season and went head to head against each other for the big awards. *La Cage* won the Tony, but *Sunday* won a Pulitzer Prize. This rivalry did not go unnoticed at *Forbidden Broadway*.

Although I personally thought George Hearn's performance in *La Cage* was stellar, I couldn't help turning "I Am What I Am" into "I Ham What I Ham." I knew it was an easy jab and not a very clever turn of phrase, but there are some parody titles I just can't resist. Certainly, I enjoyed the gales of laughter that the number earned every night. And it was great fun to see the super-talented hams of our own company—Patrick Quinn, and later Herndon Lackey and Craig Wells—going way over the top themselves.

As for *Sunday in the Park with George,* I avoided ribbing Mandy Patinkin and Bernadette Peters specifically. (In my heart of hearts, I must have deeply regretted this, because I tortured them relentlessly in later years.) But Sondheim was such a force in this era that it seemed appropriate to make him the subject of ridicule. *Forbidden Broadway* had previously had a spoof called "Too Many Sondheims." In that version, our genius pianist/musical director Fred Barton performed the number, bemoaning the many young musical theatre writers who imitated Sondheim. Now I created a

The *Forbidden Broadway* company (including Jason Alexander, far left in bottom row) celebrates the show's fifth anniversary.

little parody that had Steve himself bemoaning his lack of mass appeal. The title for that seemed obvious: "Send in the Crowds."

The first time Sondheim attended *Forbidden Broadway,* he told me he felt that my parody lyric about him was "kind and gentle." I took that to mean I should be sharper and funnier. Years later, after he had seen our other spoofs of him and his work, he told me with a twinkle in his eye that he regretted what he had initially said because, ever after, I had "mercilessly slashed" him. He also once advised me, "The meaner, the funnier"—but I was never sure if he meant I should be meaner to him or to the likes of John Stamos. In any case, I'm mean to everybody, so the bases are covered. I hope you're happy, Steve!

Of course, Sondheim wasn't the only contemporary musical theatre writer I lambasted. Right from the start, Andrew Lloyd Webber was a fun target. When Fred Barton left *Forbidden Broadway* to do the *Zorba* tour with Anthony Quinn, his excellent replacement was Mark Mitchell—a superb musical director who didn't look anything like Sondheim. One day at rehearsal, I was staring at Mark's profile and thinking, "Who does he look like?" Suddenly, it occurred to me: Andrew Lloyd Webber! (Not *Sir* Andrew; he hadn't been knighted yet.)

I must have said this aloud, because Roxie Lucas screamed, "Yes! Yes!" She found a graduation robe in the dressing room and got Mark into it. Roxie and I looked at each other and exclaimed, "Lloyd Webber's *Mass*!" So, for nearly a year, we said high mass at *Forbidden Broadway* every night—*Cats, Evita,* and *Joseph*–style.

Many people ask me if Lloyd Webber himself is put off by *Forbidden Broadway.* I suppose they assume that's the case because it seems as though he would be the easily offended British type. In fact, I find he has a wonderful sense of humor; he has seen the show more than once and has always been delightful to me, full of fun stories and *Forbidden Broadway*–like observances about theatre in New York and London.

Thinking it through, it occurs to me that Andrew Lloyd Webber and Stephen Sondheim can afford to be big about their parodies because they are secure in their art and they clearly know what they're doing. Nothing I could say in *Forbidden Broadway* can shake that basic foundation. I also think both men are intelligent enough to understand that I have the greatest admiration for writers and know that the most important ingredient for theatrical success is a brilliant score.

The summer of 1986 was the first time we did a "Summer Shock" edition of *Forbidden Broadway.* We introduced Barbra Streisand to the show, because her *Broadway Album* had recently been released. One Broadway musical that gave us a lot

Above: Fred "Sondheim" Barton and Nora Mae "Bernadette" Lyng. Below: Mark Mitchell as "Andrew Lloyd Superstar."

of mileage was *Singin' in the Rain;* even though it was an also-ran, everybody knew the songs from the movie. So we did a number called "Spinnin' Down the Drain," and another one called "You Are My Yucky Star." The finale was a ballet featuring Twyla

Left: The 1986 cast: Roxie Lucas (as Edwin Rude), Mark Martino (as Don Correia), Susan Terry (as Bernadette Peters), and Craig Wells (as Rum-Dum-Tugger). Right: Roxie Lucas (as our fantasy version of Twyla Tharp), Craig Wells (singing "Make 'Em Leave"), and Mark Martino go "Spinnin' Down the Drain."

Tharp as a neo-Nazi in a tutu and running shoes; to the tune of "Broadway Melody," the cast wailed, "That's the Broadway malady!"

The theatre scene was about to change dramatically, and so would the focus of our show. As one of my old friends in Boston used to tell me, "The British are coming! The British are coming!"

"Ya Got Trouble"

ROBERT PRESTON AS THE MUSIC MAN

FOLKS, LISTEN!
MAY I HAVE YOUR ATTENTION, PLEASE?
ATTENTION, PLEASE!

WELL, I'M HAPPY TO BE HERE MY FRIENDS,
BACK ON THE STAGE AND OFF THE SCREEN.
I'M NO SAINT LIKE CHARLTON HESTON;
I'M THE SWINGING ROBERT PRESTON,
AND I'M HERE TO TALK ABOUT THE
CONTEMPORARY THEATRE SCENE.

WELL, YA GOT TROUBLE, MY FRIENDS,

RIGHT HERE, I SAY TROUBLE RIGHT HERE IN NEW YORK CITY.

WHY SURE I'M A THEATREGOER,

CERTAINLY—MIGHTY PROUD T' SAY,

I'M ALWAYS MIGHTY PROUD T' SAY IT.

I CONSIDER THE HOURS I SPEND AT A BROADWAY SHOW ARE GOLDEN;

HELP ME CULTIVATE CULTURE,

AND A SENSE OF HUMOR AND A DRAMATIC FLAIR.

BUT JUST AS I SAY, IT TAKES JUDGEMENT, BRAINS, AND MATURITY

TO MAKE A GOOD BROADWAY SHOW.

I SAY THAT ANY BOOB CAN PUT A TWO-BIT PLAY IN A THEATRE.

AND I CALL THOSE FLOPS,

THE FIRST BIG SHOWS OF THE YEAR ARE LEADIN' TO DEGREDA . . .

I SAY, FIRST . . . IT'S LILY TOMLIN AT THE PLYMOUTH,

THEN CHER AT THE SHUBERT.

AND THE NEXT THING YA KNOW,

YOUR TICKETS ARE COSTIN' MORE MONEY THAN IN CITIBANK!

'CAUSE PRODUCTION COSTS ARE OUTTA CONTROL

TILL PRODUCIN'S NOT AN ART.

IT'S MORE LIKE GAMBLIN'—

AND THE ONLY SHOWS IN THE BLACK,

ARE THE SHOWS THEY DO ON HBO!

LIKE TO SLAP DOWN FIFTY BUCKS WHEN YA COULDA WATCHED TV?

MAKE YOUR BLOOD BOIL? WELL, I SHOULD SAY.

NOW, FRIENDS, LEMME TELL YOU WHAT I MEAN.

YA GOT ONE, TWO , THREE, FOUR,

FIVE, SIX QUALITY PRODUCTIONS,

BUT NONE OF THEM FROM THIS SEASON,

AND NOTHIN' MUCH COMIN' UP.

AND THAT ENDS WITH "P"

AND THAT RHYMES WITH "D"

AND THAT STANDS FOR DULL!

NOW I KNOW ALL YOU FOLKS ARE LOVERS OF THEATRE.

YOU ALL HATED *PERFECTLY FRANK.**

WOULD YOU LIKE TO KNOW WHAT KINDA CONVERSATION GOES ON

AT A TYPICAL SARDI'S LUNCH?

PEOPLE TALKIN' 'BOUT BONO, TALKIN' 'BOUT MADONNA!

EMULATIN' BOY GEORGE AND HIS CULTURAL CLUB.

AND JEERIN' ALL ABOUT, HOW ABOUT THE THEATRE'S PASSÉ

AND THE MUSICAL'S DEAD!

NOW ONE FINE NIGHT WE'LL BE WALKIN' DOWN BROADWAY

LOOKIN' FOR A GOOD SHOW TO GO TO

BUT ALL'LL BE GONE AND ALL YOU'LL HEAR IS PUNK ROCK,

SHAMELESS MUSIC FROM A BIG HOTEL HIGH-RISE

WITH MTV. AND VIDEO PLAYERS—

MASS MEDIA!

FRIENDS, THE IDLE THEATRE IS THE DEVIL'S PLAYGROUND.

TROUBLE!

CHORUS

OH, WE GOT TROUBLE

PRESTON

RIGHT HERE IN NEW YORK CITY

---

*Perfectly Frank was a short-lived revue of the songs of Frank Loesser. It is also the actual phrase used in "Trouble" from *The Music Man,* so I couldn't resist picking that show title.

CHORUS

RIGHT HERE IN NEW YORK CITY

PRESTON

WITH A CAPITAL "T" AND THAT RHYMES WITH "D"
AND THAT STANDS FOR DULL!

CHORUS

THAT STANDS FOR DULL!

PRESTON

WE SURELY GOT TROUBLE

CHORUS

WE SURELY GOT TROUBLE

PRESTON

RIGHT HERE IN NEW YORK CITY

CHORUS

RIGHT HERE

PRESTON

GOTTA FIGURE OUT A WAY
TO GET THIS BROADWAY SEASON
OUTTA THIS LULL!

CHORUS

THIS BROADWAY SEASON'S REALLY IN TROUBLE,
TROUBLE, TROUBLE, TROUBLE . . .

PRESTON

Theatregoers of America, heed this warning before
it's too late. Watch for the tell-tale signs of Broadway's
destruction. Are intimate little theatres being torn
down and replaced with huge, modern theatrical
barns? Are comic strips being turned into musicals?
Are performers so heavily miked they might as well
play a tape—and do? Are foreign actors creeping into
our Broadway shows? Actors like Lea Salonga?

CHORUS

TROUBLE! TROUBLE!

PRESTON

Aha! And Mandy Patinkin?

CHORUS

TROUBLE!! TROUBLE!!

PRESTON

Well, if so my friends . . .

WE GOT TROUBLE

CHORUS

OH, WE GOT TROUBLE

PRESTON

RIGHT HERE IN NEW YORK CITY

CHORUS

RIGHT HERE IN NEW YORK CITY

PRESTON

WITH A CAPITAL "T" AND
THAT RHYMES WITH "D" AND
THAT STANDS FOR DULL

CHORUS

THAT STANDS FOR DULL!

PRESTON

WE SURELY GOT TROUBLE

CHORUS

WE SURELY GOT TROUBLE

PRESTON

RIGHT HERE IN NEW YORK CITY

CHORUS

RIGHT HERE

PRESTON

REMEMBER *MAME, MACK AND MABEL,* AND *CAGE AUX FOLLES*!

CHORUS

THIS BROADWAY SEASON'S REALLY IN TROUBLE, TROUBLE, TROUBLE . . .

PRESTON

OH, WE GOT TROUBLE,

WE'RE IN TERRIBLE, TERRIBLE TROUBLE.

'CAUSE BROADWAY LOOKS LIKE IT'S HEADIN' FOR AN ARTISTIC LULL.

CHORUS

ARTISTIC LULL

PRESTON

OH, WE GOT TROUBLE, TROUBLE, TROUBLE . . .

CHORUS

OH YES, WE GOT TROUBLE. HERE. WE GOT BIG, BIG TROUBLE

PRESTON

WITH A CAPITAL "T"

CHORUS

WITH A CAPITAL "T"

PRESTON

THAT RHYMES WITH "D"

CHORUS

THAT RHYMES WITH "D"

PRESTON

AND THAT STANDS FOR DULL!

CHORUS

THAT STANDS FOR DULL!

"Sondheim Tonight"

BERNADETTE PETERS

[*She enters dressed as Dot from* Sunday in the Park with George.]

Ladies and gentlemen, this restaurant is a temple, and we are here to worship the gods who write Broadway musicals. Tonight, I am pleased to announce Stephen Sondheim.

[*As she sings, she displays and changes window cards of various Sondheim shows.*]

SOMETHING ELITIST, SOMETHING DEFEATIST,
SOMETHING THAT'S CONTROVERSIAL:
SONDHIEM TONIGHT!

SOMETHING DRAMATIC, SOMETHING CHROMATIC,
SOMTHING THAT'S NON-COMMERIAL:
SONDHEIM TONIGHT!

NOTHING WITH TUNES, NOTHING WITH NOUNS
SEND IN THE ROSES, RAZORS, AND CLOWNS
NOTHING THAT'S FORMAL, NOTHING THAT'S
    NORMAL
NOTHING YOU'D WANT TO UNDERWRITE . . .
CLARITY TOMORROW, SONDHEIM TONIGHT!

[*She holds up piano lid, revealing a color picture of Stephen Sondheim. She lowers the lid. The pianist is now bearded a la* SONDHEIM. BERNADETTE *leaves as* SONDHEIM *sings.*]

"Send in the Crowds"

SONDHEIM

I COULD BE RICH,
FAMOUS AS SHAW.
WITH MORE COMMERCIAL APPEAL,
MY NAME WOULD DRAW.
SEND IN THE CROWDS.

WHY WON'T THEY COME?
DON'T THEY APPROVE?
EVEN THE SETS ARE IDEAL;
SEE HOW THEY MOVE!
WHERE ARE THE CROWDS?
SEND IN THE CROWDS.

JUST WHEN I START
WRITING MY BEST,
EVERYONE SAYS I LOOK GRUMPY
AND I NEED A REST.

THOUGH I KEEP WRITING MY SCORES
WITH MY USUAL FLAIR,
AFTER ACT ONE,
NO ONE IS THERE.

DON'T YOU LIKE ART?
MY FAULT, I KNOW.
I THOUGHT YOU'D LIKE GEORGE SEURAT'S
TWO ACT TABLEAU.
BUT WHERE ARE THE CROWDS?
QUICK, SEND IN THE CROWDS.
WELL, MAYBE NEXT SHOW.

[*A copy of* The New York Times *miraculously appears.*
SONDHEIM *gets up from the piano to read the review
of one of his shows as the piano continues to play by
itself.*]

THANK YOU, FRANK RICH,
YOU'RE SUCH A DEAR.
THIS IS THE GREATEST REVIEW
OF MY CAREER.
NOW, THERE ARE CROWDS
AND LOT'S OF AWARDS,
AND BACKING NEXT YEAR!

"I Ham What I Ham"

[GEORGE HEARN *is discovered, rouged and lipsticked
but imperious as hell, in* La Cage *wig, necklace, and
boa. Suddenly, he breaks into tears, overcome by the
injustice of it all.*]

GEORGE HEARN

I HAM WHAT I HAM,
AND WHEN I HAM, I GET OVATIONS.
THOUGH I MAKE YOU GAG,
DRESSING IN DRAG VENTS MY FRUSTRATIONS.
IT'S MY CHANCE
TO DRESS MYSELF IN PEARLS AND ERMINE,
MY CHANCE
TO BECOME THE WORLD'S NEXT ETHEL MERMAN.
IN PANTS, I'M A LAMB,
BUT IN A DRESS,
HEY, WORLD, I HAM WHAT I HAM!

I HAM WHAT I HAM,
AND WHEN I HAM, I AM A PHONY.
WHO CARES IF I SWISH?
IT'S WORTH THE DISH TO WIN A TONY!
IT'S MY PART,
SO I'LL RANT AND RAVE LIKE MUSSOLINI.
SO WHAT
IF I PLAY IT LIKE A QUEENIE SWEENEY?

[*Suddenly, he whips out a bracelet and fastens it
around his arm. He shouts.*]

At last, my arm is complete again!

THIS LYRIC'S A SHAM—
LIKEWISE, I AM.
THAT'S WHY I HAM WHAT I HAM!

[*He rips off the wig and strikes a defiant pose.*]

"The Catchy Tune is Now"

MALE CAST MEMBER

WE MURDER EV'RY BROADWAY SHOW & EV'RY STAR
BUT IF YOU THINKING THAT YOUR THROUGH
STAY WHERE YOU
THERE STILL IS ONE SHOW THAT NEEDS FURTHER
    MUTILATION IT'S
LA CAGE AUX FOLLES

ALL

LA CAGE AUX FOLLES
DID WE FORGET TO SPOOF
LA CAGE AUX FOLLES
NO SHOW IS SLANDER PROOF

CAST MEMBER

WE COULD TRASH ITS GAUDY DISPLAYS
OR THE WAY THAT IT HOMOGENIZED GAYS

ANOTHER ACTOR

WE COULD DISCUSS THE WAY THEY WATERED
    DOWN THE PLOT

YET ANOTHER ACTOR

WE COULD DISCUSS THE ORCHESTRATIONS

THIRD ACTOR

BUT LET'S NOT

ALL

HERE'S OUR COMPOSER JERRY HERMANN
TO ELABORATE ON HIS WEAK SPOT

JERRY HERMAN

THE CATCHY TUNE IS NOW
I'LL STOP THE PLOT TO HAVE A SING ALONG
THE CATCHY TUNE IS HOW
I GET SINATRA TO RECORD A BROADWAY SONG

SO HOLD YOUR EARS & BREATH
WE'LL SING TEN REPETITIONS ANYHOW
AND BEAT THIS SONG TO DEATH
BECAUSE THE CATCHY TUNE IS NOW

ALL

LOUD!

JERRY

IT'S TRUE WE SING LOUD ANYWAY

ALL

LOUD!

GIRL (UP THE OCTAVE)

. . . LOUD!

GIRL & MAN

THE BALCONY'S SO FAR AWAY

JERRY

SO LEARN THIS LYRIC FAST
BECAUSE WE'LL TEST YOU
AND YOU MUST COMPLY
YOU CAN'T LEAVE TILL YOU PASSED
YOU LEARN THIS CATCHY TUNE
OR DIE OR DIE OR DIE

ALL

THE CATCHY TUNE IS NOW

WE'LL STOP THE PLOT TO HAVE A SING ALONG

THE CATCHY TUNE IS HOW

JERRY

WE GET SINATRA TO RECORD A BROADWAY SONG

ALL

SO HOLD YOUR EARS & BREATH
WE'LL SING TEN REPETITIONS ANYHOW
AND BEAT THIS SONG TO DEATH
YOU'LL THE CATCHY TUNE OR DIE
OR DIE! OR DIE!
GOODBYE! GOODBYE!

"RSC Gavotte"

CHORUS

EV'RYONE WHO SHOULD BE HERE IS HERE
EV'RY STAR AND THEATRE QUEER IS HERE
WHAT A GRIPPING
ABSOLUTELY RIPPING
EV'NING AT A ROYAL SHAKESPEARE PLAY.

ALL THE THEATRE CONNOISSEURS ARE POSING IN
    THEIR FURS,
LOOKING *TRES BLASÉ*.
THEY SAY, "THEATRE REALLY ISN'T THEATRE
IF IT'S NOT A ROYAL SHAKESPEARE PLAY."

THRILLING FICTION,
FLAWLESS DICTION
BROADWAY, WAKE UP!
THEY DO EVEN BETTER MAKEUP.

LAST YEAR *NICKLEBY*
HAD A SMASHING RUN,
THIS YEAR *MUCH ADO*—
THERE IS THE CUE,

THEY'RE STARTING, LOOK!
IT HAS BEGUN!

[*We hear a mish-mash of noise: British garble,
swordplay, grunts of death, a scream, and polite
applause.*]

THAT WAS CULTUR'LLY ORGASMIC;
JACOBY OUTDID LORD OLIVIER.
WITH HIS CRONIES
HE'LL WIN ALL THE TONYS
ACTING IN A ROYAL SHAKESPEARE PLAY.

THOUGH A FELLOW ACTOR'S JOB THEY STEAL,
IT'S OUR ONLY SOURCE OF SNOB APPEAL,
SO WE CHEER THEM
EVEN THOUGH WE FEAR THEM
AND CONNOT DECIPHER WHAT THE SAY.
[Alternate lyric: EVEN THOUGH THEY MIGHT OWN
    ALL BROADWAY.]
BUT TO BE "IN,"
SEE THE RSC IN
ANY BRITISH ROYAL SHAKESPEARE PLAY!

"Hey, Bob Fosse"

[*Silhouetted against the back wall, with their backs
to the audience, are a* WOMAN *and two* MEN. *The*
WOMAN *is center, in a red sequined dress and
carrying a shoulder bag; the* MEN *wear bowlers,
white gloves, and sequined jacket, but with no ties.
Advancing downstage, spreading their fingers, they
sing.*]

ALL

THE MINUTE WE WALK ON THE STAGE,
YOU CAN TELL WE HAVE A STYLE OF DISTINCTION,
A GOOD DIRECTOR.
BOB FOSSE, YOU'RE OUR GUY.

WOMAN

SAY, WOULDN'T YOU LIKE TO KNOW WHAT'S GOIN'
　　ON IN MY THIGH?

[*She kicks.*]

ALL

YOUR DANCES ARE RIGHT TO THE POINT,
AND ALTHOUGH THEY'VE GOT THAT RAZZLE-
　　DAZZLE LOOK,
HEY, BOB FOSSE!

SPEND . . . A LITTLE TIME ON THE BOOK.

MAN #2

DON'T YOU WANT A GOOD PLOT, PLOT, PLOT?

MAN #1

DON'T YOU CARE ABOUT LAUGHS, LAUGHS,
　　LAUGHS?

[*Repeat.*]

WOMAN

YOU FORGOT 'EM IN . . .

AN #2

PLOT . . .

MAN #1

LAUGHS . . .

WOMAN

BIG DEAL.

MAN #2

PLOT.

MAN #1

LAUGHS . . .

WOMAN

BIG DEAL.

MAN #2

PLOT . . .

MAN #1

LAUGHS . . .

WOMAN

BIG DEAL!!!

MAN #1

Yeah, the lights are cool, but how about turning 'em on
　　so we can see the . . .

ALL

PLOT!

WOMAN

All those sexy bods, but . . .

MAN #2

We're ready for some . . .

ALL

LAUGHS!

MAN #1

Why don't you use an original score . . .

WOMAN

. . . that has something to do with the . . .

ALL

STORY!

MAN #2

Instead of *Sweet Charity,* let's revive . . .

WOMAN

DAMN YANKEES

ALL

AND FORGET ABOUT
BIG DEEAALL!!!

THE MINUTE WE WALK ON THE STAGE . . .

[*Blackout.*]

YOU START CHANGING LIGHTS
AND RAISING SMOKE SCREENS
AND SPINNING SCEN'RY.

[*Lights up.*]

MAN #2

[*Disoriented.*]

SO CLEVER . . .

MAN #2

[*Likewise.*]

SO REFINED . . .

WOMAN

BUT EVERYTHING IS SO WILD,
YOU LEAVE THE ACTORS BEHIND.

ALL

THE STORY GETS WAY OFF THE POINT.

[MAN #2 *slams into the others.*]

AND YA HAVE TO DO A REWRITE, HOOK OR CROOK.
HEY, BOB FOSSE!

[*Each does a signature Fosse move.*]

HEY, BOB FOSSE!

[*They run upstage, waving their arms.*]

HEY, BOB FOSSE!!!

WOMAN

SPEND . . . A LITTLE TIME ON THE BOOK.

THE MEN

[*As they sidestep off, doing Fosse hands.*]

PLOT, LAUGHS, STORY,
PLOT, LAUGHS, STORY,
PLOT, LAUGHS, STORY.

WOMAN

How's about it, Bobby? Yeah!

"Barbra: The Broadway Album"

BARBRA

MEMORIES . . . PEOPLE . . .
BARBRA . . . STREISAND . . .

THERE'S A SHOW FOR ME,
SOMEDAY A SHOW FOR ME
FUNNY GIRL WAS A BROADWAY PLAY.
I'LL BE BACK SOMEDAY . . .

THERE'S A SCORE FOR ME,
A SONDHEIM SCORE FOR ME.
IF HE WON'T WRITE IT, THE BEE GEES WILL
SONGS LIKE THIS, SONGS LIKE "BILL"

BACK ON BROADWAY!
NO ONE WITH TALENT RESIDES THERE;
I'LL BE THE PRINCESS OF TIDES THERE
SOMEDAY . . .

[*Wild reverb.*]

SOMEDAY . . . SOMEDAY . . . SOMEDAY . . . SOMEDAY

THERE'S A ROLE FOR ME,
A JUICY ROLE FOR ME.
MAYBE SYBIL, GEORGE SAND, OR TESS,
MAYBE PORGY AS WELL AS BESS!
BARBRA . . . BROADWAY . . . SOMEDAY . . .

"76 Hit Shows" (with "Trouble" Reprise)

ROBERT PRESTON

FOLKS, LISTEN!
MAY I HAVE YOUR ATTENTION, PLEASE,
YOU ATTENTION, PLEASE.
I CAN DEAL WITH THIS TROUBLE, FRIENDS,
WITH A WAVE OF MY HAND, THIS VERY HAND.
YOU CAN ARGUE IF YOU WILL,
BUT WHEN I PLAYED HAROLD HILL
THERE WERE PLENTY OF SHOWS,
AND ALL WERE IN DEMAND.

WELL, A MIRACLE'LL DO IT, MY FRIENDS
OR MAYBE JUST A REAL SHOW,
DO YOU HEAR ME?
BROADWAY'S GOTTA HAVE A GOOD SHOW
AND I MEAN WE NEED IT TODAY!
WITH BOOK AND SONGS THAT MAKE YOU SMILE,
DONE WITH CRAFT AND LOTS OF STYLE.

[*He speaks as he changes from his tux jacket into his* Music Man *jacket.*]

As sure as the Nederlanders print little green tickets, the Broadway I knew and loved will come back. And you'll see the glitter of lights and the flashing of neon. You'll hear the magic of soaring music and the shimmer of trumpets.

[*He sings the first few notes of the* Gypsy *overture.*]

TA TA TA TA!

And you'll feel something akin to the electric thrill I was once a part of, when Judy Holliday, Alfred Drake, Mary Martin, Rodgers and Hammerstein, Lerner and Lowe, Cole Porter, and the great Ethel Merman all had shows on Broadway in the same historic decade!

76 HIT SHOWS ON THE GREAT WHITE WAY,
WITH 110 HIT PLAYS DOWN THE STREET.
EV'RY THEATRE HAD ROWS AND ROWS
FILLED WITH FOLK IN FANCY CLOTHES,
EV'RY SONG WOULD BRING THEM TO THEIR FEET.

[*Offstage whistle.* MAN *and* WOMAN *enter, similarly dressed.* WOMAN *puts hat on pianist.*]

ALL

76 HIT SHOWS RAN FOR YEARS AND YEARS,
WITH 110 REVUES RIGHT BEHIND.

MAN

ALTHOUGH ACTORS WOULD COME IN MOBS

ALL

THERE WERE LOTS AND LOTS OF JOBS

MAN

THERE WERE SHOWS OF EV'RY TYPE AND KIND!

WOMAN

THEY WOULD START THE THRILLING OVERTURE
AT HALF PAST EIGHT

MAN

THUNDERING, THUNDERING TUNES FROM *MUSIC
    MAN*

WOMAN

MY FAIR LADY, WEST SIDE STORY, KISS ME KATE . . .

MAN

. . . WERE SO GREAT, THEY OUTRAN *PETER PAN*.

WOMAN

ETHEL MERMAN STARRED AS ANNIE OAK AND
    MAMA ROSE—
THUNDERING, THUNDERING, LOUDER THAN A ROAR!

ALL

EVERYBODY DID THEIR PART
WHEN SHOWS HAD BOOKS WITH LOTS OF HEART
AND FIVE STANDARD SONGS IN EVERY SCORE!

76 HIT SHOWS ON THE GREAT WHITE WAY,
WITH 110 HIT PLAYS DOWN THE STREET.
EV'RY THEATRE HAD ROWS AND ROWS
FILLED WITH FOLK IN FANCY CLOTHES
EV'RY SONG WOULD BRING THEM TO THEIR FEET!

76 HIT SHOWS RAN FOR YEARS AND YEARS,
WITH 110 REVUES RIGHT BEHIND.
ALTHOUGH ACTORS WOULD COME IN MOBS,
THERE WERE LOTS AND LOTS OF JOBS,
THERE WERE SHOWS OF EV'RY TYPE AND KIND.

ETHEL MERMAN STARRED AS ANNIE OAK AND
    MAMA ROSE
THUNDERING! THUNDERING! LOUDER THAN A ROAR,
BUT IF WE LOOK STRAIGHT AHEAD,
WE'LL SEE THAT THEATRE ISN'T DEAD
AND MIGHT YET BE GREATER THAN BEFORE!

Barbara Walsh

I had done *Forbidden Broadway* briefly as a fill-in, and then in 1986 I went into the show for about a year and a half. I auditioned with a piece I had written about Barbra Streisand doing a musical version of *Out of Africa,* and Gerard subsequently wrote the Barbra "Somewhere" parody for me: "There's a show for me, someday a show for me . . ."

Part of the madness of *Forbidden* was the confined space. There were no wings whatsoever, and the dressing room was the size of my pinky. We had four adults in there, throwing things around and changing costumes for ninety minutes. It was a whole other show backstage.

A really wacky experience that sticks in my mind was one night when I was doing "Chita/Rita." After that, I had to do the Merman number. So I was wildly changing backstage, and somehow the Chita wig got caught under the tulle of my Merman dress. I was in the middle of the number before I realized there was something wrong—so I reached into the dress, pulled the wig out, and improvised for a few seconds. There were always things going wrong like that, but it was a blast.

I loved doing Bernadette Peters. Gerard wrote this very funny number to the tune of "Tell Me on a Sunday" from *Song and Dance;* it was called "See Me on a Monday," and it was all about Bernadette telling the audience to come see the show when she was rested, because she was having vocal problems.

It was fun to meet all the celebrities who came to the show. I met Mary Tyler Moore, Diane Sawyer, Shelley Winters! At one point, our opening number had a reference to Mary Beth Hurt, of all people. So there we were, belting out her name over and over, and I noticed her sitting in the audience. It was so odd.

For me, one of the greatest things about *Forbidden Broadway* was that I got a Hirschfeld in Enid Nemy's column in the *New York Times.* The reviews for the show had been terrific, and the press rep called me up and said, "You're going to have a Hirschfeld!" It was a really big deal. I spoke with Margo Feiden, whose gallery handled

Barbara Walsh spoofs Bernadette Peters in *Song and Dance*.

all of his art. She called me and said, "I can't wait to show you this gorgeous portrait." I said, "How much would it cost me to buy it?" She said, "Are you sitting down? It's twenty-five hundred dollars." That was a lot of money for me back then, so I put away $25 a week, and about three years later I was able to buy the Hirschfeld. I'm glad I did, because it's pretty stunning; you can see the pencil line where he sketched it, and he got my eyebrows and posture really well.

I'm very proud that I'm in the select group of people who were in *Forbidden Broadway* and later had someone else parody them in the show. Janet Dickinson did a great job of imitating me as Joanne in *Company*. I went to see the show with Raúl Esparza, and he seemed to enjoy his parody—but I think I laughed at it a little more than he did!

Cats, Phantoms, and More Misérables: The British Invasion: 1988–90

At the end of the '80s, most of the good shows on Broadway had been running for years, and that laid the groundwork for the British invasion. Cameron Mackintosh and Andrew Lloyd Webber had become tremendous creative forces, plus it was much cheaper to produce shows in London at that time. The dollar was very strong, and a lot New Yorkers were visiting London and talking about what was going on there: "Have you seen *Les Miz*? Have you seen *Phantom*?"

We thought we should move *Forbidden Broadway* to a different venue and make it more of an Off-Broadway show than a cabaret entertainment. So we closed the show for a while; it wasn't running in New York from September '87 to September '88, but it continued to play in Boston at the Park Plaza Hotel. We introduced a lot of new material there, including the first versions of the *Phantom* and *Les Miz* numbers. I was dating a very talented man named Phill George, and when I went to Boston to work on the show, I asked him to come along. He subsequently took over one of the roles and started to help choreograph some of the numbers.

Meanwhile, in New York, I was trying to put together a new production company. I negotiated to move *Forbidden Broadway* to

David B. McDonald, Michael McGrath, and Roxie Lucas spoofing British musicals.

Left: David B. McDonald, Roxie Lucas, Michael McGrath, Toni DiBuono, and Phil Fortenberry. Right: David B. McDonald and Toni DiBuono in "The Phantom of the Musical."

the Village Gate, which in the '70s had been popular with shows like *Scrambled Feet*, but that deal fell through. I went to my lawyer, the brilliant Mark Sendroff, who has

guided the show and my career since 1983, and asked him for advice. He suggested that we move to Theatre East, a little-used venue on East 60th Street, and that Jonathan Scharer should take over as producer. Jonathan set up a production company, brought Glenna Freedman in as our press agent—and in no time at all, we were hanging our Mylar curtain at Theatre East, ready to spoof the British invasion.

Obviously, *Les Miz* and *Phantom* and the other British shows struck a chord with people. I think that's largely because they were operettas, although that dirty word was never used in the marketing. No one had done operettas on Broadway for decades, and there's something to be said for them. All of the British shows have the weight of operas in terms of their dramatic stories and huge scenic productions, but the music is easily digestible, so the audience can readily pick up the tunes. You don't have to listen to those scores ahead of time in order to

Left: Toni DiBuono (as Patti LuPone), Michael McGrath (as M. Butterfly), and Roxie Lucas (as Little Bad Riding Hood). Right: Gerard and the 1988 cast.

appreciate them. Also, because the Brit shows are through-sung and don't have to pause for spoken dialogue, it's easy for them to keep up a high level of energy for the entire performance.

Of course, the tone of *Forbidden Broadway* changes with the type of shows that are spoofed, according to whether they're fluffy or dark or very broad. During the British invasion, our show seemed very British. That was the first time people suggested we should bring it to London.

I think *Forbidden Broadway* really came of age in the late '80s; the production values increased and the comedy became more exact. What we lost in terms of "Hey, kids, let's put on a show" charm, we gained in terms of sharpness and focus. For example, we had spent years honing the Merman-Martin number, but it really "hit the heights" when Toni DiBuono and Roxie Lucas did an exact character analysis and vocal imitation of those two great stars. Among the other Broadway luminaries we spoofed were

Elaine Stritch, Madonna, and B. D. Wong. We also had a devastating lampoon of Patti LuPone in *Anything Goes,* singing "I Get a Kick Out of Me."

But stars were becoming less integral to the Broadway scene as the big-budget Brit musicals became the stars. Though people loved *Cats, Les Miz, Phantom,* and *Miss Saigon,* all of those shows were ridiculous in a way, because they were so huge and melodramatic. In other words, they were just perfect for spoofing. That was a major reason why we felt we should move our show into an Off-Broadway theatre and add more costumes; *Forbidden Broadway* was an established hit, and it looked like we were going to be around for a while.

"Fugue for Scalpers"

I GOT THE SHOW RIGHT HERE,
IT WON A PRIZE LAST YEAR,
ABOUT A CHINESE COMMUNIST GEISHA QUEER.
HALF PRICE. HALF PRICE.
JOHN LITHGOW IS OUT;
HALF PRICE.
THE STANDY IS NOT AS NICE,
NO DICE! HALF PRICE.

I GOT TWO TICKETS HERE
FOR *PHANTOM* IN THE REAR,
BUT YOU CAN SEE REAL FINE THROUGH THE
   CHANDELIER.
TOP PRICE! TOP PRICE!
GOOD SEATS ONLY TWICE THE PRICE;
MY WIFE KEPT THE SEATS ON ICE.
TOP PRICE! TOP PRICE!

FOR JUST A SERVICE FEE,
SEE MISER-ABL-EE;
IT'S JUST A LITTLE LONG, BUT YOU'RE OUT BY THREE.
GOOD DEAL! GOOD DEAL!
LES MIZ TICKETS AT A STEAL.
INCLUDES SLEEPING BAG AND MEAL
AND TOY BASTILLE.

YOU'RE GONNA SEE JUST FINE
ABOVE THE STEEP INCLINE
BECAUSE THE MEZZ IS EMPTY AT *CHORUS LINE.*
ONE FREE. ONE FREE.
BUY ONE AND YOU GET ONE FREE.
OR JUST SELL IT BACK TO ME—
NO FEE. ONE FREE.

[*Additional verses added in later years.*]

AND THERE'S A FAIRY FEAST
AT *BEAUTY AND THE BEAST,*
A BLOCK OF STUDENT TICKETS HAS BEEN
   RELEASED.
ONE PAIR: TWO GRAND!
OF COURSE, YOU MIGHT HAVE TO STAND.
TWO TICKETS TO DISNEY-BLAND!
ONE PAIR: TWO GRAND!

AND IF YA GOT A DATE
OR COUSIN THAT YOU HATE,
WHY DON'T YOU TAKE THEM OVER TO *KISS ME, KATE*?
TWO PAIRS! TWO PAIRS!
OKAY, THEY'RE ON FOLDING CHAIRS.
IT'S THAT OR SIT ON THE STAIRS;
FOR *KATE,* WHO CARES?

AND IF YOU WANNA BRING
THE FAM'LY FOR A FLING,
I GOT SOME RED HOT TICKETS TO *LION KING.*
TOP PRICE! TOP PRICE!
I WON THEM WITH LOADED DICE;
I RIPPED OFF SOME MICKEY MICE.
TOP PRICE! TOP PRICE!

CHORUS LINE! CHANDELIER! COMMIE QUEER!
I GOT THE SHOW RIGHT HERE!

"Cameron Mackintosh"

CAMERON

I'M CAM'RON MACKINTOSH,
NAPOLEON OF BROADWAY,
I'VE PRODUCED EV'RY NEW HIT SHOW.
I'M CAM'RON MACKINTOSH,
THE EMPEROR OF BROADWAY,
BUT THERE'S SOMETHING YOU OUGHT TO KNOW:
THOUGH I CAME, I SAW, I CONQUERED
WITH MY SHOW BUSINESS FINESSE,
AND MY *MISS SAIGON* MIS-CASTING
PUT THE UNION IN DISTRESS,
IT'S MY MARKETING OF SOUVENIRS
THAT'S MORE OF A SUCCESS . . .

SWEATSHIRTS AND T-SHIRTS
AND BLANKETS AND MITTENS,
WHISKERS AND CAT EARS
AND LITTLE STUFFED KITTENS,
OLD *LES MIZ* BODICES HELD UP BY STRINGS:
THESE ARE A FEW OF MY SOUVENIR THINGS.

RECORDS AND CDS
AND VOCAL SELECTIONS,
CAT GLOVES AND CAT TAILS
FROM CAT VIVISECTIONS,
LLOYD WEBBER DOLLS AND COLM WILKINSON RINGS:

THESE ARE A FEW OF MY SOUVENIR THINGS.

WHEN A SHOW FLOPS,
WHEN THE GROSS DROPS,
WHEN A WEEK IS SLOW,
I MARKET AND MERCHANDISE SOUVENIR THINGS,
AND GROSSES DON'T SEEM SO LOW!

KEY CHAINS AND WALLETS
AND CHANDELIER CRYSTALS,
COFFEE CUPS, PLAYING CARS,
JEAN VALJEAN PISTOLS,
TOY HELICOPTERS AND TURNTABLE SPRINGS:
THESE ARE A FEW OF MY SOUVENIR THINGS.

LEZ MIZ CHOC'LATES
SHAPED LIKE ORPHANS,
PATCHES FOR YOUR SLEEVE—
IT'S ONE HUNDRED DOLLARS
TO COME SEE THE SHOW,
AND ONE HUNDRED MORE TO LEAVE!

"Never, Never Panned"

MARY MARTIN

MY NAME IS MARY MARTIN AND
AS PETER PAN I'M GRAND.
SOME CRITICS HESITATE
BUT THEY ALWAYS THINK I'M GREAT.
I'M NEVER, NEVER PANNED.

TO BE A CRITICS' DARLING, SING
IMPECCABLY BUT BLAND.
JUST KEEP AN OPEN THROAT
AND THEN SCOOP ON EV'RY NOTE,
YOU'RE NEVER, NEVER PANNED.

YOU'LL WIN A TONY IF YOU'RE COY-LIKE,
MORE PRECIOUS FAR THAN GOLD.

AND, IF YOU DRESS UP BOY-LIKE,
YOUR AUTBIO'S PRESOLD.

SO COME WITH ME WHERE CRITICS RAVE
AND MEANIES UNDERSTAND.
YOU TOO CAN BE A STAR
LIKE MY SON, WHO PLAYS J.R.
ON *DALLAS*.
WE'RE NEVER, NEVER PANNED!

"I Get a Kick Out of Me"

[*Two* SAILORS *are discovered holding up a life preserver that reads* Anything Goes. *The life preserver frames the face of* PATTI LUPONE. *The sailors sing.*]

SAILORS

IN OLDEN DAYS, THIS SHOW WAS SHOCKING
'CAUSE MERMAN WOULD KEEP THEM ROCKING
BUT NOW THEY PHONE . . .

PATTI

PATTI LUPONE.

SAILORS

GOOD CRITICS, TOO, WHO USED FOUR-LETTER
    WORDS,
NOW HAVE TO SEARCH FOR BETTER WORDS.
HOW SHE'S GROWN!

PATTI

PATTI LUPONE!

[*She sings with typical, mush-mouthed diction.*]

AN' SO IF MY HAY (HAIR) YOU LIKE
OR MY HEH (HEAD) YOU LIKE
OR MY NEH (NECK) YOU LIKE
OR MY LEH (LEGS) YOU LIKE

OR MY AH (ARMS) YOU LIKE
ALIKE ALIKE YOU LIKE,

[*She brushes the life preserver aside.*]

JUST LIKE EVA PERON!

[*Dance break to prerecorded tape, into which* PATTI, *bored to death, puts minimal effort. The* SAILORS, *of course, chorus-boy-smile up a storm.*]

PATTI LUPONE!

ONE SAILOR

PATTI LA . . .

OTHER SAILOR

PATTI LA . . .

ALL

PATTI LA . . . PONE!

[SAILORS *exit as* PATTI *shoos them off.*]

PATTI

[*She returns to the mike and throws her arms up in the Evita pose; lights dim to spot as she sings.*]

MY STORY IS MUCH TOO SAD TO BE TOLD:
I'VE PLAYED NEARLY EVERYTHING, AND I'M NOT
    VERY OLD.
THE ONLY EXCEPTION I KNOW IS THE CASE
WHEN I'M ACTING FOR BOURGEOISIE,
FIGHTING VAINLY THE OLD ENNUI,
AND I SUDDENLY TURN AND SEE
MY FABULOUS FACE!

I GET NO KICK IN A SHOW.
A BROADWAY SONG DOESN'T THRILL ME FOR LONG;
EVITA WAS NO HAPPY SPREE.

BUT I GET A KICK OUT OF ME.

SOME SNORT COCAINE WHEN THEY'RE LOW;
I NEED NO SNIFF, 'CAUSE I THINK, "WHAT'S THE DIFF?"
I'M ALREADY TERRIFIC TO SEE,
AND I GET A KICK OUT OF ME.

I GET A KICK WHEN I SNARL AND SNEER
AND PEOPLE CHEER OUT FOR ME.
I GET A KICK, THOUGH MY VOICE IS SHRILL
'CAUSE FRANK RICH WILL STILL ADORE ME.

I GET NO KICK ON A STAGE.
FLASHING SOME GUY WITH MY STUBBY KAYE THIGH
ISN'T WHY I AM IN THIS DEBRIS.
IT'S—I GET A KICK OUT OF ME!

I GET A KICK WHEN I FIRE MY MACHINE-GUN-LIKE
    VIBRATO.
I GET A KICK WHEN THE LYRIC'S CRUSHED INTO MY
    RUSHED OBLIGATO.
I GOT NO KICK IN "LES MIZ."
DYING FOR ART
IN THE PART OF A TART
BROKE MY HEART
AT THE SMART R.S.C.
BUT I GET A KICK OUT OF ME!

"Into the Words"

[*Pulsating music. Lights up on a bearded man at the side of the stage. He is* STEPHEN SONDHEIM.]

STEPHEN

Once upon a time, there was a great songwriter called Stephen Sondheim. He had many, many hit shows, among which were *Sunday in the Park with George*. [DOT *enters.*]

FEMALE 2

I WISH . . .

[*A* SWEENEY TODD *enters.*]

STEPHEN

Sweeney Todd . . .

MALE 1

I WISH . . .

STEPHEN

. . . and the fairy tale musical of 1988, *Into the Woods*.

[*A* LITTLE RED RIDING HOOD *enters.*]

FEMALE 1

I WISH . . .

STEPHEN

All the characters in all the shows were very happy to be in a prestigious Sondheim musical, except for a few things . . .

FEMALE 1

I WISH.
I WISH THIS SHOW WAS MORE MELODIC!
I WISH.

MALE 1

I WISH.
I WISH THIS SHOW WAS NOT SO BLOODY.
I WISH.

FEMALE 2

I WISH.
I WISH THE LYRICS WEREN'T SO WORDY.
I WISH.

STEPHEN

You see, with Sondheim shows, people sometimes miss the point. They're supposed to listen and go . . . into the words.

FEMALE 1

INTO THE WORDS

MALE 1

INTO THE WORDS

FEMALE 2

INTO THE WORDS

ALL

INTO THE WORDS

STEPHEN

THE METAPHORS, THE SYNONYMS, THE PERFECT
    SCAN

ALL

INTO THE WORDS

STEPHEN

THE DETAIL AND THE TRICKY LITTLE PHRASES

ALL

INTO THE WORDS

MALE 1

THE WHAT, THE WHERE, THE WHEN, THE WHY
THE PLOT BEGAN

ALL

INTO THE WORDS

FEMALE 2

THE WORK, THE CRAFT

FEMALE 1

THAT GARNERS ALL THE PRAISES

ALL

INTO THE WORDS!
INTO THE WORDS!

FEMALE 2

THE MUSIC WAITS

ALL

INTO THE WORDS!
INTO THE WORDS!

STEPHEN

THE LYRIC STATES THAT

ALL

INTO THE WORDS

STEPHEN

YOUR CONTENT ALWAYS COMES BEFORE YOUR
    FORM AND STYLE

ALL

INTO THE WORDS

STEPHEN

INTERNAL RHYMES THAT EVEN BAFFLED MERMAN

ALL

INTO THE WORDS,
A QUICK EXCHANGE,
SO VERY STRANGE, YOU'LL CRY AND SMILE

STEPHEN

AND NEVER REPEAT A VERSE OR BRIDGE;
THIS ISN'T JERRY HERMAN

ALL

INTO THE WORDS

INTO THE WORDS

STEPHEN

THEY ALWAYS TEACH

ALL

INTO THE WORDS

INTO THE WORDS

STEPHEN

TO HEAR ME PREACH

THE THOUGHTS ARE CLEAR

(IF UNDERSTOOD).

I HAVE NO PEER,

'CAUSE I'M SO GOOD.

THE SCORE IS THE STAR

THE STARS ARE JUST WOOD,

I SORT OF HATE TO ASK IT

BUT WHAT'S A RYHME FOR BASKET?

ALL

INTO THE WORDS

THAT TRIP YOUR LIP AND FRY YOUR BRAIN

AND SPRAIN YOUR TOUNGE,

INTO THE WORDS—

A CAVE SO DARK, YOU'D BETTER BRING A TORCH IN.

INTO THE WORDS

THAT FLY AND TRY TO MAKE YOU CHOKE

THE JOKE YOU'VE SUNG.

INTO THE WORDS—

MORE VOWELS THAN THEY SELL

ON *WHEEL OF FORTUNE.*

STEPHEN

Now, some people say that my songs aren't catchy. But that's not true. And to prove it, I'll conduct a Sondheim sing-along. Now everybody sing and just follow the bouncing razor. Ready? One-two-twelve-eight.

[ALL *repeat the two verses, with the audience.*]

Very good. You all graduate! So now let's do it up to tempo. One-two-twelve-eight.

ALL

[*Repeat the two verses double time, with the audience.*]

WE'RE INTO THE SYLLABLES

INTO THE ANTONYMS

INTO THE METAPHORS

INTO THE SYNONYMS

FEMALES	MALE 1	SONDHEIM
INTO THE SYLLABLES	ARE YOU SURE	CAREFUL! YOUR
INTO THE ANTONYMS	YOU UNDERSTAND?	DICTION
INTO THE METAPHORS	ARE YOU SURE	CAREFUL! YOUR
INTO THE SYNONYMS	THAT YOU VERSTEH?	DICTION
INTO THE SYLLABLES	ARE YOU SURE	CAREFUL! YOUR
INTO THE ANTONYMS	THAT YOU CAPISH?	DICTION
INTO THE METAPHORS	AWAY WE GO	CAREFUL OF
AND THE . . .	INTO THE . . .	THE . . .

ALL

WORDS!

"M. Butterfly"

[*Lights up on an actor dressed in a bright yellow kimono and geisha wig. He sings in high falsetto voice.*]

M. BUTTERFLY

I'M M. BUTTERFLY,

I'M A CHINESE SPY

DRESSED IN A DRESS.

I MUST CONFESS,

FOR YOU'D NEVER GUESS;

I BLUSH TO LIE . . .

[*His voice changes to a husky male baritone.*]

I'M M. BUTTERFLY

[*Now the music changes.*]

M. BUTTERFLY,

STRANGEST SHOW SINCE *EQUUS.*

M. BUTTERFLY,

COMMIE SPIES IN DRAG.

JOHN LITHGOW THINKS HE'S A SHE,

THE SHE-HE DRIVES LITHGOW WILD,

AND WHEN HE SAYS HE'S WITH CHILD

YOU MURMUR "GEE . . .

I CAN'T GET BY

WHERE'D HE PUT HIS PEE-PEE?

THAT WEIRDO GUY

CAN'T TELL BOYS FROM GIRLS!"

AND SO HE CRUMBLES IN GRIEF

WHILE YOU WATCH IN STUNNED DISBELIEF.

IT'S ONE SWELL LIE:

M. BUTTERFLY!

[*The music changes, and* M. BUTTERFLY *stabs himself.*]

"Madonna's Brain"

[*Lights up on* MAID *with feather duster.*]

MAID

QUIT, PROFESSOR MAMET.

QUIT, PROFESSOR MAMET.

TEACH MADONNA HOW TO SPEAK?

PLEASE, QUIT, PROFESSOR MAMET!

THOUGH YOU WROTE

SPEED-THE-PLOW,

YOU CAN'T TEACH MADONNA HOW—

HOW TO MOVE,

HOW TO WALK,

NEVER MIND TO TALK!

And now, a scene from the Broadway play *Speed-the-Plow,* which starred Madonna.

[MAID *exits;* DAVID MAMET *and* RON SILVER *enter.* MADONNA *follows, script in hand.*]

MADONNA

Okay, how's this? [*Reads from script.*] "I know what it's like to be bad. I've been bad."

DAVID

Try again.

RON

Try again.

MADONNA

"I know what it's like to be bad. I—'ve been bad."

[*She throws the script offstage, crosses to mike and vogues with her hands.*]

DAVID

I strain in vain to train Madonna's brain.

MADONNA

I strain in vain to train Madonna's brain.

DAVID

Again.

MADONNA

[*Music begins.*]

I STRAIN IN VAIN TO TRAIN MADONNA'S BRAIN.

DAVID

I THINK SHE'S GOT IT.
I THINK SHE'S GOT IT.

MADONNA

I STRAIN IN VAIN TO TRAIN MADONNA'S BRAIN.

DAVID

SHE'S FUCKIN' GOT IT!
SHE'S FUCKIN' GOT IT!
NOW ONCE AGAIN, WHERE DO YOU STRAIN?

MADONNA

IN MY BRAIN!
IN MY BRAIN!

DAVID

AND WHAT'S YOUR TINY BRAIN?

MADONNA

INSANE! INSANE!

ALL THREE

WE STRAIN IN VAIN TO TRAIN MADONNA'S BRAIN!

DAVID

HA-HA!

ALL THREE

WE STRAIN IN VAIN TO TRAIN MADONNA'S BRAIN!

RON

AND WHAT ARE YOU DOING ON BROADWAY?

MADONNA

PRACTICING TO BE A [*sic*] ACTRESS
[RON *plunks out a tune on the piano.*]

MADONNA

HOW *KIND* OF YOU TO LET ME ACT.

ALL

NOT!

DAVID

NOW ONCE AGAIN, WHERE DOES IT RAIN?

MADONNA

IN MY BRAIN!
IN MY BRAIN!

RON

WHO WED YOUR SOGGY BRAIN?

MADONNA

SEAN PAIN!
SEAN PAIN!

ALL THREE

WE STRAIN IN VAIN TO TRAIN MADONNA'S BRAIN!
WE STRAIN IN VAIN TO TRAIN MADONNA'S BRAIN!

[RON *grabs* MADONNA; *they tango.* RON *spins her to* DAVID *and exits. Suddenly,* MADONNA *rips her dress off, revealing a sexy Merry Widow with tassels dangling from the breasts. Under it, she wears fishnet stockings. She uses the dress to play bullfighter with* DAVID *as the bull, then throws the dress offstage.*]

MADONNA

[*Flexing.*]

Justify my love!

DAVID

Justify your acting!

[*Aided by* DAVID, MADONNA *leaps atop the piano on her knees and throws a few bumps, then slides down to end with a leg in the air as* DAVID *slides to the floor, hands in the air.*]

BOTH

OLÉ!

"Phantom of the Musical"

[*Loud organ music. A pulsating disco beat. Lights up on a cloaked, masked figure, his cape spread like a bat. A chandelier lurks above. He steps forward.*]

OFFSTAGE CHORUS

THE PHANTOM OF THE MUSICAL IS HERE!

THE PHANTOM OF THE MUSICAL—

PHANTOM

I'M HERE!

HOW DOES MY MAGIC WORK,

YOU'RE BOUND TO ASK?

WHAT GOD-LIKE GIANTS LURK

BENEATH THIS MASK?

BUT NONE WILL EVER SEE

THE SECRET ME!

THE PHANTOM OF THE MUSICAL IS I—

ANDREW LLOYD WEBBER

[*He crosses right and drags out a terrified* WOMAN *in a wedding dress.*]

AND NOW I HAVE A LOVELY BRIDE

NAMED SARAH BRIGHTMAN AT MY SIDE.

I TRAPPED HER HERE,

KIDNAPPED HER HERE TO SING!

SHE

SQUEAK!

HE

SING!

SHE

SQUEAK!

HE

SING!

SHE

SQUEAK!

HE

SING!

SHE

SQUEAK!

[*As she turns to us, we see that she is wearing bunny teeth.*]

SHE

YOUR SCORES POUR FORTH A VEIL OF MELODY,

JUST LIKE A NIGHTINGALE ON LSD.

YOUR SOARING STRINGS SO LUSH, I GET A RUSH . . .

THE PHANTOM OF THE MUSICAL IS YOU,

ANDREW, MY DEAREST.

THE PHANTOM OF THE MUSICAL, BUT OOH,

THAT MASK IS THE QUEEREST.

HE

DON'T TOUCH!

SHE

WHY NOT? IT MUST BE HOT. ONE PEEK . . .

HE

HANDS OFF. YOU'LL ONLY SCOFF. NO!

SHE

YES!

HE

NO! THE PHANTOM OF THE MUSICAL IS . . .

[*She sneaks up behind him, goes for his mask, shrinks back, goes again and rip! Underneath, he is Mickey Mouse.*]

SHE

AAAAAHHHH!
HOW HIDEOUS! INSIDIOUS!
I MARRIED MICKEY MOUSE!

[*She makes as if to flee, but he grabs her wrist.*]

HE

DAMN YOU, SARAH! DAMN YOU, SARAH!
NOW YOU KNOW WHAT'S REALLY UNDERNEATH
THE GREATEST WRITER OF BROADWAY SHOWS.
SO YOU MUST DIE!

[*He hurls her upstage, under the chandelier.*]

GO!

[*He gestures to the chandelier. It falls. She screams as it impales her.*]

HE

BEWARE, THE PHANTOM ALWAYS LURKS ABOVE.
TAKE CARE, I EVEN KILLED THE GIRL I NEARLY LOVE
AS MUCH AS I!

[*He laughs hysterically as the lights fade to black.*]

FORBIDDEN MEMORIES: **Brad Oscar**

Brad Oscar.

I remember that we were in previews for the '93 edition at Theatre East—or "Theatre Beast," as it was affectionately known. Numbers came and went as they were tried and refined.

For two performances, the show included a real treasure of a number: Annie and Daddy Warbucks want to take in a Broadway show, but the ABCs are full of shows dealing with homosexuality and the AIDS epidemic, *Angels in America* being the leader of the pack. Daddy must explain to Annie why he can't take her to see these shows, and he does so in a song sung to the tune of "NYC," called . . . "HIV." Then I came out as Roy Cohn and chewed Annie out over something I can't recall.

Let's just say that this was our "Springtime for Hitler" moment. The audience on the first night—which happened to include a group from the New York City Gay Men's Chorus—just sat there, stunned that such a thing would ever be sung about. And the second night wasn't much better. So out the number went, but I still think it was rather brilliant in its reflection of what was going on in the American theater at the time. It was a brave move on Gerard's part.

In the same edition, I had to play Gregory Hines as Jelly Roll Morton in a tight Afro wig. Need I tell you that number also didn't last through previews?

I remember the evening when, during our *Spider Woman* number, Susanne Blakeslee somehow got cut and started to bleed all over her white Chita outfit. The audience thought it was part of the act. And I'll always remember the sound of Carol Burnett laughing from the audience when we performed at the Tiffany Theater in L.A. during the summer of '94. That distinctive laugh was the highest compliment one could receive.

Teeny Todds and Grim Hotels: 1991–95

One of the joys of writing Broadway parodies is that I have to see every show, but one of the burdens of writing Broadway parodies is that I have to see every show. Mind you, I'm rarely given comp tickets; I almost always have to pay my way in. So when I don't get my money's worth, I'm really not a happy camper. Perhaps this gives me an outlook that's more or less in line with that of the average theatregoer. It also helps if I bring along someone who's not a showbiz insider, so I can get another opinion.

While visiting my parents in Boston in late 1989, I thought it might be fun to bring my mother to see the out-of-town tryout of *Grand Hotel*. We had lovely box seats; that was a good thing, because my mother's theatre etiquette was never very good, and she'd often make comments during a show. As you might have heard, *Grand Hotel* had a rough time in Boston. My mother was rather confused by the minimalist staging and by the sets, which consisted largely of chairs and not much else. When one of the actors said, "People come, people go, nothing ever happens at the *Grand Hotel*," she retorted: "People come, people go, people move chairs." I immediately put that line into *Forbidden Broadway*. I mean, if you can't steal from your mother, who can you steal from?

Jeff Lyons, Susanne Blakeslee, Marilyn Pasekoff, and Herndon Lackey in "Grim Hotel."

Susanne Blakeslee, Jeff Lyons (as Jerome Robbins), and Bob Rogerson sing "Jerome, Jerome, a Helluva Guy!"

While our show was playing at Theatre East, revivals were really taking hold on Broadway. *Guys and Dolls* was a major revival of the early '90s, so big a hit that it was almost like a new show. There was the "Teeny Todd" take on *Sweeney Todd* at Circle in the Square, and there was *Gypsy* with Tyne Daly. *Jerome Robbins' Broadway* was a wonderful show, but it smacked of an era that had gone by. In the air, there was a general feeling of "We don't know how to do great new shows, so we'll just revive and revue the old ones."

Speaking of days gone by, Little Orphan Annie was struggling to make a comeback: *Annie 2* tried to come in from out of town, but failed in its first incarnation. A new version of the sequel came in later as *Annie Warbucks,* but it played Off-Broadway, not on. So it seemed appropriate that we now had a new and more durable spoof of *Annie:*

I'M THIRTY YEARS OLD

TOMORROW,

AND I HAVEN'T WORKED SINCE I DID *ANNIE*

WHEN I WAS TEN.

BUT MAYBE THERE'S HOPE TOMORROW,

MAYBE SOMEONE SOMEDAY MIGHT

BRING "ANNIE" BACK AGAIN!

REVIVE ME! REVIVE ME!

PLEASE SOMEONE REVIVE ME!

BEFORE MY RED HAIR TURNS GREY.

LAST TIME I WAS ROTTEN,

NOW "ANNIE'S" FORGOTTEN,

TOMORROW IS YESTERDAY!

There were also some great revivals of straight plays at that time, such as *Orpheus Descending* with Vanessa Redgrave. And there were some excellent London imports of straight plays, like *Lettice and Lovage* with Maggie Smith.

City of Angels was a classy, wonderfully clever addition to Broadway. Of course, it was itself a spoof or takeoff on *films noir* from the '40s, and I have since learned that

PLAYKILL*

PALSSON'S SUPPER CLUB

FORBIDDEN BROADWAY

Top: The original cast of *Forbidden Broadway:* Gerard Alessandrini, Nora Mae Lyng, Bill Carmichael, Chloe Webb, and Fred Barton. Bottom: Gerard, Bill, and Nora parody *The Pirates of Penzance*.

Top: Chloe, Bill, Nora, and Gerard spoof *Fiddler on the Roof*. Bottom: Roxie Lucas as Mary Martin and Toni DiBuono as Ethel Merman.

David B. McDonald, Michael McGrath,
Toni DiBuono, and Roxie Lucas:
Forbidden Broadway '88.

The British Invasion: Michael McGrath, David B. McDonald, Toni DiBuono, and Roxie Lucas slam *Les Miz*.

Susanne Blakeslee, Herndon Lackey, Mary Denise
Bentley, and Jeff Lyons have a go at *Miss-cast Saigon.*

Clockise from top left: The tenth-anniversary cast: Alix Korey, Patrick Quinn, Leah Hocking, and Michael McGrath; Christine Pedi, Brad Oscar, Susanne Blakeslee, and Craig Wells: *Forbidden Broadway '93;* **Phillip George, co-director of** *Forbidden Broadway.*

Gerard with the cast of *Forbidden Broadway 1991*: Herndon Lackey (as "Swill Rogers"), Susanne Blakeslee (in "The Secret Deodorant Garden"), Jeff Lyons (again forced to play Lea Salonga), and Mary Denise Bentley (in *Once on This Island*).

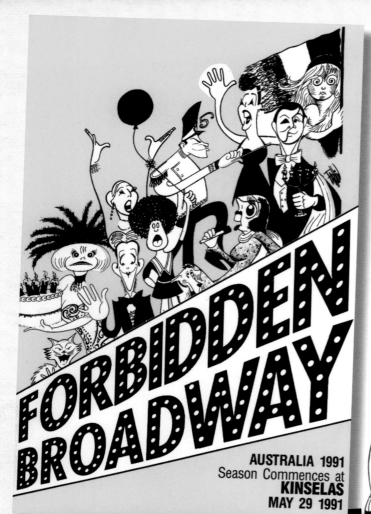

FORBIDDEN BROADWAY

AUSTRALIA 1991
Season Commences at
KINSELAS
MAY 29 1991

FORBIDDEN BROADWAY

ALL SINGING!
ALL LAUGHTER!
ALL HOLLYWOOD!

"NOT-TO-BE-MISSED!"
Hollywood Reporter

FORBIDDEN HOLLYWOOD

CREATED AND WRITTEN BY
GERARD ALESSANDRINI

The Smash Hit
Musical Spoof of the Movies!

Forbidden Broadway around the world.

Forbidden Broadway in Boston, Japan, and L.A.

Forbidden Broadway Backstage—Where the Real Show Is! Clockwise from top left: Chloe Webb as Mary Martin and Dee Hoty as Ethel Merman (but looking more like Lypsinka); Stephen Flaherty, when he was our pianist. Little did we know!; Gerard, buffed and waxed for Yul; and Christine Pedi, pushed by Gerard to the point of suicide.

Clockwise from top left: Chloe and Nora dress Bill in the busboys' area at Palsson's; Dee Hoty modeling her *Evita* costume; Rachel James, our stage manager's daughter, learned to sing "I Sleep with Everyone" for her second-grade class; and Dorothy Kiara, relegated to "Forbidden Fantine" after having starred on Broadway in *Nine*.

Clockwise from top left: Gerard, dressed and hyped to play Kurt in *"The Sound of Music* Part II"; Danny Gurwin and Felicia Finley, so crammed backstage at *Forbidden Broadway 2001* that they are forced to have sex in their *Aida* costumes; Andrea McArdle, the original Annie, gets into character backstage to play Forbidden Annie at a benefit; Phill George as King Arthur prepares to sing "I Wonder What the King is Drinking Tonight?"; Nora and Gerard backstage.

Forbidden Broadway
20th Anniversary Edition
Created and Written by GERARD ALESSANDRINI
FALLIN
17 Classic Selections *Plus* 8 PREVIOUSLY UNRELEASED TRACKS

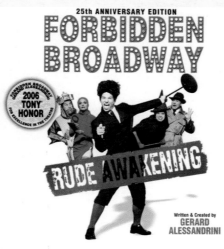

25th ANNIVERSARY EDITION
FORBIDDEN BROADWAY
2006 TONY HONOR FOR EXCELLENCE IN THE THEATER
RUDE AWAKENING
Written & Created by GERARD ALESSANDRINI

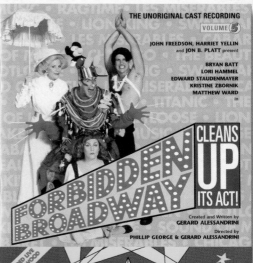

THE UNORIGINAL CAST RECORDING
VOLUME 5
JOHN FREEDSON, HARRIET YELLIN and JON B. PLATT present
BRYAN BATT
LORI HAMMEL
EDWARD STAUDENMAYER
KRISTINE ZBORNIK
MATTHEW WARD in
FORBIDDEN BROADWAY
CLEANS UP ITS ACT!
Created and Written by GERARD ALESSANDRINI
Directed by PHILLIP GEORGE & GERARD ALESSANDRINI

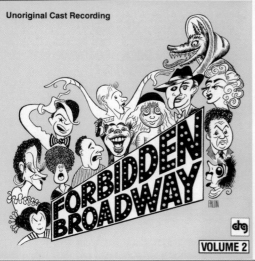

Unoriginal Cast Recording
FORBIDDEN BROADWAY
FALLIN
drg
VOLUME 2

ORIGINAL CAST RECORDING
drg RECORDS
FORBIDDEN BROADWAY
THE HIT MUSICAL REVUE

RECORDED LIVE IN HOLLYWOOD
FORBIDDEN HOLLYWOOD
THE HILARIOUS MUSICAL SPOOF OF TINSELTOWN
ORIGINAL CAST RECORDING
Fallin

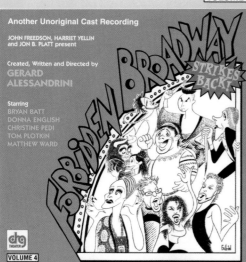

Another Unoriginal Cast Recording
JOHN FREEDSON, HARRIET YELLIN and JON B. PLATT present
Created, Written and Directed by GERARD ALESSANDRINI
FORBIDDEN BROADWAY STRIKES BACK!
Starring
BRYAN BATT
DONNA ENGLISH
CHRISTINE PEDI
TOM PLOTKIN
MATTHEW WARD
drg THEATER
VOLUME 4

The Unoriginal Cast Recording
Special Guest Vocal by Carol Channing
drg
FORBIDDEN BROADWAY
FALLIN
Vol 3

FORBIDDEN BROADWAY
SPECIAL VICTIMS UNIT
POLICE LINE
Created and Written by GERARD ALESSANDRINI

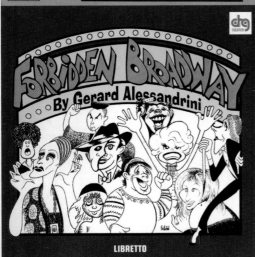

Forbidden Broadway
By Gerard Alessandrini
drg THEATER
LIBRETTO

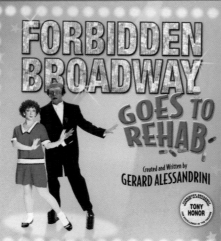

FORBIDDEN BROADWAY
GOES TO REHAB
Created and Written by GERARD ALESSANDRINI
TONY HONOR FOR EXCELLENCE IN THE THEATER

THE UN-ORIGINAL CAST RECORDING
JOHN FREEDSON, HARRIET YELLIN and JON B. PLATT present
VOLUME 7
FORBIDDEN BROADWAY 2001 A SPOOF ODYSSEY
starring
FELICIA FINLEY   DANNY GURWIN
TONY NATION   CHRISTINE PEDI
CATHERINE STORNETTA
Created and Written by GERARD ALESSANDRINI
Co-Directed by PHILLIP GEORGE

**Donna English (as Beauty) and Bryan Batt (as the Beast)
display Disney's new design for the Tony Award.**

Donna English, as Glenn Close in *Sunset Boulevard*, gets a "Master Class" in singing from Patti LuPone in the person of Christine Pedi.

Gerard surrounded by his *Cats/Chorus Line* cast. Clockwise from top left: Bryan Batt, Christine Pedi, David Hibbard, and Donna English.

it's nearly impossible to spoof a spoof. Also, *City of Angels* was very well written by comedic genius Larry Gelbart (book), the great wordsmith David Zippel (lyrics), and one of Broadway's all-time best composers, Cy Coleman. Being so well done, it was impossible to top. (I had the same problem later with *The Producers*.) But *City* was one of the few new book musicals of the '90s, so we had to take a crack at it. Our version did get a few laughs, mainly because of the clever costumes, which were half black and white, half color—an exaggeration of the premise of the real show.

Our audience tolerated my rather lame *City of Angels* parody, but you could tell they really wanted to see us attack shows that took themselves too seriously. Sir Andrew Lloyd Webber came to our rescue by delivering *Aspects of Love,* straight from London. That show became even more of a target when Sarah Brightman stepped into it; she was one of our most beloved voodoo dolls at *Forbidden Broadway,* and we were always happy to stick a few pins into her shapely bodice and attempt to adjust her overbite. Our *Aspects* number was "I Sleep with Everyone," to the tune of "Love Changes Everything." It was a big hit, partly because who is sleeping with whom in showbiz is always of great interest to the entire world. (We could do a whole sidebar on that subject. . . .)

Miss Saigon was a big hit of the early '90s, but it wasn't as spoofable as *Les Miz* because the songs weren't as hummable. We did have some fun with all the hoopla

Attend the tale of *Teeny Todd*! Jeff Lyons and Marilyn Pasekoff.

Left: Susanne Blakeslee as a jaded, chain-smoking Orphan Annie. Right: Herndon Lackey, Susanne Blakeslee, and Jeff Lyons confess: "I Sleep with Everyone." (On Broadway, who doesn't?)

about the race-blind casting of Jonathan Pryce as the Engineer in that show. Equity objected to bringing over a British star for the part, especially because the role was Eurasian. We spoofed Equity president Colleen Dewhurst objecting to Pryce's casting—and what made it really hilarious was that we had Mary Denise Bentley, an African-American actress, playing Dewhurst. She appeared onstage and said, "In order to protest Cameron Mackintosh bringing Jonathan Pryce over from London to play this role, I have now become black." It was one of the biggest laughs we ever got. Then we had "Jonathan Pryce" come out and sing "I'm an Asian, Too." That number was Phill George's idea, and he wrote most of the lyric:

JUST LIKE HO-CHI-MINH,

CHIANG-KAI-SHEK,

MAO-TSE TUNG,

LIKE THOSE CHINAMEN,

I'M AN ASIAN TOO,

A SOO-OO-OO,

JACK SOO-OO-OO!

JUST LIKE CONNIE CHUNG,

B. D. WONG,

NANCY KWAN,

IN A MUSICAL,

I'M AN ASIAN, TOO.

SO SUE –OO-OO,

GO SUE-OO-OO.

IF EQUITY TRIES TO SAY,

"THAT JUST WON'T WASH,"

I WILL RUN AWAY . . .

WITH CAMERON MACKINTOSH!

AND WE'LL DO *TURANDOT,*

KING AND I,

FLOW'R DRUM SONG,

WHICH WILL GO TO PROVE

I'M AN ASIAN, TOO!

Herndon Lackey as Jonathan Pryce in *Miss Saigon*: "I'm an Asian, Too!"

At the time, Phill and I used to work out at the same gym; it was a Bally's on Broadway at 76th Street, located over a D'Agostino's supermarket. We called it "Fags Over Dag's." I was in aerobics class one day when he came running in, yelling, "Gerard! Gerard!" The aerobics teacher turned off the music, and Phill shouted, "Colleen Dewhurst just died!" The teacher said, "I'm so sorry, was she a friend of yours?" And I said, "No, we just lost the biggest laugh in our show!"

"Grim Hotel" was one of my favorite spoofs of that or any year. *Grand Hotel* was so easy to make fun of because of all that German *Sturm und Drang.* A lot of the music is in minor keys, and there were all those people moving chairs and shaking milk cartons. We also spoofed the revolving door of the hotel; each actor would go through the door, change costumes, and come back through the door as a completely different character. We rehearsed it down to the nanosecond, and that was when I realized actors could make any costume change in twenty seconds.

We also got a lot of mileage out of "Teeny Todd," because we realized that this was the beginning of an era of downsizing on Broadway. I remember thinking that, even in the case of the *Gypsy* and *Guys and Dolls* revivals, the orchestras sounded noticeably smaller than they should have.

The Will Rogers Follies and *Miss Saigon* were among the few major hits of the era. There were some huge flop musicals back then, including *Nick and Nora* and *Anna Karenina*. I wouldn't normally have bothered to spoof a show with a brief run, but I had few other options. One of our funniest numbers was our take on the expensive flop production of *The Threepenny Opera* that starred Sting. We called it "The 300 Million Penny Opera."

Jeff Lyons, "Somewhat Overindulgent" as Mandy Patinkin.

This was a transitional period for Broadway—and, of course, for *Forbidden Broadway* as well. Even though *Cats, Les Miz,* and *Phantom* were British shows, they had given Broadway a sense of resurgence. But *Miss Saigon* was the only British blockbuster of the early '90s, and my sense was that it didn't create the same excitement as the others.

Fortunately, this was around the time of our tenth anniversary, so we assembled a show of old-favorite numbers performed by a cast that consisted of three of our most talented veterans (Patrick Quinn, Michael McGrath, Leah Hocking) plus one newcomer (to us anyway), the powerhouse singer-actress Alix Korey. Once, I asked Alix why she was raising her arm during the final bow as if to indicate that someone was standing beside her. She said, "That's for the other two actors who should be in this show!" Ever since then, in every edition, we've had all of the cast members raise their outside arms in respect of Alix's keen observation. She was absolutely right that we should have six actors to get through all of the exhausting material in *Forbidden Broadway*.

Even if there were few new shows for us to target at the time, celebrities were a different matter, and I felt it was a good opportunity to get to work on Mandy Patinkin. He certainly had been a star on Broadway, but we had never tackled him, so to speak. By the '90s, he was doing studio recordings and was still quite popular. His performances were always very intense and passionate, so it was clear what our spoof should be. Phill George and I listened to his recording of "Somewhere Over the Rainbow" again and again, and Phill commented, "It's somewhat overindulgent." That was enough. I picked up a pen, and the rest of the parody lyric wrote itself.

The Who's Tommy, Kiss of the Spider Woman, and *Blood Brothers* opened in 1993, but they didn't run all that long. It was particularly hard for us to spoof *Tommy* because that show was so much about the high-tech production.

In addition to the shows mentioned above, the early and mid-'90s brought us such huge flops as *Ain't Broadway Grand* and *The Best Little Whorehouse Goes Public*. Even

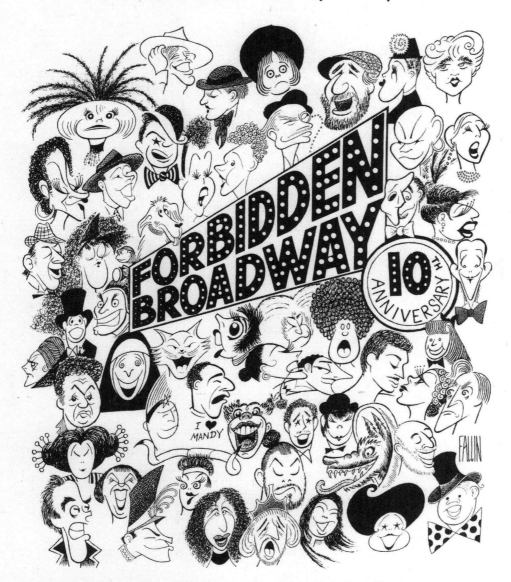

A newspaper ad for the last edition of the show at Theatre East.

Sondheim's brilliant *Passion*, which won the Best Musical Tony, only lasted about six months. Broadway was trying to find a new voice, but it couldn't. One of the few minor exceptions was *Once on This Island*, by Stephen Flaherty and Lynn Ahrens, but that show wasn't a major commercial hit.

Like Broadway, *Forbidden Broadway* was in transition. Our East Side venue wasn't as popular as it had been in 1988. The theatre district was being cleaned up, and most New York theatregoers and tourists were likely to want to see shows there; the era of people going downtown, uptown, or crosstown to see an Off-Broadway show was ending. Jonathan Scharer, our producer at Theatre East, tried valiantly to create a new market for us by using outlandish ads and gimmicks, and the pressure was on me to write more new editions of the show. In hindsight, I think those editions came too close together, because there wasn't enough activity on Broadway to warrant them.

Forbidden Broadway needed a rest, and so did I. We took the last edition of the show that we did at Theatre East to L.A. for a run there. The cast was stellar: Brad Oscar, Christine Pedi, Susanne Blakeslee, and Craig Wells. We hadn't been in L.A. since 1983, so I was able to build an edition using all of the best material from the previous twelve years.

Ironically, the big new musical of the day was also playing in L.A. at the time: *Sunset Boulevard,* starring Glenn Close. No sooner had we added an elaborate spoof of that show than Miss Close and the entire cast showed up to see *Forbidden Broadway.* Our spoof made fun of many aspects of the show, including the star's high hairline: "The audience response is so hot, it's nearly scalding / I'm perfect for this part because I'm balding." After the performance, Miss Close was very gracious with the cast, but when introduced to me, she said: "So, you think I'm balding?" I blurted out, "Oh no, Miss Close, I just needed a word to rhyme with 'scalding.'" All she said was "Mmm-hmmm," then she nodded and walked away.

At this time, John Freedson and Harriet Yellin took over producing *Forbidden Broadway* from Jonathan Scharer, who had apparently lost interest. We followed our successful run in L.A. with *Forbidden Hollywood.* Our time on the West Coast turned out to be incredibly creative and tremendously fun, especially with Susanne and Christine as part of the family, later joined by Jason Graae and Gerry McIntyre.

It was also around this time when the legendary Alvin Colt became our costumer. He had joined us part-time in 1991, but by 1994 he was our full-time designer. Alvin's costumes for *Forbidden Hollywood* were among the most spectacular he ever created.

Phill George and I continued to collaborate closely, even through the rocky years of our personal relationship and despite whatever backstage drama there was. At one point, I remember, we were trying to strangle each other over some Broadway minutiae regarding Des McAnuff. We ended up knocking over the costume rack and rolling around on the floor in a pile of dirty costumes. Mary Denise Bentley, one of the sweetest girls we ever had in the show, suddenly turned into a prison matron and screamed at us: "YOU BOYS STOP THAT RIGHT NOW!" Phill and I were very embarrassed—but somehow we always managed to maintain our friendship and come up with a show that was full of laughs and love.

"Teeny Todd"

[SWEENEY TODD *enters and sings solemnly.*]

SWEENEY TODD

ATTEND THE TALE OF TEENY TODD;
THE CAST IS SMALL AND THE STAGING ODD.
ALTHOUGH THE MUSICAL'S BARELY TEN,
SOMEBODY DECIDED TO DO IT AGAIN,
BUT IN THREE-QUARTER PROMENADE
IT'S *TEENY TODD*,
THE SMALLER VERSION OF *SWEENEY*.

[BEGGAR WOMAN *enters and sings.*]

BEGGAR WOMAN

THERE IS NO SHOP IN LONDON TOWN,
EXCEPT TWO FLATS THAT ARE PAINTED BROWN.
BUT THINK OF ALL THE CASH THEY SAVE,
THE PHYSICAL BUDGET'S IMPECCABLY SHAVED.
IT'S TEENY,
IT'S *TEENY TODD*.

[THE BEADLE *and* MRS. LOVETT *enter and join in singing.*]

ALL

THE SMALLER VERSION OF *SWEENEY*.
SWING YOUR RAZOR LOW, TEENY!
KEEP IT POCKET-SIZED.
AND, WHAT'S MORE, THE SONDHEIM SCORE IS
SYNTHESIZED!

MRS. LOVETT

OUR NEEDS ARE FEW, THE STAGE IS BARE.
WE USE A MIN'ATURE BARBER CHAIR.
THE MUG OF SUDS AND THE LEATHER STROP
ARE TINY TOY PROPS FROM A TINY TOY SHOP.
IT'S *TEENY TODD* ...

ALL

THE SMALLER VERSION OF *SWEENEY*.

BIG AND EPIC LIKE *SWEENEY* WAS,
HUGE AND BULKY THE SCEN'RY WAS.
TWENTY-TON BRIDGE, TWENTY-TON BARGE,
HAL PRINCE'S VERSION WAS UGLY BUT LARGE.

NOW THE BIGGER GUY SWEENEY'S GONE,
AND HIS KID BROTHER TEENY'S ON.
TEENY IS CUTE, EVEN MORE SUBTLE
WHEN TEENY BLINKS, THE ROACHES SCUTTLE.

[*The actors begin a round of the last few lines as they menacingly advance on the audience. The* BEADLE *grabs one end of the* BEGGAR WOMAN'S *shawl; they hold it up in front of* SWEENEY *and* MRS. LOVETT.]

ALL

TEENY! TEENY! TEENY! TEENY!
TEEEEEEEEEENNNNEEEEY!

[*The terrifying puppet* TEENY TODD *emerges over the top of the shawl; the* BEGGAR WOMAN *and the* BEADLE *quiver with fear.*]

TEENY

[*In a high-pitched puppet voice.*]

ATTEND THE TALE OF TEENY TODD.

THE OTHERS

ATTEND THE TALE OF TEENY TODD.

TEENY

THOUGH STEPHEN SONDHEIM'S A DEMIGOD ...

THE OTHERS

THOUGH STEPHEN SONDHEIM'S A DEMIGOD ...

[*A* MRS. LOVETT *puppet rises and sings in a similar voice.*]

MRS. LOVETT

. . . TO BRING BACK ONE OF HIS SHOWS TODAY,
NO ONE CAN AFFORD THE ORIGINAL WAY.

ALL

THEY SHRINK IT.

[*Even smaller puppets pop up and push* TEENY *and* MRS. LOVETT *down; they pop up behind and sing in a whisper, plotting revenge.*]

LIKE *TEENY TODD,*
THE *SWEENEY* VERSION THAT'S TEENY!

[TEENY *and* MRS. LOVETT *decapitate the smaller puppets with one blow.* TEENY *cuts* MRS. LOVETT'*s throat; she sinks down out of sight. On the musical button,* SWEENEY *cuts his own throat. Blackout.*]

"Grim Hotel"

[*Darkness; on tape, a phone rings and an* OPERATOR'*s voice is heard.*]

OPERATOR

Grand Hotel? Grand Hotel? No, this is the *Grim* Hotel. What number are you calling? Oh, you want Dr. Von Shrapnel Limplegg? Would you mind calling back? He's in the lobby, shooting up.

[*During this, a tympani roll begins. A* DOCTOR *with a patch over his eye, a limp, and a cane enters, crosses right, rolls up his sleeve, takes out a hypodermic needle, and holds it in the air. As the* OPERATOR *finishes speaking, he injects himself in the butt with morphine while the music pounds and the lights flash.*]

DOCTOR

Aaaaaahhhh! Das good!

METAL STAIRS, RIGID CHAIRS,
SETS WITH BLACK GIRDERS SHOWING . . .
MISSING WALLS, DUSKY HALLS,
SOMBER LIGHTS FAINTLY GLOWING . . .

WHORES AND THUGS, MORPHINE DRUGS
DEATH WITH BLOOD OVERFLOWING . . .
SEX AND SIN IN BLEAK BERLIN,
YOU'RE IN THE GRIM HOTEL!

[ALL *sing second verse as* FLAEMMCHEN *enters through the revolving door with a chair. She comes center, opens the chair, puts it down, bows, and exits. The* BARON *enters, looking dashing with perfect hair, a little mustache, and a cape. He bows center, picks up the chair, closes it, then exits with it. A* LILIANE MONTEVECCHI *type in furs enters with a chair, opens it, puts it down, bows, and exits.* RAFFAELA *does the same, taking the chair with her.*]

ALL

GRIM HOTEL, GRIM HOTEL.
ART AND ANGST IN PROFUSION.
GRIM HOTEL, LIVING HELL,
GIVES YOUR HEAD A CONTUSION.
SONGS ARE SWELL—WHO CAN TELL
WITH THE CONSTANT CONFUSION?
SETS ARE SLIM AND JUNGLE GYM
AND DIM IN GRIM HOTEL!

DOCTOR

It's always the same here at Grim Hotel. Nothing ever happens.

[*As he speaks,* SCULLERY MAN *enters with chair, opens it, puts it down, glares at the audience, picks it up, closes it, exits.*]

People come, people go, people move chairs.

[*He announces them as they enter.*]

Raffaela, the six-foot-two-pseudo-Italian-American lesbian confidante with the designer haircut.

[*She crosses left.*] Ah, Kringelein the bookkeeper, here to enjoy his last few days before he dies of terminal symbolism.

[KRINGELEIN *comes center and coughs, then crosses to* RAFFAELA *and coughs on her.*]

And Liliane Monte-Grushinskaya, the fading Russian ballerina, who's really a French cabaret singer from Off-Broadway.

LILIANE

Bonjour, l'amour!

ALL

SEX AND SIN IN BLEAK BERLIN—
YOU'RE IN THE GRIM HOTEL!

[ALL *strike poses on the button;* KRINGELEIN *exits.*]

LILIANE

[*Taking off her fur, revealing a tutu.*]

Raffaela! What kind of hotel is this? There are no walls in my room— only a row of chairs.

RAFFAELA

This is a concept hotel. It's German Expressionistic. You have to imagine the walls.

LILIANE

Pooh!

[*Noticing the* DOCTOR, *posed downstage right with his elbow up.*]

Who is he?

RAFFAELA

He is your door.

[LILIANE *opens and closes the "door," smashing the* DOCTOR's *face into the right proscenium; the* SCULLERY MAN *enters with a box of silverware.*]

LILIANE

Who is *he*?

[*He shakes his box of silverware menacingly and exits.*]

RAFFAELA

Ask Tommy Tune. That reminds me . . .

[*She pulls music from her pocket.*]
. . . Tommy and Maury Yeston want to add a new song to the show . . .

[*She begins to cower, fearing* LILIANE's *wrath.*]

. . . and they want it in next fall!

LILIANE

What? So soon?

I CAN'T LEARN THIS SONG SO QUICKLY.
MAURY MUST BE DREAMING;
LOOK AT ALL THESE LYRICS!

[RAFFAELA *tries to make a suggestion, but* LILIANE *cuts her off.*]

NO! DON'T CALL HIM TO APPROACH ME.
IT'S NO USE TO COACH ME;

I'LL GET LOST COMPLETELY.

[*She has missed the final pitch by a wide margin. The pianist gives it to her. She misses it again.*]

EEEEE!

[*He gives it to her again; she hits it, but only by howling like a coyote.*]

AH-OOOOOO!

RAFFAELA

[*Holding* LILIANE*'s coat.*]

Liliane, that was wonderful.

[*Lifting her up.*]

I—I—I love you!

LILIANE

Put me down, you big dyke!

[*She does.*]

I have tutus straighter than you!

[RAFFAELA *exits through revolving door. Under* DOCTOR*'s speech,* JOEL GREY *enters as the* MC *in* Cabaret.]

DOCTOR

It's always the same at Grim Hotel. People come, people go . . .

JOEL

WILLKOMMEN, BIENVENUE, WELCOME
FREMDE, ETRANGER—

LILIANE

Hey, you!

JOEL

[*Mightily irritated at having been interrupted.*]

What?

LILIANE

This is the Grim Hotel! The cabaret is down the street!

JOEL

[*Very apologetic.*]

Oh, sorry! This *looked* like a quasi-Nazi musical!

[*He laughs his evil laugh, and then the* DOCTOR *shoots him up. In a stupor, he exits through the revolving door, singing ad lib. As* LILIANE *and* RAFFAELA *come through the revolving door, the* DOCTOR *shoots them up. In the following section,* LILIANE *and the* DOCTOR *sing while* RAFFAELA *sings in counterpoint.*]

ALL

FEELING GRIM?
(YOU ARE AT THE GRIM)
FEELING GRIM?
(YOU ARE AT THE GRIM)
FEELING GRIM?
YOU ARE AT THE
AT THE GRIM
AT THE GRIM
AT THE GRIM HOTEL.

DOCTOR and LILIANE

FADED CLOTHES, DUSTY ROSE,
SHADES OF BROWN NEVER VARY.
BALLET BARRES, FACIAL SCARS,
CHAMBERMAIDS SLIGHTLY SCARY.
GASPS OF BREATH, DANCING DEATH . . .

ALL

[*They slap themselves on the downbeat.*]

IT'S THE MOST FUN SINCE *CARRIE*!
SEX AND SIN IN BLEAK BERLIN
WE'RE STUCK IN GRIM HOTEL!

[*All raise their arms menacingly as if in a Nazi salute
that turns, at the last moment, into a cheery Gallic wave.*]

BONJOUR!

[*Blackout.*]

"The Trolley Song Nightmare"

[*Three* Meet Me in St. Louis *people are discovered on the
stage in straw hats; they sway and sing in harmony.*]

TRIO

DID YOU SEE *ST. LOUIS*, LOUIS ?
DID YOU LEAVE FORLORN?
ISN'T IT ALL OOEY-GOOEY,
LAWRENCE WELK REBORN?
THOUGH THE WHOLE IDEA IS GROOVY,
USE YOUR CASH TO RENT THE MOVIE
'CAUSE THEY BLEW *MEET ME IN ST. LOUIS*, LOUIS.
IT'S BEEN CANNED LIKE CORN!

[*A grade-B Judy Garland-type dressed as* ESTHER
enters and sings.]

ESTHER

WITH MY CHIPMUNK HAIRDO
AND MY WEIRD ROLLED BANGS
AND MY HAIR A SORT OF PURPLE-RED,
I WENT TO SING A JOLLY
SONG UPON A TROLLEY
AND LOST MY LUNCH INSTEAD.

AS THE CAR WAS SPINNING AT A BRISK HIGH SPEED
ON THE HUGEST SET I'VE EVER SEEN,
TRUE, I CHERISHED THE PART,
BUT THE PROP STOPPED MY HEART
FOR THE OPULENCE WAS OBSCENE!

CLANG! CLANG! CLANG! WENT THE MUSIC,
CLUNK! CLUNK! CLUNK! WENT THE BOOK,
CHUG! CHUG! CHUG! WENT THE SCENE'RY;
IT'LL RUN YOU DOWN IF YOU DON'T LOOK!

CHORUS

CLANG! CLANG! CLANG!
OOH-OOH-OOH!

ESTHER

THUMP! THUMP! THUMP! WENT THE DANCERS,
TKST! TKST! TKST! WENT THE SOUND,
OOGH! OOGH! OOGH! WENT THE GEORGE HEARN,
AND THE SHOW NEVER GOT OFF THE GROUND!

CHORUS

OY! OY! VEY! AHHH!

ESTHER

THE WHOLE IDEA WAS RATHER SWEET:
TO PUT THIS CHARMING MOVIE UP UPON ITS FEET.
BUT ARTHUR FREED WOULD BE APPALLED
TO SEE HOW TERRIBLY HIS CLASSIC FILM WAS
    MAULED!

[*The* CHORUS *begins to "ah" and "ooh" behind her.*]

SCREAMS! SCREAMS! SCREAMS! AS THE TROLLEY
ROLLED! ROLLED! ROLLED! OFF THE STAGE
STOP! STOP! STOP! SAID THE CRITICS!
FRANK RICH JUMPED FROM HIS SEAT
BUT THE WHEELS CAUGHT HIS FEET
AS HE SCREAMED,
BUT TOO LATE, HE WAS CREAMED!

STILL IT'S WELL WORTH IT
AND IT WAS GRAND
GETTING PANNED
IN THIS BLAND VEGAS CRAP
JUST TO PUKE IN HIS LAP!

CHORUS

PUKE, PUKE, PUKE, ON THE TROLLEY
OOH-AHH . . .

[*Fadeout.*]

"Barbra II: Back to Broadway"

BARBRA

MEMORIES . . . PEOPLE . . . BARBRA . . . STREISAND . . .

BACK TO BROADWAY
TO RECORD SOME SLOW TUNES;
THEY'RE MY DULLEST SO FAR.

BACK TO BROADWAY
TO DESTROY MORE SHOW TUNES,
AND I CAN, 'CAUSE I KNOW I OUTSHINE EVERY STAR.

TELL DICK RODGERS
"SOME ENCHANTED EVENING"'S FIXED!
I IMPROVED HIS SAPPY TUNE
AND HAD HIS ORCHESTRATION NIXED.

'CAUSE I GET MY WAY
BACK ON BROADWAY:
EV'RY SONG'S REWRITTEN, REMASTERED,
AND OVERMIXED.

TELL LLOYD WEBBER
SUNSET BOULEVARD'S A BORE.
AND WATCH OUT! I'VE GOT MORE CLOUT
'CAUSE I'M GOOD FRIENDS WITH TIPPER GORE.

AND IF I REALLY
WENT BACK TO BROADWAY,
I WOULD RUN FOREVER
AND EVER AND EVER
AND EVER . . . MOOOOOOOOOOORE!

"'s Tommy Tune"

CHORUS

'S WONDERFUL, 'S MARVELOUS.
WHAT A GUY—HE'S SO HIGH!

[TOMMY *enters.*]

TOMMY

'S TOMMY TUNE! YES, THAT'S ME.
HERE'S MY PHILOSOPHY:

WHEN A LIBRETTO'S HOLLOW,
PUT ON A SAPPY SHOW,
MUSTER YOUR PRIDE AND SWALLOW,
PUT ON A SAPPY SHOW.
THROW OUT THE BOOK AND DROWN THE
    ORCHESTRA.
NOW, THAT'S MY STYLE . . .
THROW IN A DOG ACT, NAKED WOMEN,
AND YELL, "TAP AND SMILE!"

HIRE A HANDSOME CHORUS,
NOBODY WITH A BRAIN
AND IF THEY DON'T ADORE US,
GIGGLE AND ACT INSANE
AND SPREAD CONCEPT OUT TO THE BACK ROW,
JUST PUT ON A SAPPY . . .

. . . Thank y'all for coming to my one-man musical . . .

PUT ON A SAPPY SHOW!

Thank you, everyone. Now I'd like to sing one of my fav'rite songs, and I hope you'll like it too.

I SAW YOU, SIR,
EYEING MY FULL-LENGTH FUR
AS I WENT DANCING BY,
AND WHEN I GO TAP-TAP
TIPPY-TIPPY-TAP,
NOW, DIDN'T YOU SIGH A SIGH?

I WARN YOU, SIR,
EVERYONE MUST CONCUR
THAT I'M A SWELLISH GUY,
OR IT'LL BE BOOM-BOOM
BOOM-BA-BOOM-BOOM-BANG
AND KISS YOUR CAREER GOODBYE!

OH, ONCE IN LOVE WITH TOMMY,
ALWAYS IN LOVE WITH TOMMY.
I'M SO BELOVED,
SKINNY, TALL, AND BONEY,
AND I WIN A TONY EACH JUNE.

OH, ONCE YOU'RE CAST BY TOMMY,
YOU'LL STARE AGHAST AT TOMMY.
GRINNING AND GUSHING,
LATELY I'VE BEEN PLANNING
TO BE CAROL CHANNING REAL SOON.

IF I DON'T STAR MYSELF AS A PERFORMER,
I STILL STEAL THE SHOW
BY NEVER CASTING ANYONE WHO'S WARMER
THAN TEN BELOW!

OH, ONCE IN LOVE WITH TOMMY,
YOU'LL SELL YOUR SOUL TO TOMMY.
YOU BETTER LOVE ME,
'CAUSE NO ONE'S ABOVE ME,
AND IF YOU TRY TO SHOVE ME AROUND,
I'LL TAP AND TRAMPLE YOU INTO THE GROUND.

Oh, ev'rybody. I feel so happy, I want you all to experience my happiness with me. So sing along, ev'rybody. The words are "Once in love with Tommy . . ." Here we go!

[*He happily leads the audience in a brief sing-along to the first part of the song, then abruptly cuts them off.*]

Wonderful! That's enough, I'll take over . . .

MY HEIGHT MAKES MY DIZZY,
BUT I'M NEVER CHANCING
TO FALL DOWN WHEN I'M DANCING, YOU SEE,
'CAUSE EVERYONE IN TOWN FALLS OVER ME!

Goodbye, I love you all for loving me!

[*Blackout.*]

"I Couldn't Hit That Note"

JULIE ANDREWS

DEAD, DEAD, MY FILM CAREER IS DEAD,
AND WHEN I SING, YOU WON'T BELIEVE YOUR EARS;
SLEEP, SLEEP, MY TECHNIQUE IS ASLEEP
FROM NOT DOING MUSICALS FOR YEARS.

I COULDN'T HIT THAT NOTE
I COULDN'T HIT THAT NOTE
UNTIL THEY DROPPED THE KEY.

[*She sneakily signals to the pianist and, with a smug and satisfied look on her face, modulates down a key.*]

NOW THAT I'M SIXTY-SIX,
MY VOCAL CORDS PLAY TRICKS
AND WHEN I PUSH, I PEE!

I'LL NEVER KNOW WHY FREDERICK LOEWE SAID,
    "JULIE,
YOUR UPPER LIP IS MUCH TOO TIGHT."
AND SO I . . .

[*She modulates down again, quite
happily and triumphantly.*]

. . . MODULATE
A WHOLE KEY DOWN TO STATE
I COULDN'T HIT THAT NOTE ALL . . .

[*She modulates down yet again, and finishes in
exquisite delight.*]

. . . NIGHT!

Topol: "If I Sing it Slower"

TOPOL

[*Enters and looks up, as if speaking to God.*]

Dear Jerry Robbins, you made many, many roles in
Fiddler on the Roof. I realize of course, that I, Topol,
have the biggest role. But what would have been so
terrible if my part was just a little bit longer?

IF I SING IT SLOWER,
DAIDLE DEEDLE DAIDLE
DIGGUH DIGGUH DEEDLE DAIDLE DUM,
I COULD FIX THIS SILLY FLUFFY SHOW
IF I SING ADAGIO.

IF I SING IT SLOWER,
DAIDLE DEEDLE DAIDLE
DIGGUH DIGGUH DEEDLE DAIDLE DUM,
I'D STRETCH OUT MY TIME ON STAGE ALONE,
LENGTHENING IT TILL I MAKE YOU GROAN.

IF I GO SLOW, I'D ADD MORE WEIGHT TO THE
    JOKES
AND PLAY TEVYE LIKE DE NIRO WOULD;
ALL THE FUNNY LINES WOULD NOW MAKE YOU
    CRY.
I'D TAKE MY TIME AND PAUSE AND HOLD FOR
    APPLAUSE
AND MUMBLE TILL NOTHING'S UNDERSTOOD,
TAKING FORTY SECONDS JUST TO SIGH . . .

Aaaaaaaaaaaaaaaaaaaahhhhhhhhhhhhhhhhhhhhhh!

IF I SING IT SLOWER,
DAIDLE DEEDLE DAIDLE
DIGGUH DIGGUH DEEDLE DAIDLE DUM,
CURTAIN DOWN ELEVEN-FORTY-THREE
IF THE TEMPO'S SET BY ME.
YOU'LL NEVER GET TO GO HOME.

[*He gets wildly involved in melismatic flourishes.*]

DAIDLE DEEDLE DAIDLE
DIGGUH DIGGUH DEEDLE DAIDLE
DIGGUH DIGGUH DEEDLE DAIDLE
DIGGUH DIGGUH DEEDLE DAIDLE
YABBA DABBA DO!

JERRY ROBBINS, YOU'RE AS GOOD AS GOD;
BOCK AND HARNICK THINK IT'S RATHER ODD.
MORE OF ME AND LESS THIS STUPID SHOW
IF I SING THIS SONG REAL SLOW!

"Aspects of Lust"

MAN #1

I, I SLEEP WITH EVERYONE
SLEEP WITH JENNY. SLEEP WITH ROSE
SHE, SHE SLEEPS WITH EVERYONE

GIRL

[*Entering with a sheet & a teddy bear*]

WITH MY UNCLE AND MY BEAUS
I, I SLEEP WITH EVERYONE
WHILE I LUST FOE JUILIETTA

MAN #1

[*Disrobes & gets behind sheet with girl*]

WHILE I, I SLEEP WITH EVERYONE
WITH HER DAUGHTER
AND MY NIECE

BOTH

EVERYONE GETS GOOD SONGS AND
A JUICY PIECE!

MAN #2

[*Popping up from behind a blanket*]

I, I SLEEP WITH EVERYONE
WITH YOUR GIRLFRIEND

GIRL

WITH YOUR DAD

MAN #2

SAY, SAY DID I SLEEP WITH YOU?

GIRL

I DON'T THINK SO

MAN #2

THAT'S TOO BAD

BOTH MEN

HEY! I BETTER SLEEP WITH YOU
TO MAKE SURE I DIDN'T MISS YOU

ALL THREE

YES WE, WE SLEEP WITH EVERYONE
ONE BY ONE AND TWO BY TWO
[*They pull out a pillow*]

AND IF YOU'RE IN THE AUDIENCE
THEN YOU'LL SLEEP TOO!

[*They all fall asleep*]

"Somewhat Overindulgent"

MANDY PATINKIN

MY NAME IS MANDY, MANDY "CHE" PATINKIN,
AND I'VE BEEN THINKIN' I MIGHT
BE KNOWN MORE AS A MALE CHANTEUSE.
SO IF YOU LIKE MY TWENTY SONGS ON CD,
YOU SHOULD COME AND SEE ME EV'RY NIGHT,
DRESSING CASUAL AND LOOSE
AND TURNING ON THE JUICE
WHILE EMOTING LIKE A GOOSE . . .

SOMEWHAT OVERINDULGENT, LIKE I'M HIGH.
I INTERPRET A LYRIC LIKE I'M ABOUT TO DIE.
SOMEWHAT OVERINDULGENT, I SING BLUE,
AND YOU WON'T RECOGNIZE THE TUNE
AFTER I GET THROUGH.

SOMEDAY I'LL DO A ONE-MAN SHOW,
SING JOLSON SONGS LIKE "OLD BLACK JOE"
AND "MAMMY."
I'LL TWITTER LIKE A LITTLE BIRD
AND EMPHASIZE MOST EV'RY WORD
TO PROVE I'M HAMMY!

SOMEWHAT OVERINDULGENT—WATCH ME CRY!
BARBRA DID IT IN *YENTL*, WHY, THEN, OH, WHY
    CAN'T I?

IF BARBRA STREISAND GETS TO BE BEYOND
   INDULGENT,
WHY, OH, WHY NOT ME?

Ooh-La-La-La, *Les Misérables*!

Of all the shows *Forbidden Broadway* has ever spoofed, none is more identified with us than *Les Misérables*. It's ripe for parody because it takes itself so seriously, it's through-composed, and it's endless. Also, any show about a horrifically bloody revolution in which all of the characters wear fabulous costumes strikes me as hilarious.

When *Les Miz* show opened in London at the RSC, it was such a hit that we knew it was bound to come to New York sooner rather than later. I thought I'd better get right on it, so I made a special trip to London to see the show—and by the end of the first act, I was totally confused. I thought the singing and diction were questionable; I had a hard time following the story and understanding the lyrics. At intermission, I opened my Playbill and found the synopsis. I started reading it and I was literally thinking, "Oh, I see! Now I get it! It's not the big, famous French Revolution, it's the little, later one!" Everything became clear, and then I was into it—but if I hadn't read that thorough synopsis, I would have been lost.

I was impressed by the scale of the show, and I was somewhat moved by the story in the second act because I could follow it better. The whole thing seemed completely new, yet it somehow made my mind feel closed; it wasn't like the Sondheim musicals, which take you to someplace different but in an enlightening way.

When it came time to actually write a parody of the show, I listened to the cast album till I felt my ears would burst. Although the music was often lovely, it really doesn't have the drive of a classic Broadway score. I thought to myself, "I need to get some good, old-fashioned show tunes into this parody!" One day, while walking through Shubert Alley, I

Roxie Lucas dreamed a show in days gone by . . .

noticed someone wearing a button that said, "*Les Misérables, c'est magnifique.*" Inspiration struck: "*Les Miz*, French. French, *Can-Can.*" There's nothing like a Cole Porter song to kick off a revolution.

The first show *Forbidden Broadway* spoofed in an all-out mini-version was *Les Miz*. Before that, we had been spoofing individual stars and trends. One of the reasons we took a new approach for *Les Miz* was because there really were no huge names in the cast. That was another major change on Broadway at the time.

The idea for the "turntable" didn't come to us immediately. We worked up the *Les Miz* number for the Boston production of the show, during our hiatus in New York. We were actually considering having a Lazy Susan sort of turntable built into the stage in Boston; Harriet Yellin, our producing manager at the time, reluctantly called in carpenters to figure out how to do it. They said, "We can have it ready in about three weeks," which seemed like a long time. Phill George, who was helping stage some of the numbers, said, "Well, until the turntable comes, why don't we just mime it?"

So the cast mimed it—and, of course, it was hysterically funny. We immediately realized that was the way to go. So we called off the carpenters, saved a lot of money, and put into the show one of the funniest bits ever. At the time, we had no idea we'd be able to use and update that number for year and years, because we had no idea that *Les Miz* and/or our show would run for years and years.

After that, for each new edition of the show, I would add a spoof of another character or song from *Les Miz*. I think if we ever strung all of the parodies together, we would have a show as long as the original.

"More Misérable"

[*A sultry* FRENCH CHANTEUSE *is discovered atop the piano, wearing a pink boa and a beret. She is smoking a cigarette through a long holder. She sings.*]

FRENCH CHANTEUSE

WHAT SHOW TAKES YOU UP IN THE AIR
WHEN YOU COME TO CALL?
IT'S BROADWAY'S BIG LOVE AFFAIR,
BUT NOT REALLY BROADWAY'S AT ALL.

BUT I SAW IT AND I DIDN'T MIND:
COMPARE IT TO OTHER SHOWS AND YOU'LL FIND,

JUST LIKE THE POSTER SAYS, GOD KNOWS,
IT'S LESS MISERABLE THAN OTHER SHOWS.

GO TRY GET IN TO WATCH THE PEOPLE SPIN!
OO-LA-LA-LA, *LES MISÉRABLES.*
JAVERT GETS SUNK AND EPONINE GOES PUNK.
OO-LA-LA-LA, *LES MISÉRABLES.*
VALJEAN GETS CAUGHT AND EVERYONE GETS SHOT
OO-LA-LA-LA, IT'S NOT *HEDDA GABBLER.*
IT'S HOT, IT'S CHIC,
C'EST TRES, TRES MAGNIFIQUE:
LES MISÉRABLES.

[*She fades away as three ragged actors, two men and one woman, enter as if on a turntable. Very intense, very miserable, they sing.*]

LES MIZ ACTORS

AT THE END OF THE PLAY WE'RE ANOTHER YEAR
    OLDER,
AND WE'RE OFTEN EXHAUSTED FROM PLAYING THE
    POOR.
RANDY GRAFF FELL IN THE BAND,
AND THE TURNTABLE'S MAKING US DIZZY;
TREVOR NUNN YELLS A COMMAND
AND HE'S THROWING US ALL IN A TIZZY
AND THERE'S GONNA BE HELL TO PAY
AT THE END OF THE PLAY.

[*The turntable jerks to a stop, spilling them every which way.*]

MOST MISERABLE ACTOR

AT THE END OF THE PLAY, SEE THE AUDIENCE
    SMOLDER,
SITTING FLAT ON THEIR BUTTS FOR THREE HOURS
    OR MORE.
THEY CAN'T WAIT TO GET BACK HOME
AND TO READ THE LIBRETTO IN BED
TO DECIPHER WHATEVER WENT ON . . .

FORBIDDEN FANTINE

. . . AND WHAT WE SAID,

ALL

BETTER READ YOUR SYNOPSIS
AT THE END OF THE PLAY!

[*One of the male actors is carried away by the turntable; female is carried upright. The other male actor,* COLM WILKINSON, *manages to stay at the microphone. He sings.*]

COLM WILKINSON

GOD, IT'S HIGH,
THIS SONG'S TOO HIGH.
PITY ME, CHANGE THE KEY.
BRING IT DOWN! BRING IT DOWN!
IT'S TOO HIGH, IT'S TOO HIGH,
MUCH TOO . . .

[*Dubbed by female offstage.*]

HIGH!

[COLM *spins off; female spins to mike and emotionally prepares herself as she becomes* FANTINE. *She sings very dramatically.*]

FORBIDDEN FANTINE

THERE WAS A TIME WHEN SHOWS WERE FUN
AND THEY USED BRIGHT LIGHTING
AND THE SHOWS WEREN'T SO LONG
AND THE SONGS WEREN'T SO BITING.
THERE WAS A TIME . . .
THEN IT ALL WENT WRONG.

I DREAMED A SHOW IN DAYS GONE BY
WHEN ALL THE SCEN'RY LOOKED SO PRETTY.
I DIDN'T SING ONE SONG, THEN DIE,
AND ALL MY COSTUMES WEREN'T SO GRITTY.

I DID A TAP DANCE AND I SMILED,
AND PATHOS WASN'T OVERSTATED.
MY LIPS WERE RED, MY HAIR WAS STYLED,
I DIDN'T ACT SO CONSTIPATED.

BUT NOW THAT MISERY'S IN STYLE,
IT'S ARTISTIC IF YOU SUFFER.
SO THEY TORE MY DRESS APART
AND THE CHORUS GIRLS WALK LAME.

I DREAMED A SHOW IN DAYS GONE BY;
NEIL DIAMOND DIDN'T SING MY HIT SONG.
A PRETTY GIRL THEY'D GLORIFY,
AND ACT I WASN'T SO DAMN LONG . . .

COME WATCH US GROVEL IN THE DIRT,
THEN BUY A SOUVENIR AND DON IT.
RICH FOLKS PAY TWENTY BUCKS A SHIRT
THAT HAS A STARVING PAUPER ON IT!

I DREAMED A SHOW IN DAYS GONE BY,
WHERE ALL THE SETS WEREN'T PILES OF RUBBLE.
I DIDN'T HAVE TO BELT HIGH E
AND BE AS MISERABLE AS ME.

[FANTINE *rotates offstage as* ENJOLRAS *and* ETIENNE *rotate on. They take a few moments to steady themselves and regain their equilibrium.*]

ETIENNE

IF I SEEM TO BE GRIEF STRICKEN
WHEN THIS SONG GOES ON AND ON,
EMPTY SONGS WITH EMPTY LYRICS
ALL ABOUT THE DEAD AND GONE . . .

ENJOLRAS

[*Recitative; very fast.*]

OH, NO, ETIENNE, YOU'RE SIMPLY A CONFUSED
AND WORRIED CHILD. LET ME EXPLAIN THE PLOT
OF THE SHOW TO YOU, SO YOU CAN UNDERSTAND
THE WAY IT'S STYLED: JEAN VALJEAN IS A CONVICT
WHO'S BEING CHASED BY THE POLICEMAN JAVERT,
WHO DOESN'T KNOW THAT HE IS NOW A MAYOR
AND HAS ADOPTED COSETTE, THE LITTLE WAIF
DAUGHTER OF FANTINE WHO DIES IN ACT 1. THAT'S
WHY JEAN VALJEAN MUST RUN.

ETIENNE

Ah, yes.

ENJOLRAS

[*Faster.*]
THEN HE BECOMES INVOLVED IN THE FRENCH
REVOLUTION—BUT NOT THE BIG FAMOUS ONE,
THE LITTLE LATER ONE YOU THOUGHT YOU DIDN'T
KNOW ANYTHING ABOUT—WHEN JEAN VALJEAN
WATCHES EVERYONE GET CAUGHT, EXCEPT FOR . . .

ETIENNE

[*Taking a good guess.*]

Marius!

ENJOLRAS

YES, MARIUS! WHO LOVES COSETTE INSTEAD OF
EPONINE, WHO JOINS THE REVOLUTIONARIES AND
RUNS OVER THE BARRICADE, WHERE SHE GETS . . .

ETIENNE

Pregnant?

ENJOLRAS

SHOT! AFTER SHE SINGS A LONG BALLAD. VERY
MUCH LIKE JEAN VALJEAN, WHO DIES PEACEFULLY,
KNOWING HE'S DRIVEN JAVERT TO JUMP OFF A
BRIDGE AND HAS SIGNIFICANTLY CHANGED FRANCE
BY BEING AN ALL-AROUND NICE GUY AND *C'EST
FINIS* OUR STORY'S DONE. HOW DID YOU LIKE THAT?

[ETIENNE *begins snoring as he sleeps.*]

DO YOU HEAR THE PEOPLE SING,
SINGING THE HIT SONGS FROM *LES MIZ*?
IT IS THE BEST SHOW OF A CLASSIC
SINCE THEY MODERNIZED *THE WIZ.*

BETTER LEARN THE SONGS BY HEART,
AND IF YOU DON'T, THEY'LL CALL YOU DUMB.
THEY'LL BE ATOP THE RECORD CHART
WHEN THE BRITISH COME!

NO MORE GERSHWIN, NO MORE KERN,
WE DON'T NEED OLD SHOWS ANYMORE.
WE'LL SET ABLAZE AND BURN
MOST EV'RY STEPHEN SONDHEIM SCORE!

[OTHER MISERABLES *enter from very odd places and
join in singing.*]

OTHERS

COME JOIN WITH THE FEW
WHO HAVE STARTED A MUSICAL WAR!

ALL

DO YOU HEAR THE PEOPLE SING
ALL OF THE NEW SONGS FROM *LES MIZ*?
EVEN THE GREAT ANDREW LLOYD WEBBER
WISHED THE SONGS WERE REALLY HIS.
YOU'LL BE TICKETED AND PINCHED
IF A *LA CAGE* SONG YOU SHOULD HUM;
POOR JERRY HERMAN WILL BE LYNCHED
WHEN THE BRITISH COME!

[*The British and French flags are handed to the
miserable revolutionaries. They march toward the
audience, militantly singing.*]

DO YOU HEAR THE PEOPLE SING
ALL OF THE NEW SONGS FROM *LES MIZ*?
NOW, WITH OUR NEW FRENCH REVOLUTION,
WE'LL DECAPITATE THE BIZ.

NOW *LES MIZ* IS HERE TO STAY,
AND *MISS SAIGON* WILL LEAVE YOU NUMB,
PHANTOM WILL HAUNT THE GREAT WHITE WAY
WHEN THE BRITISH COME!
AH! AH! AH!
THE BRITISH COME!

[*They raise the flags and strike a dramatic tableau, then
they turn the French flags over and they are British.*]

FOR BRITAIN BROADWAY!

COSETTE

[*Entering with a huge broom, as in the original
illustration.*]

I'M AN OBNOXIOUS SINGING WAIF.
MY CLOYING STRAIGHT TONES GRATE AND CHAFE.
LOST IN THE LABYRINTH OF THIS PLOT
YOU'LL BE RELIEVED WHEN I GET SHOT.

[MADAME THENARDIER *enters.*]

MADAME THÉNARDIER

Enough of that, my dearie. Now get off the stage!

[THÉNARDIER *enters. He and* MME. THÉNARDIER *take*
COSETTE*'s broom, throw her offstage and scream at
her.*]

And next time, we won't be so nice to you!

"Half an Empty House"

THÉNARDIER

WELCOME, MY FRIENDS.
DON'T GIVE US GRIEF;
WE ARE *LES MIZ*'S COMIC RELIEF.

MADAME THÉNARDIER

COVERED WITH DUST,
CRUSTY WITH MUD . . .

THÉNARDIER

. . . BUT EV'RY PUNCH LINE
LANDS WITH A THUD.

BOTH

SELDOM DO YOU SEE

LAUGHLESS CLOWNS LIKE WE
PERFORMING WORN-OUT JOKES
NO ONE COMES TO SEE.

HALF AN EMPTY HOUSE,
NO ONE IN THE BACK;
WE PUT VICTOR HUGO
ON A TORTURE RACK.
HOLDING FOR APPLAUSE,
MUGGING WITH OUR FACE,
LENGTHENING OUR PARTS BY STRETCHING OUT
    THE PACE.

THÉNARDIER

TRYING TO GET LAUGHS IS DISMAL . . .

MADAME THÉNARDIER

. . . WHEN THE FUNNY LINES AREN'T THERE . . .

BOTH

AND NOTHING GETS YOU NOTHING,
'SPECIALLY WHEN YOU'RE PLAYING TO THE AIR.

THÉNARDIER

HALF AN EMPTY HOUSE,
STILL WE NEVER CLOSE.

MADAME THÉNARDIER

COUNT THE ROACHES LIVING IN OUR
WORN-OUT CLOTHES.

THÉNARDIER

SPIDERS IN THE WIGS

MADAME THÉNARDIER

RODENTS IN MY DRESS

THÉNARDIER

NO WONDER CAM'RON MACKINTOSH
KEEPS OUT THE PRESS!

SO I PLAY A CARDBOARD CUTOUT

MADAME THÉNARDIER

AND A WRETCHED CARTOON SPOUSE.

THÉNARDIER

FLATTER THAN A PHOTOGRAPH . . .

MADAME THÉNARDIER

WHAT A LOUSY EPITAPH!

THÉNARDIER

BEGGING FOR A LITTLE LAUGH

BOTH

WHEN THERE'S HALF AN EMPTY HOUSE!

"On My Phone"

EPONINE

ROTATING UPSTAGE, WHERE IT'S DARK,
THERE ISN'T ANYONE TO TALK TO.
I SAY MY LINES, I HIT MY MARK,
BUT I KEEP LOOKING AT THE CLOCK, TOO.
UNTIL I ENTER NEXT,
THERE'S LOT'S OF TIME TO SEND A TEXT . . .

ON MY PHONE,
I CHECK UP ON MY VOICE MAIL;
ON MY PHONE,
BEHIND THE *LES MIZ* RUBBLE.
WITHOUT LIGHTS,
THE MURKY SHADOWS HIDE ME.
IN CASE I'M FEELING BORED,
I KEEP MY IPHONE CLOSE BESIDE ME.

ON MY PHONE,
WHILE JEAN VALJEAN IS WEEPING,
I CAN CALL

THE JERK WITH WHOM I'M SLEEPING.

IN THE DARKNESS, I STILL CAN TEXT A MESSAGE

AND GOSSIP WITH MY GIRLFRIEND

WHILE I'M SINGING "ON MY OWN."

[*Her phone rings.*]

Hello? Oh, hi! Where are you guys? Oh, you're in Act II? We're still in Act I. I'll call you back after I die.

ROTATE ME, THEN SHOOT ME.

I'M DYING TO CALL YOU . . . ON MY PHONE.

"Scars"

JAVERT

THERE, OUT IN THE DARKNESS,

AN AUDIENCE WATCHES

MY UGLY FACE

GRIMACE AND CHASE

PRETTIER PEOPLE

WITH PRETTIER SONGS

THAN A MIDDLE-AGED BASS

EVER GETS TO EMBRACE . . .

AND AFTER YEARS

OF LES MIS'RABLE HELL

HERE'S MY REWARD . . .

SCARS

ON MY VOCAL CORDS,

MOUNTED AND MOUNTING,

SWELLING MY TONSILS.

MY THROAT IS SO TIGHT,

I CALLED UP EQUITY.

THEY DIDN'T CARE;

THEY SAID, "GOSH, WHAT A SHAME.

DID YOU THINK THIS WAS *MAME*?"

BUT AFTER YEARS

OF TOURING THROUGH HELL,

MY CORDS AFLAME!

SCARS!

NOT JUST ON MY CORDS

SCARS ON MY EGO.

ONCE I PLAYED *HAMLET*!

NOW, NIGHT AFTER NIGHT,

I JUMP OFF A PLASTIC BRIDGE.

I SWEAR, SINGING "STARS"

GIVES ME MORE VOCAL SCARS!

[*He mimes jumping off a bridge. His last note trails off into an echo.*]

"Thank Heaven There Is *Lez Miz*"

MAURICE CHEVALIER

[*Entering, he speaks directly to the audience.*]

Bonjour, monsieur. Bonjour, madame. Things are getting a little melodramatic around here, so I have dropped by to add a little Gallic charm.

[*He sings to the tune of "Thank Heaven for Little Girls."*]

REMEMBER ALL THOSE FRENCHIE SHOWS FROM
   1957

GIGI AND *CAN-CAN* HAD TO CLOSE, THAT'S WHY I
   SAY . . .

THANK HEAVEN THERE IS *LES MIZ*!

IT GETS MORE MIS-ER-A-BLE EV'RY DAY.

THANK HEAVEN THERE IS *LES MIZ*!

IT'S NOT THE FOLIES BERGERE, BUT 'S OK.

THOSE STARVING PAUPERS ALWAYS MAKE ME
   SHIVER,

AND IT'S A SMASH WHEN JAVERT CRASHES IN THE
    RIVER!

[*Alternate version of bridge.*]

AND WHEN IT'S CLOSED, IT'S ALWAYS REASSURING
TO KNOW WE'LL JOIN THEM IN DES MOINES
WHERE THEY'RE STILL TOURING.

THANK HEAVEN THERE IS *LES MIZ*!
THANK HEAVEN FOR THE PLOT
AND FORTY SONGS THAT RUMBLE BY;
WITHOUT IT, HOW WOULD JEAN VALJEAN DIE?

GET A TICKET TO GO; IT'S BY VICTOR HUGO.
THANK HEAVEN THERE IS *LES MIZ*!

THERE'S EPONINE AND COSETTE SO APPEALING;
WHEN THEY ESCAPE, WE'LL HAVE TO SCRAPE YOU
    OFF THE CEILING.

THANK HEAVEN THERE IS *LES MIZ*.
THANK HEAVEN FOR THE SONGS,
SO OVERBLOWN THEY RAISE THE ROOF,
WITHOUT IT, WHO AND WHAT WOULD WE SPOOF?

"Ten Years More"

VALJEAN

TEN YEARS MORE!
ANOTHER DECADE IS OUR DESTINY,
THIS NEVER-ENDING RUN OF INFAMY.
THE PUBLIC DOESN'T MIND THE FACT
THIS CRUSTY SHOW HAS BEEN SHELLACKED.
TEN YEARS MORE!

FANTINE

I DREAMED THAT I WAS IN *LES MIZ*;
NOW, EV'RY NIGHT, I WAKE UP SCREAMING.

VALJEAN

TEN YEARS MORE!

FANTINE

MY TEETH ARE BLACK, MY HAIR IS FRIZZ,
I WALK AROUND ONSTAGE BLASPHEMING.

VALJEAN

WE'VE BECOME A THEME PARK RIDE.

FANTINE and JAVERT

WE'RE THE VICTOR HUGO RIDE

VALJEAN

BRITISH SHOWS ARE STUFFED AND MOUNTED

FANTINE and JAVERT

LIKE A TAXIDERMIST SHOW

VALJEAN

YOU CAN SMELL FORMALDEHYDE!

FANTINE and JAVERT

DON'T SIT TOO CLOSE WHEN YOU GO

VALJEAN

ALL THE ACTORS ARE EMBALMED!

FANTINE and JAVERT

NEW SHOWS, BEWARE:
WE'LL STILL BE THERE!

VALJEAN

TEN YEARS MORE!

JAVERT

TEN YEARS MORE IS UNDERSTATING
ALL THE YEARS WE HAVE AHEAD.
CHANCES ARE WE'LL STILL BE RUNNING
WHEN MOST PEOPLE HERE ARE DEAD!

MADAME THÉNARDIER

ONCE A PIECE OF ART,

NOW A PIECE OF CRAP.

JUST WHAT NEW YORK NEEDS:

ANOTHER TOURIST TRAP!

CROSS IT OFF THE LIST,

GET BACK ON THE VAN.

ONLY BROADWAY SHOW

WITH OUR OWN PENSION PLAN.

ALL

PHANTOM, MISS SAIGON, AND *CATS,*

(PRAISE THE LORD, THEY JUST CLOSED *CATS!*)

THEY'LL ALL CLOSE, AND WE'LL BE RUNNING.

(NOTHING ELSE WILL LAST AS LONG.)

WE'RE THE RULING AUTOCRATS

(INDESTRUCTIBLE AS RATS).

DO YOU HEAR THE PEOPLE SING?

THE SAME OLD SONGS GO ON AND ON.

[*They repeat the lyrics above, singing together. Then . . .*]

TOMORROW I'LL BE MUMMIFIED,

TOMORROW I'LL BE OSSIFIED,

TOMORROW YOU'LL BE TERRIFIED.

THERE'S NOTHING REALLY NEW IN STORE.

WHAT A BORE!

YOU'RE IN FOR

TEN YEARS MORE!

Parody Tonight: 1996–97

After the break in the show's New York run and our stints in L.A. and San Diego, we were very excited about opening a new edition in New York at the Triad Theatre on West 72nd Street. Does that location sound familiar? Well, the Triad is the new incarnation of Palsson's Supper Club, the very same venue where *Forbidden Broadway* was originally done in 1982.

The 1995-96 season was particularly interesting and varied: *Rent* was big news, Julie Andrews was back on Broadway in *Victor/Victoria*, and Carol Channing was back with her last revival of *Hello, Dolly!* There was that smash revival of *The King and I* with Donna Murphy and Lou Diamond Phillips, and other noteworthy shows like *Big* and *Bring in Da Noise, Bring in Da Funk*. *Show Boat* was playing at the Gershwin, and Nathan Lane had done a revival of *A Funny Thing Happened on the Way to the Forum*.

Then there was *A Delicate Balance* with Rosemary Harris, George Grizzard, and Elaine Stritch; even though it was a play, it was almost like a musical in its hype. And most importantly there was *Master Class,* eminently spoofable because it was about Maria Callas and it was so operatic—especially when Patti LuPone replaced Zoe Caldwell after having been fired from *Sunset Boulevard.*

So there was a lot for us to "reflect upon," which led to *Forbidden Broadway Strikes Back!* That was the perfect title because we had been away for a while. It was also a great time for a new edition because American musicals were back in a big way. It felt like Broadway was finally starting to come out of the British "operacals" era; *Les Miz, Phantom,* and *Cats* were all still running, but they weren't the new, trendy shows anymore.

One of the major occurrences of the time was that *Cats* passed *A Chorus Line* as the longest-running show in Broadway history. In our show, we had a "Stop Cats!" number. The point was, "Enough is enough!" It was all right for *Cats* to still be running, but for it to break *A Chorus Line*'s record was just wrong.

Left: Donna English (as Julie Andrews), Bryan Batt (as Lou Diamond Phillips), David Hibbard (as Nathan Lane), and Christine Pedi (as Elaine Paige). Right: Donna English, Bryan Batt, Christine Pedi, and Tom Plotkin lead the protest to "Stop *Cats!*"

Phill George and I agree that creating *Forbidden Broadway Strikes Back!* was one of our most enjoyable experiences in the show's history. Phill did an incredible job with the staging, and that freed up a lot of time for me to go home and hone the lyrics. Although Phill and I were no longer in a romantic relationship at that point, we continued to work together fruitfully through the many editions of the show that followed. You could say our professional relationship was an Off-Broadway version of the one between Gwen Verdon and Bob Fosse—although Phill always reminded me, "I'm no Gwen Verdon, and you, Gerard, are no Bob Fosse."

As Fred Ebb might have said, that year at *Forbidden Broadway* was The Happy Time. Heaven knows, we had a lot to work with. Sondheim's *Passion* had opened and closed while we were in California, but the show was too juicy for us to skip over: So we had Donna Murphy playing Anna in *The King and I* as if she were Fosca from *Passion,* singing "I Whistle a Sondheim Tune."

I was particularly proud of the *Master Class* sketch. Patti LuPone was the teacher, and her students were the people who had wronged her: Madonna, who had done the movie version of *Evita;* Glenn Close, who had stolen Patti's role in *Sunset Boulevard;* and Andrew Lloyd Webber, who had fired her from that show. It was all about gossip and hearsay, and it came out like a sharp little one-act play.

Ms. LuPone came to see the show while we were doing that sketch. I think she liked it; she hung around afterwards and took pictures with the cast. But I remember her saying to me, "That was much better than the last number you wrote about me [meaning "I Get a Kick Out Of Me"]. Thanks, Gerald!" Now, I'm pretty sure she knows my name is Gerard. So maybe that was her way of getting in a little dig.

We had previously spoofed Julie Andrews with a number called "I Couldn't Hit the Note (Until They Dropped the Key)." I had heard through the grapevine that she knew about it and was very upset. But for the *Victor/Victoria* spoof, we focused on the whole drama of her turning down her Tony Award nomination. That spoof was far less mean—you could even say it was supportive—so we tried to get her to come see the show. But it never happened.

Phill George and Gerard Alessandrini give 'em the ol' glossy Fosse.

I did get to meet Julie through my talented friend Rachel York, who was in *Victor/Victoria.* I went backstage after the show and asked Julie to sign my *My Fair Lady* cast album, on which I already had Rex Harrison's signature. He had written, "Congratulations, Gerard, for a job well done." Julie asked me, "Why was Rex congratulating you? What do you do?" I said, "Well . . . I'm the writer and director of *Forbidden Broadway.*" She gasped, "Oh!"—and just for a moment, she looked as if someone had squirted a lemon in her face. But she immediately recovered, said "That's wonderful," and signed the album: "Love, Julie Andrews."

Our show had a tremendous cast at the time: Bryan Batt, Donna English, and Christine Pedi at her peak. That edition was a lot of people's favorite *Forbidden Broadway,* partly because we had so much great material to work with. Michael Crawford was doing a concert tour, so we razzed him with a number called "Put On Your Phony Voice," to the tune of "Put On Your Sunday Clothes" from *Hello, Dolly!*

Our parody of *Rent* was an eye-opener for me. We had spoofed rock musicals before, and I had found that the original lyrics were pretty loose as far as how well they scanned and rhymed, how little subtext they contained, and so on. I assumed *Rent* was going to be more of the same, and it wasn't until I actually started working

"Seasons of Hype": Bryan Batt, Christine Pedi, Donna English, and Tom Plotkin.

on the parody that I realized how well crafted Jonathan Larson's lyrics and libretto are. It's tragic that he didn't live to write more shows.

In the summer of 1997, we moved the show to the cabaret space at Ellen's Stardust Diner on Broadway—right next to the Winter Garden, where *Cats* was playing. That was where Elaine Stritch came to see Christine "do" her. As I remember, we weren't very nervous about her coming. I guess we figured anyone who's that uncensored and direct about life could probably take being made fun of, and besides, I don't think we said anything all that bad about her.

Donna Murphy came to see the show, and I remember that she was practically under the table—either from embarrassment or because she was laughing so hard, I'm not sure which. The number was about the sexual subtext in *The King and I;* we did "Shall We Boink?" to the tune of "Shall We Dance?" I liked that it was all about sex but we used the silly, sophomoric word "boink" instead of something more explicit. I had realized that we could put the f-word into the show fifteen times and get fifteen laughs, but they'd be cheap laughs. (Years later, I saw an old Groucho Marx interview in which he said exactly the same thing.)

Later in the '96 edition, we added a *Titanic* number. That was such a spoofable musical. It had an elaborate opening sequence with the whole cast singing about the ship, except there was no ship onstage. Not even a tiny part of it. So I wrote a parody of the song "Ship of Dreams," called "Ship of Air."

We never got around to *Steel Pier,* because it closed so quickly. It had become clear to us that you really can't spoof the quick-closing flops—not only because it's mean to kick people when they're down, but also because our audience needs to have seen a show, or at least have read and heard a lot about it, in order for us to spoof it. Maybe the one exception is when something is a huge hit in London and then flops on Broadway, but I don't think that has happened for a long time. (Of course, the best type of show for us to target is a flop that runs for a while, like *The Little Mermaid* . . .)

During this period, *Forbidden Broadway* became a veritable parade of Alvin Colt's costumes. I'll never forget what Alvin came up with for the Julie Andrews number: Julie would come out in her robe for "Le Jazz Hot," but under that was her *Mary Poppins* costume, and under *that* was her *Victor/Victoria* tux with tails. It was brilliant work on Alvin's part. With this great artist now a more vital part of our mischievous crew, we were all set for the next stage in *Forbidden Broadway*'s evolution.

Christine Pedi, Bryan Batt, Donna English, and Tom Plotkin go down on the *Titanic*.

"Parody Tonight"

[*Fanfare.* NATHAN LANE *enters, wearing a Roman tunic and headband over a tux.*]

NATHAN

Playkillers, I bid you welcome. I'm Nathan Lane. Thank you. This cabaret is a temple, and we are here to make a sacrifice to the gods of Broadway. Tonight, I am pleased to announce a parody. We shall steal a little bit of every show in our desire to abuse them.

SOME SONGS FROM SONDHEIM,

SOME SETS FROM SUNSET,
SOMETHING ON EVERYONE,
A PARODY TONIGHT!

SOMETHING INCISIVE,
SOMETHING DERISIVE,
SOME DIRT ON EVERYONE,
A PARODY TONIGHT!

NO DISNEY DROPS,
NO SATIN GOWNS—
SEND IN THE LITTLE NIGHT MUSIC CLOWNS.

CLASSIC SHOWS CUT DOWN,
LESSER ONES SHUT DOWN.
WE'LL SHOOT OUT EV'RY BROADWAY LIGHT!
THEATRE WING TOMORROW,
PARODY TONIGHT!

[LIZA *bounces out of the wings, yelping and screaming for no apparent reason.*]

LIZA

Oh! Oh! Oh! I'm so happy to be here . . . oh! Nathan, I love you. I love you. It's all so terrific!

[*She suddenly stops and freezes into a typical, phony, Liza-esque pose.*]

NATHAN

TRAVESTY *TOMORROW,*
PARODY TONIGHT!

[LIZA *drops character and exits with her tail between her legs.*]

SOMETHING DRAMATIC,
GRAND, OPERATIC,
SOMETHING WITH ZOE CALDWELL,
PARODY TONIGHT!

[ZOE CALDWELL *enters grandly as Maria Callas in* Master Class.]

ZOE CALDWELL

Please, Ari, no! No! I don't want to sing. I don't want to make love. I don't want Patti LuPone to replace me in *Master Class.* However, I won't have a word said against her. But a Maria Callas from Long Island?! I ask you . . .

NATHAN

NO *GRAND HOTEL,*

NOTHING WITH CHAIRS,
ONLY THIS GUY FROM *HOLLYWOOD SQUARES* . . .

[JOHN DAVIDSON *enters.*]

JOHN DAVIDSON

I'M JOHN DAVIDSON, I STARRED IN *STATE FAIR,*
AND TO TELL YOU THE TRUTH, IT'S NOT GREAT
    FARE;
THE PLOT IS SO VAPID YOU'LL ALL GO INSANE,
BUT THAT'S PERFECT FOR ME, 'CAUSE I DON'T HAVE
    A BRAIN . . .

OH, WHAT A BEAUTIFUL MORON!
OH, WHAT A BEAUTIFUL GUY!
I'VE GOT A BEAUTIFUL HAIRDO
EVEN WITHOUT MY HAIR DYE.
OH, WHAT A BEAUTIFUL . . .

[ZOE *interrupts him.*]

ZOE

John, John, I'm sure you're a very nice person. But you don't have a look . . .

ZOE and NATHAN

Get one!

NATHAN

SUNSET'S BIG DITTY
SUNG BY A BRIT E—
LAINE PAIGE AS NORMA DESMOND:
PARODY TONIGHT!

[ELAINE PAIGE *enters, walking on her knees.*]

ELAINE

ONE FOOT MORE
AND YOU'D SEE MY FACE.
I'M TOO SHORT FOR THAT BIG STAIRCASE!

I'M A BIGGER STAR BACK HOME;
HERE IT'S SO BIZARRE, I'M A MUNCHKIN STAR.

ZOE

Elaine Paige. I won't have a word said against her. But a three-foot Norma Desmond? I ask you . . .

[ZOE *exits.*]

ELAINE

I'm not small! It's the sets that got bigger!

[ELAINE *and* JOHN *exit, leaving* NATHAN *alone onstage.*]

NATHAN

GOSSIP 'BOUT GREAT STARS,
TEN-YEARS-TOO-LATE STARS.
JULIE WILL RUN AWAY IN FRIGHT!
CAMELOT TOMORROW,
PARODY TONIGHT!

And now, in order to take you to *Forbidden Broadway,* I need you all to blow out the candles on your tables. Go ahead and blow! And now, the formally attired company!

[*The members of the company enter individually after they finish their changes into evening wear; they sing the following, some lines solo, some together.*]

SOMETHING DELICIOUS
AND SLIGHTLY VICIOUS,
RUMORS REITERATED,
PARODY TONIGHT!

LYRICS PERVERTED,
NEW WORDS INSERTED,
PHANTOM OBLITERATED,
PARODY TONIGHT!

NO STAR UNSCARRED,
NO STONE UNTHROWN,
AND WE'LL LEAVE NO SHOW TUNE ALONE.

SOMETHING THAT'S RENTED,
SOMETHING DEMENTED,
QUICK CHANGES ALL DONE OUT OF SIGHT!

MUSICAL SURPRISES,
SAVIONS AND LIZAS,
COMMUNISTS AND COOLIES,
ISABELLES AND JULIES,
THEATRE VETS, BERNADETTES,
HEART ATTACKS, JERRY ZAKS,
MISTAKES, FAKES, FLOPS, PROPS
ROCKERS, SHOCKERS, MOCKERS, KNOCKERS . . .

NO RISING SET, NO CHANDELIER,
BUT FOUR CAROL CHANNINGS, I FEAR!
DON'T CROSS THAT MEANY
ALESSANDRINI—
HE'LL PUT YOU ON A TORTURE RACK!
PARODY THIS EVENING:
FORBIDDEN BROADWAY STRIKES BACK!

"Slow Boat"

SOUTHERN BELLE CHORUS

P.C. *SHOW BOAT,* P.C. *SHOW BOAT*
HAROLD PRINCE'S FLOATING BARGE!
P.C. *SHOW BOAT,* P.C. *SHOW BOAT,*
ULTRA-STREAMLINED, ULTRA-LARGE.

FIFTY PEOPLE IN THE CHORUS,
FORTY PLAYERS IN THE PIT—
EV'RY BALLAD, EV'RY REPRISE,
EV'RY LITTLE BIT!

[GAYLORD *and* MAGNOLIA *enter as the chorus exits.*]

GAYLORD

ONLY MAKE BELIEVE YOU'RE TWENTY

MAGNOLIA

ONLY MAKE BELIEVE YOU'RE SIX FOOT TWO

GAYLORD

LET'S FORGET WHAT YOUR SET OF REVIEWS SAID:
COULDN'T SING, COULDN'T ACT

MAGNOLIA

NOR COULD YOU!

GAYLORD

MAKE BELIEVE MY BREATH IS MINTY

MAGNOLIA

AND YOUR CLUMSY FEET DON'T CRUSH MY TOES.

BOTH

MIGHT AS WELL MAKE BELIEVE, I SUPPOSE,
FOR IN [*Insert number.*] WEEKS, WE CLOSE.

OFFSTAGE CHORUS

CAPTAIN ANDY, CAPTAIN ANDY—
OLD JOHN CULLUM STEALS THE SHOW!

[JOHN CULLUM *enters as Andy.*]

JOHN

OL' SHOW *SHOW BOAT,*
BUT IT'S A SLOW BOAT,
THEY SHOULD CUT SOMETHIN'
BUT DON'T CUT NOTHIN'!
IT'S OL' SHOW *SHOW BOAT,*
AND WE DO EV'RY DAMN SONG.

THERE'S THIRTY BACKDROPS
AND TONS OF COTTON
AND SO MUCH SCEN'RY

THE PLOT'S FORGOTTEN.
IT'S ALL OF *SHOW BOAT,*
AND IT'S TWO HOURS
TOO LONG!

[CHORUS *enters and sings.*]

CHORUS

TWO HOURS TOO LONG!

"Stritch"

[ELAINE STRITCH *enters and sings.*]

ELAINE

I THOUGHT THAT I HAD HIT A LOW NOTE
WHEN I TOOK A SMALLER BIT IN *SHOW BOAT.*
I NORMALLY AVOID A LOSER,
BUT WHEN CASTING TIME IS NEAR,
THIS IS WHAT I HEAR
WHEN THEY'RE LOOKING FOR A BOOZER:

STRITCH!
NOTHING RILES YOU UP OR MAKES YOU TURN RED.
STRITCH!
YOU'RE SO DEADPAN, PEOPLE THINK THAT YOU'RE
    DEAD.

STRITCH!
WOULD YOU LIKE TO WORK AT RAINBOW AND
    STARS?
STRITCH!
THEY NEED SOMEONE DOWNSTAIRS PARKING THE
    CARS.

ONCE MY BROADWAY CREDITS TOWERED,
I DID SHOWS FOR NOËL COWARD.
STRITCH—I WAS VENERATED!
I WAS CLASSY AS DEE HOTY,

NOW I ALWAYS PLAY A THROATY
BITCH—I'VE DEGENERATED.

STRITCH!
ALL MY CO-STARS CRY OUT, "PUT ON YOUR SHOES!"
STRITCH!
WHO THE HELL DRANK ALL THE BOOZE?

AND WHEN I GET DRUNK, THE AUDIENCE
    APPLAUDS!
OH, STRITCH!
STRITCH, STRITCH, STRITCH!
I'M THE QUEEN OF BROADWAY'S BOOZING BROADS!

I'll drink to that!

[*Blackout.*]

"The King Is Her"

[*Lights up on fanfare from* The King and I. LOUIS
enters, looks out at audience, and speaks.]

LOUIS

Mother, Rodgers and Hammerstein would not have
liked this production of *The King and I,* would they?
Mother!

[DONNA MURPHY *enters, looking like Fosca from*
    Sondheim's Passion.]

DONNA

No, Louis. Rodgers and Hammerstein would *not* have
liked this production of *The King and I.* Not ever!

LOUIS

Mother, I think you're frightening when you play Anna
like Fosca from Stephen Sondheim's *Passion.*

DONNA

Yes, Louis, sometimes I frighten myself very much. Very
much indeed.

LOUIS

What do you do?

DONNA

I whistle!

LOUIS

A Richard Rodgers tune?

DONNA

Oh, no, Louis. I whistle something much more
complicated . . .

WHENEVER I FEEL AFRAID
THAT *KING AND I*'S TOO COY,
I WHISTLE A SONDHEIM TUNE
AND TAKE OUT ALL THE JOY FROM THE PLAY.

WHILE SINGING A SAPPY SONG
FROM BROADWAY'S CLASSIC SHOWS,
I WHISTLE A SONDHEIM TUNE
AND NO ONE EVER KNOWS
THERE'S A PLAY.

THE RESULTS ARE QUITE DISTURBING
AND VERY STRANGE TO TELL,
FOR EVERYBODY COWERS IN FEAR
AND SO DO I, AS WELL!

I WHISTLE A SONDHEIM TUNE,
WEAR DRESSES FULL OF FLEAS,
PLAY ANNA LIKE I'M A LOON,
AND ALL THE SIAMESE ARE AFRAID!

SCRUNCH UP LIKE A TROLL
AND THEN GROVEL WHEN YOU BOW,

WEAR AN UGLY MOLE
AND A FURRY UNI-BROW.

[ANNA *grabs* LOUIS*'s face and they badly whistle a strange melody.*]

BOTH

EVERYONE'S AFRAID,
BUT WE GET A SECOND BOW!

DONNA

Now it's time to meet the new King of Siam: Lou Diamond Phillips!

[LOUIS *exits.* KING LOU *enters grandly to music. He is wearing a* King and I *tunic and has black hair piled very high on his head.*]

KING

What manner of Mrs. An-na is this? This is no Mrs. Ann-na!

DONNA

Oh, forgive me, Your Majesty. I carry residual fear and anger from playing Fosca in Sondheim's *Passion*. It's like catching a strange sickness.

KING

Sickness? You! Go away!

DONNA

Oh, no, your majesty, please. Let me stay.

[*She throws herself at his feet and grovels.*]

I beg you. Please!

[*She tugs at his cloak.*]

I need you! I love you! Don't spurn me!

KING

You disgust me. Get away! There are no James Lapine characters in Rodgers and Hammerstein.

DONNA

Please, I know I'm pathetic, but please love me. Love me or I'll die!

KING

What is this strange passion you bring to this show?

DONNA

It's the subtext, Your Majesty.

KING

Subtext? I know nothing of acting. My big movie was *La Bamba.* You teach. Teach, teach, teach!

DONNA

THIS SHOW WAS DONE BEFORE,
AND DONE SO VERY WELL,
WE HAVE TO FIND A BRAND-NEW SLANT
SO ALL THE TICKETS SELL.
YOU'RE CERTAINLY NOT YUL . . .

KING

AND YOU'RE NO GERTRUDE L.

DONNA

LET'S MAKE THE TEXT
OVERSEXED,
LIKE THE BRITISH DID TO *CAROUSEL*!

SHALL WE BOINK?
SHALL WE PLAY ALL THE SUBTEXT ON THE TOP?
SHALL WE BOINK?
SHALL WE BREAK OUT THE CHAINS AND RIDING
    CROP?

KING

LET'S NOT DANCE;
LET'S GET LUN-THA AND TUPTIM, AND THEN SWAP.

DONNA

SHALL WE ROLL IN A HAYSTACK
WITH OUR ARMS AROUND EACH OTHER

KING

WHILE THE PIGGIES GO OINK, OINK, OINK?

DONNA

WE COULD DISCO OR SAMBA

KING

BETTER YET, LET'S DO *LA BAMBA*!

BOTH

SHALL WE BOINK?
SHALL WE BOINK?
SHALL WE BOINK?

[*They dance* La Bamba. *The* KING *gets lost under her dress.*]

DONNA

Yes, Your Majesty. No, Your Majesty. How low should I go, Your Majesty?

[*They moan ecstatically. The music stops.*]

Oh, that was good, Your Majesty!

[*The* KING *hands* DONNA *a cigarette and takes one himself. They smoke. Blackout.*]

Michael Crawford: "Put On Your Phony Voice"

MICHAEL

[*Enters wearing Phantom mask, sing very pretentiously and slightly sharp.*]

MICHAEL CRAWFORD,
PHANTOM OF THE AGES,
NOW A SINGER
ON LAS VEGAS STAGES.
WHEN MY LUNGS INFLATE,
I SING BETTER THAN JOHN RAITT,
AND THOUGH PINZA'S VOICE WAS GREAT
BACK IN HIS DAY,
MINE IS RICH AND DEEPER PEOPLE SAY.

[*He suddenly de-masks and becomes a dumb, insipid Cornelius Hackl from the movie* Hello, Dolly!]

"MICHAEL!"
PEOPLE ASK ME HOW I DO IT.
THOUGH I PLAYED CORNELIUS HACKL LONG AGO,
I'D CACKLE LONG AGO . . .

"MICHAEL,
TELL US ALL HOW YOU GET THROUGH IT."
WELL, I'LL TELL YOU,
IT'S MY TRAINING, EVERYONE.
STOP COMPLAINING, EVERYONE!

PUT ON YOUR PHONY VOICE

[*Suddenly switches back to Phantom.*]

AS IF YOU'RE ALFRED DRAKE,

[*Suddenly switches back to Cornelius.*]

TURN UP THE REVERB
WHEN THE SONG'S A BITCH.

TO SELL A MILLION RECORDS
IS A PIECE OF CAKE,

[*Back to Phantom.*]

YOU SING REAL SLOW,
JUST A TOUCH BELOW THE PITCH,

[*Back to Cornelius.*]

AND YOU'RE SUDDENLY RICH!

PUT ON YOUR PHONY VOICE
AND EVERYONE IS FOOLED.
THE STARVING PUBLIC BOWS TO ME AND KNEELS!

SING THROUGH YOUR NOSE,
AND THE EMPEROR'S CLOTHES
CAN BE YOURS IF NOBODY SQUEALS,
'CAUSE A PHONY VOICE
IS WHAT MAKES RECORD DEALS.

[*Back to Phantom.*]

SAY YOU'LL BUY MY NEXT PRETENTIOUS ALBUM!
YOU'RE A FOOL TO BUY, BUT IF YOU DO,
THIRTEEN BUCKS IS ALL I ASK OF YOU.

[*Back to Cornelius; sings in double time.*]

PUT ON YOUR PHONY VOICE
AND JUST EMOTE THE REST,
BECAUSE IT'S PUT TOGETHER BIT BY BIT.

THOUGH I'M A WEASEL,
I STILL CAN PLEASE ALL
THE FOLKS WHO THINK I'M LEGIT.

WITH MY PHONY VOICE I STILL CAN SHOVEL,
PHONY VOICE I STILL CAN SHOVEL,
PHONY VOICE I STILL CAN SHOVEL . . .

[*Reverts back to Phantom, sings reverentially.*]

SHIT.

[*The chandelier falls on his head, and he screams.*]

SHIT!

"Be Depressed"

LUMIÈRE

Mademoiselle Broadway, it is with deepest pride
and greatest pleasure that we give you a glimpse of
the world's most successful musicals. But, my dear
Broadway, they don't come from you anymore. So . . .

BE DEPRESSED, BE DEPRESSED,
'CAUSE WALT DISNEY IS THE BEST.
NOW THE BIGGEST BROADWAY MUSICAL'S
A CARTOON FROM THE WEST.

CHILDREN SAY, "IT'S A FEAST
SEEING *BEAUTY AND THE BEAST.*"
NOW, WHAT TURNS THE GREAT WHITE WAY ON
IS A DRAMA DRAWN IN CRAYON.

GUYS WHO SING, DOLLS WHO DANCE,
MOB AUDITIONS FOR THE CHANCE
TO PLAY DINNERWARE THAT SEEMS TO BE
    POSSESSED.

AND BROADWAY, WHILE YOU'RE FADING,
WE WILL BE INVADING

BE DEPRESSED—*OUI*, DEPRESSED—
BE DEPRESSED.

[*The* BEAST *enters.*]

BEAST

I'M A BEAST, I'M A TROLL
BUT AT LEAST I HAVE A ROLE.
DISNEY OFFERED ME A BONUS
SO I HAD TO SELL MY SOUL

I'M A WRECK IN THIS DRECK.
AH, BUT HECK, I GET A CHECK.

LUMIÈRE

ALL IN ALL, IT'S QUITE DELICIOUS
GETTING PAID TO DANCE WITH DISHES!

BEAST

WE HAVE SONGS, WE HAVE PLOT—
EVERYTHING MOST SHOWS HAVE NOT.

LUMIÈRE

IT'S NO WONDER VINCENT CANBY IS IMPRESSED!

BEAST

WHILE LUMIÈRE IS FLICK'RING,
BROADWAY, YOU'LL BE BICK'RING.
YOU'RE SO STRESSED, I SUGGEST
YOU RECOUP AND TAKE A REST.
BE DEPRESSED, BE DEPRESSED, BE DEPRESSED.

[MRS. POTTS *enters.*]

MRS. POTTS

WHAT A TRIP, WHAT A TRAP,
DRESSING UP INSIDE THIS CRAP.
WHEN I'M STUCK INSIDE A DOORWAY,
EV'RYBODY GIVES ME FLAP.

HOW I DREAD AND TURN RED,
ACTING WITH A SEVERED HEAD.
LITTLE CHIP IS SO REPULSIVE,
KIDDIES SCREAM AND GET CONVULSIVE.

DISNEY BRIBED, DISNEY FOUGHT,
THE NEW AMSTERDAM THEY BOUGHT;
FOR THAT DEAL, THEY SHOULD BE
SUBJECT TO ARREST.

BUT, BROADWAY, YOU WERE DYIN'
TILL THE DISNEY BUY-IN

BEAST

YOU'RE DEPRESSED.

MRS. POTTS

YOU NEED "EST,"
MAYBE PROZAC, I SUGGEST.

LUMIÈRE, BEAST, and MRS. POTTS

BE DEPRESSED, BE DEPRESSED.
BROADWAY, NOW YOU'RE DISNEY'S GUEST.
WATCH OUT! MICKEY MOUSE AND DONALD DUCK
WILL PUT YOU TO THE TEST.

IF WE LAUGH, IF WE GLOAT,
IT'S 'CAUSE THEATRE'S SO REMOTE.

[BELLE *enters as* MRS. POTTS *exits.*]

LUMIÈRE, BEAST, and BELLE

AND NOW STEPHEN SONDHEIM'S TEACHER
IS AN ANIMATED FEATURE!

BLOCK BY BLOCK, STORE BY STORE,
WE'LL ACQUIRE MORE AND MORE.
WE'LL BUY FORTY-SECOND STREET
FROM EAST TO WEST!

BUT, BROADWAY, YOU WERE DYIN'
TILL THE DISNEY BUY-IN.
SO BE DEPRESSED, BE DEPRESSED,
BE DEPRESSED, 'CAUSE WE'RE THE BEST!

[*The* BEAST *retrieves a large Tony Award from the wings. The Disney characters pose around it and then turn the center of the award around to reveal a Mickey Mouse silhouette emblazoned on the center. They point to it lovingly. Blackout.*]

"Stop Cats!"

VOICEOVER

And now, welcome to auditions for the longest-running show in Broadway history!

[*Music from* A Chorus Line. *Lights up on auditioning cats.*]

VOICE-OVER (ZACK)

AGAIN!
SCRATCH, LICK, LICK, PURR, KICK, SCRATCH!

AGAIN!
SCRATCH, LICK, LICK, PURR, KICK, SCRATCH!

AGAIN!
SCRATCH, LICK, LICK, PURR, KICK, SCRATCH!

RIGHT! THAT CONNECTS WITH
PURR, PURR, FLICK, HISS, SCRATCH, STEP,
TURN, LICK, LICK, PURR, KICK, SPRAY!

Got it? Right. Let's do the whole combination now facing downstage away from the litter box!

UH, five-six-seven-eight!

CATS

MEOW, I HOPE I GET IT!
I HOPE I GET IT!
HOW MANY KITTIES DOES HE NEED?
MEOW, I HOPE I GET IT!
I HOPE I GET IT!
DOES HE WANT STRAYS OR SIAMESE?
LOOK AT ALL THE PUSSIES,
AT ALL THE PUSSIES.
HOW MANY KITTIES DOES HE NEED?
HOW MANY STRAYS OR SIAMESE?
HOW MANY KITTIES DOES HE . . .

FEMALE CAT

I REALLY HATE THIS SHOW
BUT, GOD, I NEED THE DOUGH.
I GOTTA DO THIS SHOW!

CATS

MEOW, I THINK I GOT IT!
I THINK I GOT IT!
I'LL HAVE A JOB FOREVERMORE!

[*In counterpoint.*]

ALL THESE BRITISH EPICS
THEY RUN FOREVER
[SUSANNE:] THESE BRITISH SHOWS!
IT DOESN'T MATTER
WHO THEY BORE!
[JASON:] THEY NEVER CLOSE!

NO ONE SEEMS TO GET IT

NOBODY GETS IT

ALL OF THE TOURISTS WANNA GO
TO SEE THE BIGGEST SET
THEY KNOW

THAT'S WHY I HAVE TO GET
THIS . . .

I REALLY NEED A SIGN
[CHRISTINE:] I'VE GOT A FLEA IN MY COAT
PLEASE, GOD, GIVE ME A SIGN
{MALE CAT:] I GOT A FURBALL IN MY THROAT

WHAT WILL PASS CHORUS LINE?

[*Music changes to "One."*]

CATS! WHAT HUMILIATION,
EV'RY RECORD RUN IT BREAKS.
CATS! WHAT A DEGRADATION,
EV'RY DOLLAR IT MAKES.

ONCE *CHORUS LINE* TOPPED THE HIT LIST
OF BROADWAY SHOWS,
BUT CATS IS SO GODDAMN WITLESS,
THE PUBLIC GOES!

CATS! PROVES THAT MEDIOCRE
OFTEN PASSES FOR THE BEST.
NOW THAT IT OUTRAN THE REST,
YOU'LL GO, SO . . .

HOW ODD, BROADWAY'S DECOMPOSING.
THANK GOD! *CATS* IS FIN'LLY CLOSING!
BYE, BYE, GOODBYE
BYE, BYE, CATS!
CATS!
CATS!
CATS!
CATS!

"Rant"

[*Two* Rent *boys who look a lot like* ANTHONY RAPP *as Mark and* ADAM PASCAL *as Roger are at center microphone.*]

ANTHONY

HOW DO YOU KEEP UP WITH THE FADS
WHEN ALL THE FADS
ARE MULTIPLYING BY THREE BIG ADS?
SMALL ADS BLOW MY MIND, AND NOW, EGADS,
THIS NEW SHOW TO SEE!

BOTH

RENT!

ADAM

HOW DO WE GET INSIDE
WHEN THE PAPER LIED
AND SAID THERE ARE GOOD SEATS TO SPARE?
WITH SUCH ADULATION,
LATE CANCELLATION
FOR TWO SEATS IS EXTREMELY RARE.

ANTHONY

A BIG SNOBBY SMASH HIT . . .

ADAM

WE'RE DESPERATE TO CRASH IT!

BOTH

HOW WE GONNA GET
HOW WE GONNA GET
HOW WE GONNA GET
SEATS TO *RENT*?!

[*Music continues as* ANTHONY *reveals his 16mm camera.*]

ANTHONY

Close-up on *Rent*. We're in the East Village, looking around for some misery to photograph. Cut to Avenue B. Zoom down the street. No one is left.

ADAM

They've all moved to West 41st Street, where they are now squatting in the rarely used Nederlander Theatre.

ANTHONY

Nederlander Theatre! How are we going to get in there?!?

ADAM

There's only one thing left to do!

BOTH

Check the "Lee-Brett-Toe."

ANTHONY

Zoom in on copy of an ancient text we found buried under the crumbling marble of Lincoln Center.

ADAM

This "Lee-Brett-Toe" is a strange and wonderful book of prophecy called . . .

BOTH

L.A. Bo-heeme.

ANTHONY

It tells us what the hell is going on in this show.

ADAM

And what happens next.

ANTHONY

Check scene two.

ADAM

It says we have a "Breaking Back Into the Theatre Party" tonight.

ANTHONY

Yesssssss!!!

BOTH

NOW WE'RE GONNA GET
NOW WE'RE GONNA GET
NOW WE'RE GONNA GET
INTO *RENT*!
LET'S SEE *RENT,*
WHERE THEY RANT.
RANT! RANT! RANT! RANT! RANT!
RANT! RANT! RANT! RANT! RANT! RANT! RANT!
  RANT!
BREAK BACK INTO *RENT,*
CAUSE ALL OUR CASH IS SPENT!

ANTHONY

[*Reading from the libretto.*]

Scene three. Daphne Rubin-Vega plays Mimi. In *Bohème*, she's a sweet, shy seamstress. Now she's a nymphomaniac crack-head prostitute! YEAH!

[DAPHNE RUBIN-VEGA *leaps onto the stage.*]

"Ouch, They're Tight!"

DAPHNE

Meow!!!!!

OO-OO-OO-OO-WOE-OH-WELL!
WATCH ME GET A WINK FROM THE STAGEHANDS,
WEARIN' MY BLUE VINYL PANTS
AS SMOOTH AS SKIN; I CAN'T BREATHE IN,
AND SO WHEN I DA-ANCE, I SCREAM . . .

OOOUCH, THEY'RE TIGHT!

AH-HA! I HAVE TO SCREAM

OOOUCH, THEY'RE TIGHT!

HMMMM!

I HAVE TO SCOWL, HOOT LIKE AN OWL.

I'M IN SUCH PAIN, I GOTTA HOWL:

OUCH, THEY'RE TIGHT!

[*Third chorus.*]

IN THIS NUMBER, I GOTTA MOVE,

I GOTTA LOOK SEXY AND GET IN THE GROOVE.

I GOT A LOT TO PROVE,

WHIMP'RING SIGHS AND FAKING CRIES.

SO I'LL USE THIS BAR

AND HUMP IT LIKE SOME PORNO STAR,

BUT I GET SCARS FROM CONTORTING MY ACHING
    THIGHS

I SCREAM:

OOOUCH, THEY'RE TIGHT!

I HAVE TO SCREAM

OOOUCH, THEY'RE TIGHT

MMM-AH! AH! AH! OH!

IF I TRY SITTING, MY SEAMS START SPLITTING.

SO CALL UP WARDROBE FOR ANOTHER FITTING,

AND LET 'EM OUT TONIGHT!

OU-OUCH, THEY'RE TIGHT!

[*She strikes a pose, and we hear the loud sound of her pants splitting.*]

"Too Gay 4 U"

ANGEL

IT WAS MY LUCKY DAY, ONE DAY, ON AVENUE A

WHEN THEY TOOK ME IN A LIMOUSINE TO
    BROADWAY.

THEY SAID, "DAH-LING, YOU'RE A DEAR,

AND THE QUEER OF THE YEAR,

BUT TONE IT DOWN OR ELSE

THE STRAIGHT SUBURBAN CROWD

WILL DISAPPEAR . . .

"BE CHITA, EVITA—JUST DON'T ACT UP.

PLEASE DO AS WE SAY, YOU'RE JUST A PUP.

DON'T BE TOO FEY

ON OLD BROADWAY."

WELL, I'VE HEARD THAT BEFORE,

BUT THIS IS WHAT I SAY:

TOO GAY FOR YOU,

TOO HET'RO FOR ME!

TOO GAY FOR YOU,

TOO HET'RO FOR ME!

WE AGREED ON A FEE

AND A SIX-MONTH GUARANTEE

WITH A BONUS

IF I DRESS UP LIKE

A CHRISTMAS TREE.

NOW, WHO COULD FORETELL

I'D WIN AWARDS AS WELL?

BUT PLAYING TO THE BLUE-HAIR GIRLS

IS CANDY-WRAPPER HELL.

THEY KEEP EXPECTING EVITA

IN ALL HER GLORY,

NOT A DRAG QUEEN TALE

OR A LESBIAN STORY.

EACH BRIDGE AND TUNNEL BUBBY
SAYS, "OY, WHAT A SHOW!"
THEY TELL ME GET A GIRLFRIEND,
I JUST SAY, "NO!"

TOO GAY FOR YOU,
TOO HET'RO FOR ME!
TOO GAY FOR YOU,
TOO HET'RO FOR ME!

BACK ON THE STREET
AND MY LIFE IS SWEET,
I'M ROCKIN' AND WIGSTOCKIN'
TO THE FUNKY BEAT.
IT'S ALL RELATIVE
TO WHEN AND WHERE YOU LIVE.
IT'S THE SAME, I REPEAT,
ON THAT BROADWAY STREET.

TOO GAY FOR YOU,
TOO HET'RO FOR ME!
TOO GAY FOR YOU,
TOO HET'RO FOR ME!

[*Christmas music plays.*]

ANTHONY

PRETTY VOICES SINGING

ANGEL

[*Joins* ANTHONY.]

PRETTY VOICES SINGING

DAPHNE

[*Enters and joins in.*]

PRETTY VOICES SINGING

ALL THREE

SOMEWHERE ELSE—
NOT HERE!

"Think Punk"

KAY THOMPSON

Oh! What is this fabulous, ratty sweater! Look at those gorgeous shit-kickers! They'll look fabulous in my new *Rent* boutique at Bloomingdales. Angel, take a memo: "To the fashion scene of America—no, to the fashion scene of the world: Chuck the chiffon! Tear the taffeta! Banish the pink! And from now on, world . . .

THINK PUNK! THINK PUNK!
RUMMAGE THROUGH THE TRASH FOR CLOTHES.
THINK PUNK! THINK PUNK!
NEVER WASH AND PIERCE YOUR NOSE.
FASHION'S DEAD, NEW IS CRUDE.
BE OBSCENE; GET TATTOOED!
WEAR YOUR DREADLOCKS LONG AND LOOSE
AND DYE THEM PUCE
AND CHARTREUSE.

THINK PUNK!
WHO CARES IF THE DRAB LOOK HAS NO BUST?
THINK PUNK!
PUT ON A SHIRT WITH A DIRTY CRUST.
THE *RENT* BOUTIQUE AT BLOOMINGDALE'S
IS LOADED WITH YOUR NEIGHBOR'S JUNK,
SO IF YOU WANNA BE A HUNK,
THINK PUNK!

HORUS BOYS

THINK PUNK! THINK PUNK!
DRESSING DOWN IS *"QUELQUE CHOSE."*
THINK PUNK! THINK PUNK!
WEAR A SKIRT WITH MOLD THAT GROWS.

[DAPHNE *enters wearing a sweatshirt covered with garbage.*]

SMELLS SO CHIC WHEN YOU REEK,
FEELS SO NICE WEARING LICE.
ALL THE RICH ARE MAKING THE SWITCH,

KAY

THEY SCRATCH THAT ITCH!

CHORUS

EVERY EAST SIDE BITCH . . .

KAY

. . . WEARS EACH STITCH . . .

ALL

. . . LIKE SHE DIGS A DITCH.

KAY

THINK PUNK! THINK PUNK!
SUFFERING IS MAINSTREAM NOW.

CHORUS

SUFFER NOW!

KAY

THINK PUNK!
THE HOMELESS ARE NOW A BIG CASH COW.

CHORUS

EMULATE THE HOMELESS.

KAY

BLOOMINGDALE'S AND *RENT* ARE NOW
   COMBINING,
GUCCI AND CHANEL ARE SUNK.
SO RUMMAGE THROUGH YOUR ATTIC TRUNK.
THINK PUNK!

CHORUS

THINK PUNK! NOT PINK!
THINK PUNK! NOT PINK!
THINK PUNK! NOT PINK!

ALL

THINK PUNK!

"Seasons of Hype"

COMPANY

FIVE-HUNDRED-
TWENTY-FIVE-THOUSAND-
SIX-HUNDRED WRITE-UPS,
FIVE-HUNDRED-
TWENTY-FIVE-THOUSAND
MAGAZINE SPREADS,
FIVE-HUNDRED-
TWENTY-FIVE-THOUSAND-
SIX-HUNDRED PHOTOS:
HOW DO YOU MEASURE
OUR SWELLING HEADS?

IN RECORDS AND TV
AND MIDNIGHT ON *DAVID LETTERMAN*
AND DOZENS OF GROUPIES
IN THE FIRST ROW, IN

FIVE-HUNDRED-
TWENTY-FIVE-THOUSAND-
SIX-HUNDRED FEATURES.
HOW DO YOU MEASURE
THE WORTH OF A SHOW?

HOW ABOUT HYPE! HYPE!
LAYERS OF HYPE! HYPE!
FORGET ABOUT LOVE;
IT'S THE SEASON OF HYPE!
SEASONS OF HYPE!

SEASONS OF HYPE!

FEMALE SOLOIST

FIVE-HUNDRED-
TWENTY-FIVE-THOUSAND-
SIX-HUNDRED TONYS;
ADD ON A HIGHLY IMPRESSIVE
PULITZER PRIZE.
FIVE-HUNDRED-
TWENTY-FIVE-THOUSAND-
SIX-HUNDRED HOUSE SEATS
THERE'D BE A RIOT
IF THE PUBLIC GOT WISE!

MALE SOLOIST

FOR A HOUSE ORDER SEAT
IS ESPECIALLY SAVED
FOR THE SHOW BIZ ELITE,
NOT THE VILLAGE DEPRAVED.

ALL

HOW SADLY IRONIC
THAT A STORY ABOUT FRIENDS
IS NEVER TO BE SEEN
BY THEIR LIKE—
JUST THE RICH, WHO LIKE TRENDS.

EVERYTHING'S HYPED!
THINK OF THE HYPE!
WHERE IS THE LOVE
IN THE DECADE OF HYPE?
SEASONS OF HYPE!
SEASONS OF HYPE!

"This Ain't Bohème"

ANTHONY

THIS AIN'T *BOHÈME*!

ALL

THIS AIN'T *BOHÈME*!

ANTHONY

THERE WAS A GUY NAMED GIACOMO
WHO WROTE AN OP'RA LONG AGO,
BUT NOTHING REMAINS.
BOHÈME WE OBLITERATE.
AS WE GO AGAINST THE GRAIN,
YOU'LL GO INSANE,
AND WE'RE GLAD!

DID I MENTION THE TENSION
AND MOVES FROM FIFTH DIMENSION?
WE'RE STARVING FOR ATTENTION,
FULL OF PRETENSION,
NEED INTERVENTION.
A CONVENTION OF SPOILED TWENTY-SOMETHINGS
GOING MAD.

PRECOCIOUS, OBNOXIOUS KIDS
REINVENTING *HAIR*
AND CHER
AND *VANITY FAIR*.
AREN'T WE CUTE, TO BOOT?
HEAR THE GRUNGIES HOOT!
WE'RE SUCH A FAMOUS FAD.
WE AREN'T THE MET; FORGET
THAT MUSICAL GEM,
THIS AIN'T *BOHÈME*!

ALL

YEAH! THE SONGS!

ANTHONY

IT'S ROCK, IT'S ULTRA-BLUESY:
GALT MACDERMOT, LIZZIE SWADOS . . .

KAY THOMPSON

STEVIE WONDER, LEONARD BERNSTEIN,

RENT PUCCINI, SONDHEIM'S *SWEENEY* . . .

ALL

STYLE!

ADAM

IT'S LOUD, COMPLETELY WIRED,
HAND-HELD MIKES AND FACIAL VEGAS . . .

DAPHNE

DINGY LIGHTING, METAL PLATFORMS,
CHILDREN RAGING, MESSY STAGING . . .

ALL

PLOT!
IT'S PROSTITUTION, NO SOLUTION,
SOUND POLLUTION,
GENERATION X
IN COUNTER-COUNTER REVOLUTION!
EVERYONE HAS LOST THEIR VOICE,
IT'S TRUE . . .

ADAM

I HAVE!

DAPHNE

AND ME!

KAY

AND ME!

ALL

AND YOU AND YOU AND YOU!
IT'S ACTORS SCREAMING AND BELCHING
AND SCREECHING, BUT NOT REACHING
ANY HIGH NOTES.

ANTHONY

SO, IF SOME PATRONS QUAKE WITH FEAR,
LET'S REMIND ALL OF THEM . . .

ALL

THIS AIN'T *BOHÈME*!
THIS AIN'T *BOHÈME*!

ANTHONY

BUT NOW THAT WE ARE THE MAINSTREAM,
WHO IS OUT OF THE MAINSTREAM?
HOW DO WE OFFEND?
WHAT'S THE NEW TREND?
WE NEED A SHOW, A NEW SHOW . . .
THE OPPOSITE OF *RENT* AIN'T *BOHÈME*,
IT'S *OKLAHOMA!*

ALL

YEAH!
IT'S *OKLAHOMA!*
IT'S *OKLAHOMA!*
IT'S *OKLAHOMA!*
IT'S *OKLAHOMA!*
O-K-L-A-H-O-M-A!
VIVA LA *OKLAHOMA!* YO!

"Death and Resurrection"

DAPHNE

AHHHHH!!!!

ANTHONY

Zoom in on Daphne, now dying of exhaustion after doing *Rent* for only six months. Will Adam be able to revive her with his new hit song?

[ADAM *sings, thinking* DAPHNE *is dead; the music is Musetta's waltz from* La Bohème.]

ADAM

DAPH-NEEEEEEEEE!

[DAPHNE *revives as the music surges.*]

DAPHNE

Mooo . . .

[ADAM *and* ANTHONY *jump back and cry in horror.*]

ADAM and ANTHONY

She's back!

DAPHNE

I swear I died! I was going through a tunnel—the Lincoln Tunnel, I think—going towards a warm white light, leaving dingy New York for good.

ADAM and ANTHONY

Oh my God!

DAPHNE

. . . and I swear I saw an angel in gold lamé. She looked like Lady Thiang from *The King and I* [LADY THIANG *enters.*], and she said . . .

[LADY THIANG *speaks as* DAPHNE *mouths along.*]

LADY THIANG

Go back. Back home to Broadway. It isn't dead yet.

ADAM

Wow!

[ANTHONY *starts looking through the libretto.*]

ANTHONY

Hey! According to the *Bohème* libretto, you're not supposed to come back. You're supposed be dead!

DAPHNE

Yeah, but . . . [*She gyrates.*] . . . uh-uh-uh, this ain't Bohème . . .

[*Music chord or pickup as* DAPHNE *thrusts her pelvis.*]

DAPHNE, ANTHONY, and ADAM

THIS AIN'T BOHÈME!
THIS AIN'T BOHÈME!
THIS AIN'T BOHÈME!

[*They go off, dancing.*]

"Grand Finale"

LADY THIANG

THIS IS A SHOW THAT THINKS WITH ITS HEART;
ITS HEART IS NOT ALWAYS WISE.
THIS IS A SHOW THAT STUMBLES AND FALLS,
BUT THIS IS A SHOW THAT TRIES.
SO MANY SHOWS WE LOVE AND FORGIVE
AND SEE THEM AGAIN AS LONG AS WE LIVE . . .

BROADWAY WON'T ALWAYS DO
WHAT YOU WOULD HAVE IT DO,
BUT NOW AND THEN THEY'LL DO
SOMETHING WONDERFUL.

YOU'LL DISH OUT EIGHTY BUCKS
AND NOT GET ANY YUKS,
THEN ALL AT ONCE SAY, "SHUCKS,
THAT WAS WONDERFUL!"

[*Two* MEN *and one* WOMAN *enter, in turn.*]

MAN 1

YOU'LL HEAR A THOUSAND SONGS
THAT WON'T RING TRUE

WOMAN

THEN, ALL AT ONCE, A BRILLLIANT ONE
THAT STUNS AND TOUCHES YOU.

MAN 2

YOU'LL ALWAYS PAY THE PRICE,

FEEL LIKE YOU'RE ROLLING DICE,

ALL

THEN YOU'RE IN PARADISE
AND IT'S WONDERFUL!

LADY THIANG

THOUGH IT WILL NEVER BE
ALL THAT IT WANTS TO BE,

ALL

BROADWAY WILL ALWAYS BE
SOMETHING WONDERFUL!

FORBIDDEN MEMORIES: **William Selby**

Why did I stay with *Forbidden Broadway* for so many years, from 1985 to 2009? I wore many hats during that time, as performer, director, assistant to Gerard, understudy, dance captain, teacher to anyone who joined the show, casting director, occasional prop artist, and friend to all—I hope!

I traveled around the world performing countless numbers, directed more than ten productions across the country, did a series of interviews with members of the family for YouTube, and loved, loved, *loved* every minute of it. Of course, that was the reason why I stayed. My love for the show never wavered. In fact, my feelings are as strong today as they were the first time I saw the show in Boston in 1984.

William Selby and Steve Essner in "Grim Hotel."

Did I use the word "family"? That's what we became. When you're involved in the process of creating each new show—with ideas flying about and Gerard's brilliant lyrics being sung while you're trying to learn Phill George's terrific, zany staging—there's a definite feeling that you're all in it together. We bonded very quickly in the trenches.

And oh, the joy of performing those numbers for an audience! To take every chaotic moment of creativity in rehearsal, pull it all together, don those amazing costumes, and share it all with an appreciative crowd gave me a high I never grew tired of.

Being a part of *Forbidden Broadway* was like being on a merry-go-round, like dressing up for Halloween every night. It gave me a chance to be a kid forever. I never wanted it to end—and, in my heart, it never will.

A Jolly Holiday with Rudy: 1998–2001

The late '90s was a great era for Broadway theater. I think the freshness of *Rent,* and the fact that it was a huge financial hit, sparked a sort of renaissance for Broadway. The *Chicago* revival was another great success, and even some of the shows that weren't hits, like *The Life,* were at least tuneful and original. Also, New York City itself was having a renaissance. Under Mayor Rudy Giuliani, the city was being cleaned up, and tourists started to feel more comfortable being in midtown. This was a major reason why we had moved to Ellen's Stardust, so we could be right in the middle of the action.

Ed Staudenmayer and Bryan Batt leap for joy as they cry, "Shut *Footloose!*"

And that's when *Forbidden Broadway* began to become very tourist-friendly. For years, we had been sort of an "insider" show. Of course, we had always had some tourists in the audience, but it was mostly people with some connection to the theater. When we did *Forbidden Broadway Strikes Back!,* we got such great reviews that tourists began to come to the show in much greater numbers—and it stayed that way from then on. Which is why, fortunately or unfortunately, we still do the *Annie* number ("I'm thirty years old tomorrow") and it still brings the house down.

I think the fact that we ramped up the show with Alvin Colt's costumes also helped us appeal to tourists. His creations made such an effect that you didn't necessarily have to get the show on all levels in order to enjoy it. I remember watching the movie parodies on *The Carol Burnett Show* when I was a kid. I certainly didn't catch all the references—I didn't see most of those movies till many years later—but I was still doubled over in laughter because Bob Mackie's costumes looked so funny. That's what Alvin did for us.

We played *Forbidden Broadway Strikes Back!* very successfully at Ellen's in '97, and then we started planning a new edition. That's when Giuliani really started to clean up the theater district at an amazing rate: The porno places were all closing, Disney was gaining ground with *Beauty and the Beast* and *The Lion King,* the whole area was very quickly becoming gentrified. It was almost too much, too fast. The funny thing is, we were still getting shows that were very adult—like the revival of *Cabaret,* which was pretty filthy, and *The Beauty Queen of Leenane.* The idea behind *Forbidden Broadway Cleans Up Its Act* was, "We're gonna clean up, too!" Of course, the joke was that we were edgier and meaner than ever.

Bryan Batt, Kristine Zbornik, Lori Hammel, and Ed Staudenmayer are Von Trapped in *The Sound of Music.* It has always been a point of pride that *Forbidden Broadway* never descended to camp, as this picture proves.

We still had to be careful about audience recognition of the shows we were spoofing. I remember that when we first took a shot at *Ragtime,* our number got only a few laughs. We kept it in and, about a month or so later, it started to get more laughs. Two or three months later, it was bringing the house down. Again, people needed time to see the actual show in order for our spoof to be funny. We parodied *The Lion King,* and Alvin's costumes really made that number. Also *Swan Lake.* Although *Footloose* was a flop, it ran about a year, so we were able to do that one, too.

Chicago had opened a month before *Strikes Back!,* but it took me some time to figure out what was funny about it. As it turned out, that show was perfect for *Cleans Up Its Act.*

What else? We spoofed the production of *Follies* with Ann Miller at Paper Mill. *Sunset Boulevard* closed, so we had Andrew Lloyd Webber singing "Memory." *Jekyll and Hyde* was another show of questionable quality that ran for a while; we loved eviscerating that one. And it was fun to make fun of Bernadette Peters in *Annie Get Your Gun*—but not as much fun as we had a year later, when Cheryl Ladd went into the show.

There were so many new shows in the late '90s that we didn't always have to do *Phantom* and *Les Miz.* There were times when those parodies weren't in *Forbidden Broadway* at all. When we did revisit *Les Miz,* I wrote a new lyric called "Ten Years More," because I couldn't believe how long the show had run. The Phantom came back when we did a number about Merman trying to teach him how to project without a microphone. I loved that because it wasn't about a star being too old or singing flat; it was about the issue of sound amplification on Broadway, which is certainly still relevant.

We were lucky to have extremely gifted cast members at that time: Ed Staudenmayer, Christine Pedi, Lori Hammel. Bryan Batt was still in the show, and I think many people would agree that he was one of our greatest talents. Bryan definitely had that *Forbidden Broadway* sensibility; he always knew exactly what was funny about a show or a star, and he was always willing to go for the jugular.

Bryan was a great collaborator. I think he suggested the Mandy Patinkin/*Mamaloshen* number, and I remember he had the idea to do Rafiki in *The Lion King* as "Rafreaky." He was also responsible for one of the funniest lyrics we ever had in the show. In my original parody of "Bring Him Home" from *Les Miz,* I had Jean Valjean sing "Pity me, change the key," and then he sang, "Take it down, take it down!" Bryan was auditioning for us with that number, and he didn't quite remember the lyrics, so he sang "Bring it down, bring it down!" That was perfect, because it was closer to the original lyric and also much funnier. I thought, "How did I miss that?" Anyway, we put it and him right into the show.

As we approached the millennium, Times Square was changing drastically. I think we all had assumed it would

Left: Bryan, Donna, and Ed in our version of *Chicago*. Right: Christine Pedi as Ethel Merman tells Bill Selby as the Phantom, "You don't need amplifyin'!"

Charges that *Forbidden Broadway* has a gay sensibility are completely unfounded. Here are Ed and Bryan in our take on *Swan Lake*.

keep at least some of its character, but it was rapidly turning into a mall or a theme park—especially when Madame Tussauds opened. We did a new edition of the show called *Forbidden Broadway 2001: A Spoof Odyssey,* but honestly, I think it was a little too soon after the previous edition.

Left: Danny Gurwin, Felicia Finley, and Tony Nation in *Forbidden Broadway 2001: A Spoof Odyssey.* **Right: In 2001, Christine Pedi and Danny Gurwin spoofed Elton John's** *Aida* **while Verdi turned 'round in his grave.**

The shows that were big then, like *Aida* and the revival of *Kiss Me, Kate,* seem unimportant in retrospect. *Miss Saigon* closed, but nobody seemed to care. *Saturday Night Fever* ran for a while, so we were able to go after that one, but my parody wasn't terribly clever. Broadway was still thriving because shows like *Rent, The Lion King, Les Miz,* and *Phantom* were still going strong, but we didn't have a lot of new material to work with at the turn of the century.

Our most topical number was "Let's Ruin Times Square Again," the idea being that we should bring back some of the old grittiness and sleaze of the theater district. Fortunately, we had great people like Felicia Finley and Danny Gurwin in the show, and they really boosted whatever material I gave them. But now that I look back on it, the end of the '90s was the end of an era for *Forbidden Broadway.*

"A Jolly Holiday with Rudy"

ACTOR AS EMCEE

WILKOMMEN, BIENVENUE, WELCOME,
FREMDE, ETRANGER, SUCKERS.
I WILL ATTACK YOU AND MAKE YOU FEEL SICK,
WICKED AND RAUNCHY WHEN I GRAB MY . . .

[*Before he can go any further, a whistle blows from the back of the room.* RUDOLPH GIULIANI *enters.*]

GIULIANI

Stop right there! That lyric is polluted and the staging is obscene. I order you to stop immediately!

[ACTOR *drops* EMCEE *character.*]

ACTOR

Just a minute, please! Who are you?

GIULIANI

I'm Mayor Rudolph Giuliani! And you're in violation of New York City's new zoning laws for adult entertainment. No parody lyrics within fifty feet of the nearest church or public school.

ACTOR

Oh no! You can't close us down! What do we have to do to keep from having our door bolted?

GIULIANI

From now on, this show will have to be more than 60 percent family entertainment. From now on, I don't want to see anything on this stage dirtier than . . . than . . . *Mary Poppins.*

ACTOR

Okay, Your Honor. I think we can comply.

[*Calling backstage.*]

Julie! Oh, Julie!

[JULIE ANDREWS, *dressed as Mary Poppins, enters. The* ACTOR *exits.*]

GIULIANI

Julie Andrews! What are you doing here?

JULIE

Julie Andrews, Giuli-ani; we're a practically perfect pair.

GIULIANI

Julie Andrews, Giuli-ani. I love the way that sounds!

JULIE

And I love the way you've made the Broadway district safe and lovely again for Disney ingenues. Thank you!

[*She begins singing.*]

WHAT A REMARKABLE SIGHT,
MIDTOWN IS SUCH A DELIGHT!
AND LOOK—A BRAND-NEW GAP!

RUDY

HAVE YOU EVER SEEN
THE STREETS SO CLEAN?
WHAT A TOURIST TRAP!

JULIE

OH, IT'S A JOLLY HOLIDAY WITH RUDY;
RUDY'S CLEANING UP TIMES SQUARE.

RUDY

It's changed quite a bit.

JULIE

PORNO SHOPS ARE SELLING "HOWDY-DOODY,"
DISNEY STORES ARE EVERYWHERE!

RUDY

The crime rate has plummeted! What's wrong with that?

JULIE

YOU'LL NEVER SEE A NIPPLE OR A G-STRING,
A DAISY DUCK DISPLACES EV'RY WHORE.
WHEN RUDY TOOK COMMAND
THE TOWN WENT BLAND
AND CLOSED DOWN EVERY CORNER
HOT DOG STAND.

RUDY

They obstruct the flow of pedestrians.

JULIE

IT'S A JOLLY HOLIDAY WITH RUDY.
THE CITY ISN'T SEEDY ANYMORE!

Come along, Rudy. Spit spot!

RUDY

OH, IT'S A JOLLY HOLIDAY WITH RUDY,
BROADWAY'S DULL AS CITY HALL.
42ND STREET WAS DARK AND MOODY,
NOW IT'S JUST ANOTHER MALL!

JULIE

IT'S GONE FROM ONE EXTREME UNTO ANOTHER,

RUDY

FROM SICK'NINGLY DEPRAVED . . .

JULIE

. . . TO STICKY-SWEET

BOTH

WE HATED IT FOR YEARS,

BUT NOW ONE FEARS

THE PROSTITUTES ARE DRESSED AS
    MOUSEKETEERS!

OH, IT'S A JOLLY HOLIDAY WITH RUDY,

AND WHEN THE TRANSFORMATION IS COMPLETE . . .

RUDY

ANY DAY NOW . . .

BOTH

BROADWAY WILL BE GIULIANI STREET!

"Glossy Fosse"

[MAN *sings while* WOMAN *mouths the words as if she were a ventriloquist's dummy.*]

MAN

WHERE YA GOIN'?

WOMAN

TO *CHICAGO*!

MAN

WHAT'S CHICAGO?

WOMAN

IT'S A NEW SHOW!

MAN

IS IT BRAND-NEW?

WOMAN

WELL, NOT REALLY;

IT'S THE CHEESY CONCERT VERSION

OF GWEN VERDON'S LAST EXCURSION.

MAN

WHAT'S THE SET LIKE?

WOMAN

LIKE A BARE STAGE.

MAN

ARE THERE COSTUMES?

WOMAN

[*She actually speaks.*]

Are you kiddin'?

MAN

WHO'S THE BIG STAR?

BEBE NEUWIRTH,

BUT WHAT MAKES HER SO ENGAGING

IS BOB FOSSE'S SEXY STAGING.

OH YES OH YES OH YES SHE IS

OH YES SHE IS

BEBE IS A BIG GUN!

AND HERE AND HERE AND HERE SHE IS

AND HERE SHE IS NOW TO SHOW YOU HOW IT IS
    DONE!

And now, here she is, Miss Bebe Neuwirth!

[BEBE *enters;* MAN *and* WOMAN *exit.*]

BEBE

Hello, suckers! You know, Ann, Walter Bobbie, Barry, Fran, and me, we all won Tony Awards for *Chicago*. And you can win one too: All you have to do is a little grave robbing!

GIVE 'EM THE OLD SAUCY FOSSE,
GLOSSY-FOSSE 'EM.
TWIST AND CONTORT AND THROW SOME TRASH IN
  IT,
AND THE REVIEWS WILL ALL BE PASSIONATE.

[*Two* BOYS *in gloves, bowler hats, vests, and no shirts
  enter.*]

BOYS

GIVE 'EM THE OLD
SPREAD THE FINGERS

BEBE

WEAR A BOWLER HAT,
WIGGLE YOUR PANTS LIKE ANTS ARE IN YOUR
  THIGHS.
THOUGH THE PRODUCTION MAY BE SHODDY,
EVERYONE LIKES A NAKED BODY!
SAUCY FOSSE 'EM
AND THEY'LL NEVER CATCH WISE.

Left foot blue! Right hand red! Now, dance!

[*They are all tangled and try to dance, but collapse.
They get up and hit another Fosse pose.*]

ALL

GIVE 'EM THE OLD SAUCY FOSSE,
DIP AND UNDULATE.

BEBE

SHOW 'EM THE LIMBER BURLESQUE QUEEN YOU
  ARE!

BOYS

[*They mime fondling* BEBE*'s breasts.*]

I love ya, honey, I love ya!

ALL

RUN THROUGH YOUR DANCE LIKE GREASED
  MACHIN'RY

BEBE

THEY'LL NEVER SPOT WE GOT NO SCEN'RY.

BOYS

GLOSSY-FOSSE 'EM

BEBE

SAUCY FOSSE 'EM
AND THEY'LL MAKE YOU A STAR!

ALL

Pose!

"Gag-Time"

LITTLE BOY

In 1998, Garth Drabinsky built a theater at the crest of Broadway and 43rd Street, New York, New York.

MOTHER

And it seemed that for some years thereafter, the show he produced would run and run. He called the show *Ragtime . . .*

LITTLE BOY

. . . but we call it something else.

BOTH

WHAT SHOW IS SAD AND WEEPY?

MOTHER

EVERYONE CRIES

BOY

HALF THE CAST DIES
BOO-HOO-HOO-HOO-HOO!

MOTHER

WHAT SET IS DARK AND CREEPY?

BOY

BIG AS A BARGE

MOTHER

EV'RYTHING LARGE

BOY

LA-LA-LA-LA LARGE!

BOTH

WHAT PLOT IS COMPLICATED,
THINGS GET AS STICKY AS SLIME?

MOTHER

IT ALL ENDS HAPPY

BOY

BUT IT'S ALL SO SAPPY

BOTH

THE PEOPLE CALL IT *GAG-TIME*!
GAGTIME!

MOTHER

Now it's time to do a little gardening. Aaah! Look! A little African American baby has been buried in our garden!

WHAT KIND OF WOMAN WOULD DO SUCH A THING?

[SARAH *enters.*]

SARAH

Hello. My name is Sarah Brown-Eyes. I'm a half-crazed washer-woman who can easily belt high "C." So now they're sending me to jail.

MOTHER

No! You and the baby can live here with me.

SARAH

Oh, God bless you, white lady. How can I ever repay you for your kindness?

MOTHER

Well, you could start with the windows.

[*Looking at baby prop that looks like a Cabbage Patch Doll. She speaks to the baby.*]

My, you have an awfully big head! What shall I call you? I know—Savion Glover!

[*Knock, knock;* COALHOUSE *enters.*]

Who are you?

COALHOUSE

I'm Coalhouse Walker, that baby's father. Is Sarah here?

MOTHER

She doesn't want to see you.

COALHOUSE

May I play your piano while I wait for her to change her mind?

MOTHER

Go right ahead. Say, do you know anything from *The Lion King*?

COALHOUSE

The Lion King is children's theater! This is called *Gag-Time.*

[*FATHER enters.*]

FATHER

Mother, I'm home.

MOTHER

Welcome home, Father.

FATHER

Mother, why is that black man playing our piano?

MOTHER

He has an audition for *Smokey Joe's Cafe.*

FATHER

Why are you holding that black baby?

MOTHER

I've become a Democrat.

FATHER

My God, things have changed around here. I can hear it in the music . . .

WONDERFUL TUNE, LUSH MELODY,
DESTINED TO BE NEW MUZAK,
PLAYED WHILE IN A DENTIST'S CHAIR.

MOTHER

LILTING AND SWEET, BUT WHERE'S THE BEAT?
CAN'T TAP YOUR FEET TO MUZAK
MADE FOR ELEVATOR AIR.

COALHOUSE

WHO WANTS A TUNE TODAY?
EV'RYTHING SOON TODAY

WILL BE SUB-STANDARD RAP OR FUNK.

MOTHER and FATHER

OR A MOVIE OSCAR SONG THAT'S POPULIST JUNK.
NEW MUZAK . . .

ALL THREE

SONGS WITH CLASS ARE LABELED "FULL OF GAS."
TELL STEPHEN FLAHERTY HE'S THROUGH!

FATHER

'CAUSE, EVENTUALLY,
HE'LL END UP MUZAK TOO!

MOTHER

Look! Sarah is coming down the stairs!

[*Sound effect: Body falling down a staircase, ending with a thud.*]

SARAH

Ouch!

COALHOUSE

SARAH, PLEASE MARRY ME!
SARAH, PLEASE COMB YOUR HAIR!!

SARAH

I'll do anything if you'll stop playing that song!

COALHOUSE

Ha, ha, ha! Lets go pick up a few Tonys in my new Ford!

SARAH

Okay, honey!

COALHOUSE

IN EV'RY SHOW
THERE'S ONE BIG BALLAD

SARAH

THAT MAKES YOU WEEP
AND CLUTCH YOUR THROAT.

BOTH

WE'LL SING TILL THE RAFTERS RING
AND EMOTE TILL WE OVERBLOAT
AND THEN THIS SONG,
THIS SONG WILL END
WITH A REALLY LONG NOOOOOOOOOOOOOOOTE!

[BEN BRANTLEY *enters.*]

BEN BRANTLEY

Stop right there!

COALHOUSE

Who, sir, are you?

BEN BRANTLEY

I'm Ben Brantley, chief critic of the *New York Times*. And here's a little review from the boys down at the office!

[*He smashes the car.*]

Have you driven a Ford lately?

[*He leaves.*]

COALHOUSE

That critic just totaled our car!

SARAH

Forget about it, Coalhouse. We're getting married tomorrow!

COALHOUSE

I'm not marrying anyone until he prints a retraction.

[*He exits.*]

SARAH

Coalhouse, wait! Oh, what am I going to do now? I know—I'll go ask the President of the United States for help. Yoo-hoo! Mr. President! My fiancé won't marry me, and I got a son!

VOICE

Look out, she's got a gun!

SARAH

No! I said, "I got a son. A son!"

VOICE

Whatever.

[*Gunshot!* SARAH *dies, falling offstage and tossing the baby to* MOTHER, *who enters with* COALHOUSE *as* SARAH *is handed a Tony.*]

COALHOUSE

Noooooo! She's dead! I'm bitter and angry and disillusioned.

MOTHER

Why? Because they killed an innocent woman?

COALHOUSE

No, because they gave her a Tony and not me!

[COALHOUSE *exits.*]

MOTHER

I know what you mean.

THERE WAS A TIME IT SEEMED AS THOUGH NO ONE
    WOULD WONDER,
RAGTIME WOULD WIN THE TONY AND NOT BE
    IGNORED.
WE OPENED LATE, AND *LION KING* STOLE ALL OUR
    THUNDER;
NOW WE'LL NEVER GET BACK OUR AWARD.

THERE WAS A TIME WHEN ALL OF THE CRITICS
    WERE GUSHING,
ALL OF MANHATTAN TOLD ME THAT I'D BE ADORED,
BUT THEY WERE WRONG, AND I'LL END UP SINGING
    IN FLUSHING;
NOW I'LL NEVER GET BACK MY AWARD.
THEY CAN NEVER RE-COUNT OR RE-VOTE,
SO I'LL JUST SING A REALLY LONG NOTE!

[MOTHER *exits.* COALHOUSE *re-enters.*]

COALHOUSE

I won't stop killing innocent people until the there's
    justice for *Ragtime*!

[FATHER *re-enters, wearing a Mickey Mouse Club hat.*]

FATHER

Don't be naive, Coalhouse. You can't stop the Mouse-
ification of Broadway.

COALHOUSE

But if I surrender, they'll shoot me, and I still won't win
    a Tony.

FATHER

I promise you that they will and you won't.

COALHOUSE

I believe you. I'm coming out.

FATHER

You've made the right decision, Coalhouse.

IT'S GETTING NEAR ELEVEN
AND YOU NEED TO WRAP THINGS UP:
MAKE THEM SHOOT YOU!
MAKE THEM SHOOT YOU!

COALHOUSE

YOU NEED TO BLOW YOUR BRAINS OUT
IF YOU WANT TO WIN THE CUP.
MAKE THEM SHOOT YOU!
MAKE THEM SHOOT YOU!

GET MOWED DOWN BY MACHINE GUNS
WHILE YOU SING "STOUTHEARTED MEN,"
"YOU'LL NEVER WALK ALONE," AND
"LAWD, I'M ON MY WAY"—AND THEN

KEEP SINGING "OL' MAN RIVER"
TILL YOU'RE OUT OF OX-Y-GEN.
THEN THEY'LL SHOOT YOU.
WHEN THEY SHOOT YOU,
SING THAT LONG NOTE AGAIN!

[COALHOUSE *is machine-gunned to the ground; others
    enter.*]

OTHERS

[*Singing to the tune of the title song.*]

AND THAT'S THE PLOT OF *RAGTIME*,
SPRINKLED WITH CHAOS AND CRIME!

COALHOUSE

MURDER AND MAYHEM RIGHT FROM THE
    BEGINNING

LITTLE BOY

HOUDINIS EXPLODING

EMMA GOLDMAN

AND IMMIGRANTS SPINNING

MOTHER

IF YOU CAN DECIPHER US,
WE ARE SUBLIME . . .

LITTLE BOY

BUT IF YOU CAN'T, WE'RE *GAGTIME*.

CHORUS

RAGTIME

LITTLE BOY

GAGTIME

CHORUS

RAGTIME

LITTLE BOY

GAGTIME

CHORUS

RAGTIME!

ALL

GAGTIME! GAGTIME!

[Alternate Ending]

LITTLE BOY

The plot of *Gagtime* had run out. But we did not know
that then, because we were so confused.

MOTHER

Mother moved to Queens, where she opened a
Democratic headquarters.

COALHOUSE

Coalhouse, ended up at a dinner theater in Florida,
understudying the role of Scar in *The Lion King*.

SARAH

Sarah turned into Audra McDonald and was offered
the lead in every Broadway show for the next thirty-
eight years, winning thirty-nine more Tony awards. My
thirty-ninth was a special one for winning thirty-eight.

LITTLE BOY

And *Ragtime* survived both its *Times* review and this
obnoxious parody.

COALHOUSE

IN EV'RY SHOW THERE'S ONE BIG REPRISE . . .

SARAH

. . . THAT MAKES YOU WEEP AND CLUTCH YOUR
   THROAT.

MOTHER

WHEN *RAGTIME* IS OLD ENOUGH,
THEY WILL CALL IT A MASTERPIECE.

ALL

LIKE ALL GREAT SHOWS, OUR SHOW WILL END
WITH A REALLY LONG NOOOOOOTE!

"The Circle of Mice" (*The Lion King*)

[RAFREAKY *the baboon is discovered standing center
stage, chanting in quasi-African.*]

RAFREAKY

HOW'M I GONNA GET A TICKET
TO *THE LION KING*?

AFRICAN BALONEY,
BUT WE WON A LOT OF TONY.
HIGHFALUTIN' PUPPET SHOW
KUKLA, FRAN, AND OLLIE-O,
PINOCCHIO.

STORY SO BIZZARI:
HAMLET GO SAFARI.
I GOT A LOTTA MAKEUP ON,
JOHNNY—JOHNNY—ELTON JOHN!

You understand? No? Rafreaky translate.

[*Motions pulling the handle of a cash register.*]

Ker-Ching! Ker-Ching!

FROM THE DAY *LION KING* CAME TO BROADWAY,
THE THEATER IS NOT QUITE THE SAME.
THERE IS MORE TO SEE
THAN HAS EVER BEEN SEEN,
BUT THE BOOK
IS CHILDISH AND LAME.

BUT TO HAVE A HIT TODAY, I FEAR,
THE VISUALS OUTRANK WHAT'S PROFOUND.
AND NOW *HUNCHBACK* IS NEXT!
BUT MY HUNCH IS IT'S HEXED!
THE THEME PARK SHOWS
KEEP GAINING GROUND.

IT'S THE CIRCLE OF MICE!
DISNEY'S ALL AROUND,
AND YOU'LL PAY THE PRICE
AND YOU'LL BE SPELLBOUND.
PUPPET SHOWS REPLACE
WHAT WE USED TO CALL CONTENT.
WHO NEEDS SONDHEIM
IN THE CIRCLE OF MICE!

"Can You Feel the Pain Tonight?"

NALA

I HATE JULIE TAYMOR;
SHE DOESN'T HAVE A CLUE.
MY NECK IS BREAKING WEARING HER DESIGNS,
AND SUBLUXATED, TOO.
HER PUPPETRY IS STUNNING,
BUT NOW WE MUST CONFIDE:
ALTHOUGH IT LOOKS GREAT FROM THE AUDIENCE,
IT'S TORTURE HERE INSIDE.

SIMBA

CAN YOU FEEL THE PAIN TONIGHT,
THE STRAIN THIS HEADDRESS BRINGS?

NALA

THE CRACKING BONES, THE TEARING CARTILAGE
CAN KILL ALL LIVING THINGS.

BOTH

CAN YOU FEEL THE SPRAIN TONIGHT,
AS YOUR DELTOIDS THROB?
I CAN HEAR YOUR CRUNCHING VERTEBRAE.
WHAT A LOUSY JOB!

AND IF YOU FEEL THE PAIN TONIGHT,
LET ME CARRY YOU
TO BE WED BY MY CHIROPRACTOR, WHO
WORKS FOR DISNEY TOO!

[*They go to kiss and scream out in pain.*]

OHHHHH!

"Andrew Lloyd Webber"

CHORUS

ANDREW LLOYD SUPERSTAR!
ANDREW LLOYD, WHY ARE YOU SO BIZARRE?
ANDREW LLOYD SUPERSTAR!
OOOOO, OOOO, OOOO

ANDREW

MEM'RY, IS MY POWER A MEM'RY?
EVEN THOUGH *CATS* AND *PHANTOM*
WILL FOREVER PLAY ON,
I REMEMBER THE TIME WHEN ALL OF BROADWAY
   WAS MINE.
IS THAT ERA EVER GONE?

GREAT YEARS UNDER REAGAN AND THATCHER!
MY NEW TUNES BY THE BATCH WERE
MILLION SELLERS AT LEAST.
SARAH BRIGHTMAN
AND I ONCE SCHEMED TO CONQUER THE WORLD;
SHE WAS BEAUTY, I THE BEAST.

THEN CAME *SUNSET BOULEVARD . . .*
THE FUTURE SEEMED SO SUNNY.
THEN GLENN CLOSE LEFT, ANOTHER STAR TOOK
   OVER,
AND WE LOST ALL OUR MONEY.

HATE ME! PEOPLE INSTANTLY HATE ME;
ALAN LERNER ONCE TOLD ME
THAT'S BECAUSE IT SAVES TIME.
WELL NOW, LATELY, I UNDERSTAND WHAT MEMORY
   IS.
DISNEY, CAN YOU SPARE A DIME?

"Ethel and the Phantom"

[*The lights dim. A chandelier lowers out of the ceiling. The light from the glow reveals a silhouette of the* PHANTOM. *He sings pretentiously.*]

PHANTOM

I'M THE PHANTOM, BROADWAY'S SMOOTHEST
   CROONER
HEAR ME GURGLE IN THIS HORROR TUNER!
WHEN THE SONGS A BITCH AND I'M SLIGHTLY
   UNDER PITCH,
THEY JUST FLICK THE REVERB SWITCH FROM LEFT
   TO RIGHT
AND COVER UP MY MUCUS OF THE NIGHT.

[*A voice is heard from the back of the house.*]

VOICE

What????

PHANTOM

COME TO *PHANTOM*, THEATER'S GREAT SENSATION.

VOICE

Sing out, Louise!

PHANTOM

WHY WERE STILL HERE, THERE'S NO EXPLANATION!

VOICE

What kind of a song is that?

[*The* PHANTOM *stops, then starts again.*]

PHANTOM

I'M THE PHANTOM . . .

VOICE

What kind of a voice is that?

[*The* PHANTOM *stops. The voice belongs to* ETHEL MERMAN, *who barrels to the front of the stage and then right onto it.*]

[*The* PHANTOM *starts singing again, timidly.*]

HANTOM

. . . BROADWAY'S GREATEST CROONER . . .

ETHEL

What's that stupid mask on your face? You look like Lon Chaney. How can you sing with that thing over your mouth. Take it off!

[*She rips his mask off. He is horrified.*]

PHANTOM

How dare your de-mask me? Who do you think you are?

ETHEL

Ethel Merman. That's who.

[*Applause from the audience.*]

Thank you. Thank you. Swell.

[*She turns back to* PHANTOM.]

God, your face is uglier than I thought it would be. And what's that growth on your forehead? Oh, it's that strange Andrew Lloyd Webber disease I heard about.

PHANTOM

[*Very snottily.*]

This is my DX 445 mega voice thickener and sound propellant.

ETHEL

Well, I think they should call it the sound RE-pellant!

PHANTOM

Times have changed, Ms. Merman. This is how we sing nowadays.

I KEEP SINGING THOUGH MY VOICE IS AIR,
I KEEP GOING WHEN THERE'S NOTHING THERE.
THERE'S A BIG BLACK LUMP INSIDE MY HAIR.
YOU WONDER WHY?
I'LL TELL YOU WHY:
I KEEP WALKING THROUGH THE SHOW EACH NIGHT,
BUT IN SPITE OF THAT, YOU'LL HEAR ALRIGHT.
STARS LIKE ME SEEM EVER TIRELESS,
THANKS TO MY WIRELESS
HEAD MICROPHONE!

ETHEL

In my day, we didn't need microphones. We had voices then!

YOU DON'T NEED AMPLIFYIN'
YOU'LL BE LOUD AS A LION.
BE LIKE ME, USE YOUR DIAPHRAGM!
TAKE THAT THING OFF YOUR FOREHEAD,
IT LOOKS LIKE A NUKE WARHEAD
AND YOU SOUND SHEEPISH AS A LAMB.

IF TODAY I GOT HIRED,
I WOULD SWEAT WHEN I'M WIRED,
CAUSING SOME ELECTRONIC ZING.
COME ON, KID, AND GET SOME CLASS:
TAKE THAT MIKE OUT OF YOUR ASS . . .

[ETHEL *turns the* PHANTOM *around, rips his microphone pack out of the back of his pants, and throws it offstage.*]

. . . AND ADMIT
YOU JUST CAN'T SING!

I'll have you singing like Jolson in no time!

[*They repeat the two sections above in counterpoint. As they do so, the* PHANTOM *gains in confidence and begins to sing more forcefully. Then.*]

ETHEL

COME ON, KID, SING LOUD AND CLEAR;
WARBLE DOWN THAT CHANDELIER.

PHANTOM

[*Sings in the style of Merman.*]

THE PHANTOM OF THE OPERA IS ME!

BOTH

THAT'S THE MERMAN WAY TO SING.
SWELL!

"Swan Lake"

[CAMERON MACKINTOSH *enters in Napoleonic cape and sings.*]

CAMERON MACKINTOSH

I'M CAMERON MACKINTOSH,
NAPOLEON OF BROADWAY,
AND I'M BORED LOOKING FOR NEW PLAYS.
I'M CAMERON MACKINTOSH,
THE EMPEROR OF BROADWAY,
SO I'VE STARTED A BALLET CRAZE . . .

[*He opens his cape, revealing he is bare-chested with tons of feathers around his legs.*]

SWAN LAKE IS NOW MY LATEST SHOW,
A SHOW THAT'S RICH IN SNOB APPEAL.
AND IN *SWAN LAKE*
ALL THE SWANS ARE GAY, YOU KNOW,
AND MAKE THE CHELSEA ELSIES SQUEAL.
AND IN THE PLOT OF OUR *SWAN LAKE*,
SIEGFRIED'S ON THE MAKE.

[*Choreographer* MATTHEW BOURNE *enters, also dressed as a swan prince.*]

MATTHEW

I'M THE PRINCE OF CHELSEA,
AND I'M IN DISTRESS
'CAUSE MY LIFE'S A MESS,
'CAUSE MY TIMBERLAND
BOOTS HAVE BEEN BADLY STAINED
AT THE BIG CUP*.

CAMERON

NOW HE IS DRAINED AND HE'S FED UP!

MATTHEW

THEN HE MEETS ODETTE, THE HEAD SWAN.

[CAMERON *becomes Odette.*]

CAMERON

EYE CONTACT MADE; THERE'S A PICK-UP.

MATTHEW and CAMERON

THEY PAS-DES-DEUX SOMETHING FIERCE,

---

* The Big Cup was a popular gay hangout and pickup joint
  in Chelsea during the late '90s.

THEN THEY GO WATCH *MILDRED PIERCE.*

CAMERON

FABULOUS
THEN SIEGFRIED ASKS, "WHAT IS NEXT TO SEE?"

MATTHEW

ODETTE SAYS, "LET'S DO SOME ECSTASY."

CAMERON

GIGANTIC PILLS

MATTHEW

LA-LA-LA-LA-LA-LA

CAMERON

BALLETIC THRILLS

MATTHEW

LA-LA-LA-LA-LA-LA!
AND AT THE ROXY, THEY DANCE TILL DAWN,
THEY TWIST AND SHOUT AND THEY GET IT ON.

BOTH

FIVE HOURS OF ETERNAL LOVE!

CAMERON

MEANWHILE, SIEGFRIED, SO ELATED,
DOES A SOLO GAY PRIDE DANCE,
OVERSTATED, OVERRATED . . .

MATTHEW

. . . BUT I LOOK GREAT IN HIS SHAGGY PANTS!

[CAMERON *is pissed at* MATTHEW's *attitude. They fight.*]

THEN ODETTE THROWS A HISSY FIT
AND TORMENTS SIEGFRIED, MAKING JABS;
SEIGFRIED PULLS HIS BEAK OUT JEALOUSLY
AND PUTS A HEX ON ODETTE'S ABS.

CAMERON

AS POOR ODETTE GETS A FLABBY WAIST,
SIEGFRIED LEAVES REPULSED . . .

MATTHEW

. . . TO GO GET A CAPPUCCINO

CAMERON

POOR ODETTE GETS SO OVERWEIGHT,
HE IS NOW CONVULSED . . .

[CAMERON *lies on the piano and does sit-ups violently.*]

MATTHEW

. . . AND HE'S WRITHING AROUND DOWN ON THE
   GROUND.
HARD AS HE TRIES, CAN'T LOOSE A POUND.
LOOKS LIKE BLACK MAGIC,
AND IT ALL ENDS TRAGIC.

BOTH

SO COME AND SEE OUR NEW *SWAN LAKE*!
TCHAIKOVSKY THINKS THE BOYS ARE SWELL.

CAMERON

AFTER *SWAN LAKE*, MATHEW BOURNE AND I WILL
   DO . . .

BOTH

. . . A NEW, ALL-LESBIAN *GISELLE*.
See it *and* live to regret it!

"Mandy Patinkin: *Mamaloshen*"

MANDY

MANDY PATINKIN,

MANDY PATINKIN,

MANDY PATINKIN,

AM I FOR REAL?

I KNOW YOU'RE THINKIN',

"HAVE YOU BEEN DRINKN',

MANDY PATINKIN?

WHAT A SCHLEMIEL!"

AY-DIG-A-DIG-A-DIG-A-AY-DIE-DIE!

AY-DIG-A-DIG-A-DIG-A-AY-DIE-DIE!

These Yiddish songs were taught to me by my mother
in the Mamaloshen—that means "native tongue." They
are simple, sweet songs from a culture rich in tradition.
And I've brought them here tonight to pummel them
to death.

DREIDEL, DREIDEL, DREIDEL,

I MADE IT OUT OF CLAY,

AND WHEN YOU'RE DRY AND READY,

THE DREIDEL WE SHALL PLAY!

DREIDEL, DREIDEL, DREIDEEEEEEL!

AY-DIG-A-DIG-A-DIG-A- AY-DIE-DIE!

AY-DIG-A-DIG-A-DIG-A- AY-DIE-DIE!

SUPER-FRANTIC-HYPERACTIVE-SELF-INDULGENT
   MANDY.

WHEN I GET HYSTERICAL,

THE CRITICS SAY I'M DANDY.

WHEN THEY CAST A LUNATIC,

I ALWAYS COME IN HANDY—

SUPER-FRANTIC-HYPERACTIVE-SELF-INDULGENT
   MANDY!

AY-DIG-A-DIG-A-DIG-A-

AY-DIE-DIE!

AY-DIG-A-DIG-A-DIG-A-

AY-DIE-DIE!

BECAUSE I'M SUCH AN ODDITY,

MY MAINSTREAM DAYS ARE THROUGH,

AND SINCE I LEFT *CHICAGO HOPE*,

THERE'S NOTHING MUCH TO DO.

AND SO I BUILT A REPERTOIRE

TO PLEASE THE YIDDISH FAN,

SO, BROADWAY, WON'T YOU WELCOME BACK

THE MAMALOSHEN MAN!

SUPER-FRANTIC-HYPERACTIVE-SELF-INDULGENT
   MANDY!

AM I UNDER MEDICATION, OVERSEXED, OR
   RANDY?

PASS AROUND THE MATZO BALLS AND
   MANESCHEWITZ BRANDY!

SUPER-FRANTIC-HYPERACTIVE-SELF-INDULGENT
   MANDY!

AY-DIG-A-DIG-A-DIG-A-AY-DIE-DIE!

AY-DIG-A-DIG-A-DIG-A-AY-DIE!

THERE'S NOTHING I LIKE BETTER

THAN A LYRICAL STAMPEDE!

GESTICULATING SONDHEIM

ALWAYS MAKES MY FINGERS BLEED.

AND SO TO GET THE KUDOS

AND ATTENTION THAT I NEED,

I LIKE TO TAKE SOME SIMPLE SONG

AND DOUBLE UP THE SPEED.

SUPER-FRANTIC-HYPERACTIVE-SELF-INDULGENT
   MANDY!

MUSIC DRIVES ME CRAZIER THAN BLANCHE
   DUBOIS WITH TANDY.

I CAN BARK AND WAG MY TAIL LIKE ANNIE'S DOGGIE
SANDY,
SUPER-FRANTIC-HYPERACTIVE-SELF-INDULGENT
MANDY!
SUPER-FRANTIC-HYPERACTIVE-SELF-INDULGENT
MANDY!

[*The tempo nearly doubles.*]

SUPER-FRANTIC-HYPERACTIVE-SELF-INDULGENT
MANDY!
IF YOU EAT WHILE WATCHING ME YOU'LL THROW UP
ALL YOUR CANDY.
ALTA KAKAS LOVE ME WHEN I GET ALL HOLY-LANDY.
SUPER-FRANTIC-HYPERACTIVE-SELF-INDULGENT
MANDY!
SUPER-FRANTIC-HYPERACTIVE-SELF-INDULGENT
MANDY!

"*Cabaret* Meets *The Sound of Music*"

EMCEE

WELCOME ME BACK AGAIN, STRANGERS.
DON'T CALL THE SEX POLICE RANGERS.
WE GET SO RAUNCHY
IN THIS CABARET,
POOR ROBYN BYRD
WOULD BLUSH AND TURN AWAY.
WE'RE NC-17 RATED;
THIS CABARET IS SO RISQUÉ,
JOEL GREY TURNED GRAY!

And now, in keeping with Mayor Rudolph Giuliani's
new 60/40 family entertainment law, the Kit Kat Klub
is forced to present that international sensation direct
from the Salzburg Music Festival on their way to
America: The Von Trapp Family Singers!

MARIA and CHILDREN

DO-RE-MI-FA-SOL-LA-TI-DO!

[*The* EMCEE *pops out again. He is dressed in lederhosen
like the children, except he is not wearing a shirt.*
MARIA *and the* CHILDREN *recoil in fear with an
audible gasp.*]

EMCEE

Look! It's me!

MARIA

Come along, children, get in line—next to the freak.

[*The* EMCEE *hides behind* MARIA *in the proper
formation but sticks his head out once in a while,
mischievously.*]

MARIA and CHILDREN

WE'RE A SAD SORT OF REMNANT FROM AN
INNOCENT TIME
WHEN THE CRITICS WOULD NOT POO-POO
A SHOW FILLED WITH MELODY
OR MOUNTAINS TO CLIMB
OR CHARACTERS A BIT CUKOO.
(CUKOO, THAT'S YOU, CUKOO)
NOW *CABARET* LOOKS BRILLIANT,
BUT OUR SHOW LESS RESILIENT,
FOR SENTIMENT IS THROUGH.

CHILD ONE

SO LONG, FAREWELL,
GREAT SHOWS LIKE US HAVE VANISHED.
WE'RE SO UN-COOL,
WE'RE PRACTICALLY BANISHED.

[*The* EMCEE *pulls up her dress, revealing polka-dot
underwear. She runs off humiliated.*]

CHILD TWO

SO LONG, FAREWELL,
NEW SHOWS ARE DARK AND DISMAL,
BUT WE'RE SO SWEET,
THEY HAND OUT PEPTO-BISMAL.

[*The* EMCEE *gives him a wedgy. The boy runs off,*
painfully humiliated.]

MARIA

SO LONG, FAREWELL,
WE'RE STICKIER THAN STRUDEL.
THE CRITICS SAID
WE'RE SOGGY AS A NOODLE.

[*The* EMCEE *humiliates her and she runs offstage.*]

EMCEE

THOUGH *CABARET* IS SLIGHTLY OVERRATED,
THE TIMES HAVE CHANGED
AND *SOUND OF MUSIC'S* DATED
AUF WIEDERSEHN! A BIENTOT!

[*The* MOTHER ABBESS *enters and watches.*]

MOTHER ABBESS

GOODBYE!

[*She pulls the* EMCEE *off by the ear.*]

MOTHER ABBESS

FIND MARY MARTIN,
SEARCH HIGH AND LOW,
LOOK FOR JULIE ANDREWS
WHEN YOU DO A SHOW.

CALL ETHEL MERMAN—
GEE, SHE WAS SWELL!
TELL ME, WHAT BECAME OF
THEODORE BIKEL?

SECOND NUN

BUT BROADWAY SURVIVES
AND CONTINUES TO GIVE
STIRRING MUSIC TO SING
FOR AS LONG AS WE LIVE . . .

THIRD and FOURTH NUNS

FIND MARY MARTIN!
TELL HER TO BEAM

ALL

FOLLOW ALL OF BROADWAY
TILL YOU FIND YOUR DREAM!

Favorite lyrics from *Forbidden Broadway 2001: A Spoof Odyssey*

"Judi Dench"

JUDI

Good evening, ladies and gentle. Whenever I see a play
here on Broadway, I can't help thinking . . .

WHY CAN'T AMERICANS DO THEATER LIKE THE
BRITS?
OUR AVALANCHE OF TALENT IS CRUSHING YOU TO
BITS.
IF YOU DID A CHEKOV PLAY
AS ENGLISH ACTORS DO,
YOU MIGHT WIN A TONY OR TWO.

WE'VE PETER HALL AND TREVOR NUNN
AND MAGGIE SMITH FOR STARTERS;
YOU'VE LOT'S OF KELSEY GRAMMERS,
CHERYL LADDS, AND DIXIE CARTERS!

MOST OF YOUR ACTORS NEED A LAUGH TRACK ON
A SET.
OH, WHY CAN'T AMERICANS GO AND

GET SOME DECENT TRAINING
IN LONDON AT RADA OR AT THE RSC?
JUST LOOK WHAT WONDERS IT HAS DONE FOR ME!

WHEN I READ A PHONE BOOK,
NEW YORKERS COMPLETELY BURST WITH GLEE.
IN HOLLYWOOD, THEY ABSOLUTELY PEE!

WHY CAN'T AMERICANS DO THEATER LIKE THE
   BRITS?
WHEN GEORGE C. WOLFE DOES SHAKESPEARE,
SIR KENNETH BRANAGH SHITS.
THE RICH THEATERGOERS LOVE MY ROYAL
   ROUNDED TONES.

Americans don't notice if I'm actually acting or not, as long as I do it with an English accent!

THE BRITISH CAN DO ANYTHING
ONCE WE'VE GOT OUR DIPLOMA.
WE EVEN BEAT AMERICANS REVIVING *OKLAHOMA!*

OUR SHOWS ARE BETTER,
EVEN THOUGH WE'RE SNOBBY TWITS.
SO IMPORT YOUR THEATER,
OR DO YOUR THEATER
LIKE THE BRITS!

"Cheryl Ladd in *Annie Get Your Gun*"

CHERYL

I'M NOT ETHEL MERMAN, I'M NOT BERNADETTE;
I'M TV'S CHARLIE'S ANGEL, CHERYL LADD.
I PLAY ANNIE OAKLEY ON BROADWAY, AND YET,
IT'S OBVIOUS THE PUBLIC HAS BEEN HAD!
THE WEISSLERS PLAY THE STAR REPLACEMENT
   GAME
AND STICK IN ANY TELEVISION NAME . . .

I'VE NO BUSINESS IN SHOW BUSINESS,
BUT WHEN BUSINESS IS SLOW,
ANY TV STAR'S A GOOD REPLACEMENT,
RECOGNIZED BY ALMOST EVERYONE.
EVEN IF THEIR TALENT'S IN THE BASEMENT,
A PRETTY FACE MEANT THE SHOW WILL RUN.

THERE'S NO TALENT LIKE TUBE TALENT
WHEN NO TALENT IS THERE.
YESTERDAY THEY TOLD ME I WOULD NOT GO FAR,
THAT NIGHT I OPENED, AND THEY WERE RIGHT.
NEXT DAY OFF MY DRESSING ROOM THEY TOOK MY
   STAR,
BUT I REALLY DON'T CARE,
'CAUSE I'VE GOT PERFECT HAIR!

"Cole Porter"

[COLE PORTER *appears onstage, sitting elegantly on a silver stool. He takes a puff from a cigarette and sings.*]

COLE PORTER

I'M THE TOP,
I'M THE GREAT COLE PORTER!
FROM THE PAST,
LIKE A SILVER QUARTER,
I'VE RETURNED THIS YEAR
BECAUSE I'M REVIVED NONSTOP,
BECAUSE SONGS BY ME, COLE PORTER,
ARE THE TOP!

Yes, after many years of writing songs for motion pictures and theater, I find it very exciting to return to Broadway— what's left of it!

FROM THIS SEASON ON,
NO MORE NEW SHOWS,
ONLY TRIED AND TRUE SHOWS,
FROM THIS SEASON ON.

FROM THIS DISMAL DAY,

NO NEW TITILES,

ONLY DANCE RECITALS,

FROM THIS SEASON ON.

FOR CREATIVE ART CAN COST TOO MUCH,

MEN WITH CASH ARE OUT OF TOUCH.

WHO NEEDS BOOKS WITH SUBSTANCE OR BITE?

SWING AND *FOSSE* SELL OUT EVERY NIGHT.

FROM THIS SEASON ON,

ALL ARRIVALS

ARE REVIVED REVIVALS.

EV'RY RISK IS GONE

FROM THIS SEASON ON.

For example here's an excerpt from the current revival of my greatest hit, *Kiss Me, Kate,* starring Brian "Stokes" Mitchell and Mar . . . Mary . . . Mar . . . [*An offstage voice whispers "Marin Mazzie."*] Oh yes! Marin Mazzie!

"Would-Be Stars"

[*Lights up on* MARIN MAZZIE *and* BRIAN STOKES MITCHELL *in* Kiss Me Kate *dressing gowns.*]

STOKES

GAZING DOWN FROM A MARQUEE

MAZZIE

IS A BIG, BRIGHT PHOTO OF US

STOKES

IT SAYS "SEE *KISS ME, KATE*"

MAZZIE

BUT OUR BILLING'S NOT GREAT

BOTH

THOUGH OUR PICTURE IS ON EV'RY BUS . . .

WOULD-BE STARS, WOULD-BE STARS

STOKES

I'M THE NEW AGE ALFRED DRAKE,

JUST AS GOOD AS A RAKE,

BUT I CAN'T QUITE GET A BREAK.

BOTH

WOULD-BE STARS, WOULD-BE STARS . . .

MAZZIE

I'M AS GOOD AS BERNADETTE,

BUT MY NAME YOU'LL FORGET

'CAUSE I'M NOT QUITE FAMOUS YET.

MARIN MAZZIE, SINGER/DANCER.

STOKES

BRIAN MITCHELL; CALL ME "STOKES."

MAZZIE

DO YOU KNOW US?

STOKES

PLEASE DON'T ANSWER.

BOTH

TRUE, WE'RE SLOWPOKES.

PLEASE, NO JOKES, FOLKS!

WOULD-BE STARS, WOULD-BE STARS,

SORT OF CLOSE BUT NO CIGARS.

ONLY KNOWN IN GAY BARS—

WE'RE FOREVER WOULD-BE STARS!

"*Beauty*'s Been Decreased"

OFFSTAGE VOICES

LA-LA-LA-LA-LA,
BEAUTY AND THE BEAST . . .

BEAUTY

SHOW AS OLD AS TIME,
WORN AS IT CAN BE,
OVERSIZED AND GRAND,
THEN SOMEONE IS CANNED
UNEXPECTEDLY . . .

JUST A LITTLE CHANGE,
SAYS THE DISNEY BEAST.
PROFITS GROWING THIN,
DOWNSIZING IS IN:
BEAUTY'S BEEN DECREASED

FIRST A MISSING SPOON,
THEN A FIRED FORK
THEN THE CHORUS BOYS
ARE REPLACED BY TOYS—
EVEN IN NEW YORK!

PINK SLIPS EVERYWHERE,
NO FOOD AT THE FEAST.
WIGS ARE ALL A MESS,
NEXT THEY'LL TAKE MY DRESS . . .
BEAUTY'S BEEN DECREASED!
SINCE WE'RE IN THE RED,
LIKE A SHRUNKEN HEAD,
BEAUTY'S BEEN DECREASED.

[*She leaves as if being fired. The* BEAST *hand-holds out a tiny doll.*]

"Let's Ruin Times Square Again"

TOM HEWITT AS FRANKENFURTER

IT'S ASTOUNDING: ROCKY HORROR
WAS MAINSTREAM BROADWAY FARE.
THOUGH I'M SCARY, MIDWEST TOURISTS
LOVED MY . . . UNDERWEAR.

I REMEMBER VISITING TIMES SQUARE—
RAUNCHY, WAY BACK WHEN.
BUT SINCE SOMEONE CLEANED IT,
IT'S GETTING LIKE VEGAS.
LET'S RUIN TIMES SQUARE AGAIN!

NOW THERE'S THE GAP ON THE LEFT
AND HMV ON THE RIGHT,
AND MADAME TUSSAUDS
IS OPEN EV'RY NIGHT.
NOW, FOR THE OL' TIME SLEAZY
I GOT A REALLY BAD YEN . . .
LET'S RUIN TIMES SQUARE AGAIN!
LET'S RUIN TIMES SQUARE AGAIN!

ELTON JOHN

I'M ELTON JOHN AND I'VE SOLD OUT
TO THE MICKEY MOUSE HOLD OUT
BROADWAY'S UNDER SEDATION
FROM THIS DISNEYFICATION

BOTH

LET'S RUIN TIMES SQUARE AGAIN!

A 42ND STREET CHORINE

HEY, LOOK WHO'S TEARIN' UP THE TOWN
WITH THEIR TAPPIN' FEET!
IT'S THE NEW OLD SHOW CALLED *42ND STREET*.
WE SHAKE OUR BEHINDS AND WE BOUNCE OUR
    LITTLE TITS

AND TURN THIS BROADWAY SAGA INTO VEGAS
   GLITZ.
THE CHORUS GIRLS WILL MAKE YOU HOLD YOUR
   EARS,
AND THE CHORUS BOYS ALL THINK THEY'RE
   BRITTNEY SPEARS!

ALL

LET'S RUIN TIMES SQUARE AGAIN!
LET'S RUIN TIMES SQUARE AGAIN!

FRANKENFURTER

IT'S BURGER KING ON THE LEFT
AND AMC ON THE RIGHT.
NOW IT LOOKS LIKE A MALL,
AND A CULTURAL BLIGHT!
IT'S A NEW KIND OF PORNO
BUT MORE OBNOXIOUS TIMES TEN.
LET'S RUIN TIMES SQUARE AGAIN!
LET'S RUIN TIMES SQUARE AGAIN!

FORBIDDEN MEMORIES: **Bryan Batt**

While in college, I first saw *Forbidden Broadway* and marveled at the hysterically witty writing and the brilliant performances, never dreaming that years later I would join the ranks for two incarnations. Physically, vocally, and mentally, it was the most challenging and exhausting work I have ever experienced, and I loved every minute. Having already performed on Broadway, I think I was the only cast member to spoof two shows that I had actually been in—and they were both still running at the time!

Previews were hard, as the show was daily tweaked and perfected. For about a month of performances, new numbers were written, rehearsed, and sometimes put into the show within a day or so. The running order would change constantly, and due to the crazed state the actors were in, sometimes the only way we could remember the lineup was because the dresser had placed our costumes in order over our dressing room chairs.

There should be a CD of numbers that were cut from the show or never made it in. I loved playing "Anita Fix," the non-Equity, triangle playing waitress/Kit Kat girl in the *Cabaret* revival parody. The most twisted song we ever had—I don't think it was ever completely written, much less staged—was about the *Rent* phenomenon and Jonathan Larson: "Nice work if you can get it, and you can get it if you die." Instant red light.

Bryan Batt ruled as the King of *Forbidden Broadway* from 1996 to 1999.

We learned one big number because Carol Channing was coming to see the show. It was right when Dolly the sheep was cloned, and we played cloned "Dolly Levis" in sheep masks. That number stayed in the show for only a few days. When we spoke with Carol afterwards, the following dialogue occurred:

CAROL CHANNING: How do you do all those impersonations? It's just astounding.

TOM PLOTKIN: Actually, Ms. Channing, I'm having vocal problems and I'm on prednisone.

CAROL: Prednisone? Don't ever, ever take prednisone.

TOM: Why not?

CAROL: I used to be five foot two!

One night, Christine Pedi had a severe costume malfunction and didn't make it onstage for the end of the Disney parody. Donna English, Bill Selby, and I nobly kept trying to continue, but the number was going way south; we ran out of stalling improv lines, and we were standing onstage with egg all over our faces. Then, after a pregnant pause, Bill blurted out: "I know a joke." The rest of us ran offstage, leaving him to tell it.

I will always treasure meeting Bob Hope, Elaine May, Chita Rivera, and Stephen Sondheim at the show. Carol Burnett's iconic laughter during *Forbidden Broadway: Cleans Up Its Act* will ring in my ears forever. But my favorite memory of the show involves my friend Gerard. In 2003, my partner and I opened a business in my hometown of New Orleans. Two years later, Katrina's floodwaters devastated the city, and while I was evacuated to NYC, Gerard called and offered me a job in *Forbidden*. He was the only person to do so. I am forever grateful for the years of friendship and fun.

Wickeder: 2001–05

We moved *Forbidden Broadway* to the Douglas Fairbanks Theatre on 42nd Street in May 2001. Then 9/11 happened. That was a Tuesday, and we canceled the show that night and for the next two nights. There was a feeling that no one would want to go to the theatre anymore. I thought, "Oh my God, we're doing a comedy at this tremendously tragic time." I remember my mother saying to me, "Well, Gerard, it took a bomb to close your show."

I went to the theatre on Friday for our first performance after 9/11, because I wanted to see how the show would play. The house was about a quarter full, which was small for a Friday night. Then the show started—and it seemed funnier and better than ever. It suddenly went over like a great celebration of New York and American musical theatre. For that whole year following, all this love came forward from the audience. We did great business for the next few years.

The world situation was so serious that people seemed to be hungry for light entertainment—the lighter and fluffier, the better. This may partly explain the critical success of shows like *Mamma Mia!, Thoroughly Modern Millie,* and of course *Forbidden Broadway.* It was at this point that "meta-musicals" really began to proliferate.

Donna English, Kristine Zbornik, Michael West, and Daniel Reichard celebrate our twentieth anniversary.

I believe Broadway is at its best when there are many types of shows running. In the early 2000s, almost all the new entries were big, bright, funny meta-musicals. *Urinetown* had the look and pretense of a dark, serious piece but in fact was a spoof that

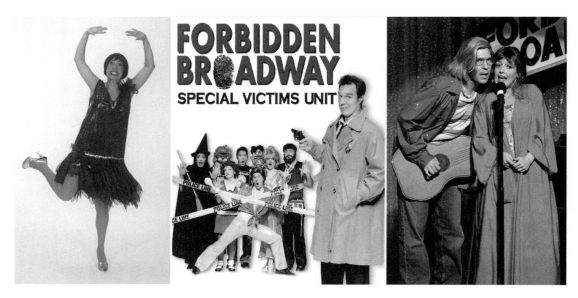

From left: Valerie Fagan as Sutton Foster in "Thoroughly Perky Millie." Poster for *Forbidden Broadway: Special Victims Unit*. Ron Bohmer and Jennifer Simard murder *Assassins*.

included allusions to *West Side Story* and other well-known musicals. *The Producers* and *Spamalot* were on the horizon, and there was even more to come.

Shows like *The Producers* and *Wicked* were great for Broadway and for us. Everyone knew them, and they had a lot of star power in Nathan Lane, Matthew Broderick, Kristin Chenoweth, and Idina Menzel. Again, the success of *Forbidden Broadway* doesn't necessarily depend on our audience having seen the shows; they just have to be aware of them and have heard all the buzz and hype.

I remember thinking that our show was like *Law & Order*: Both were New York institutions and basically trod the same path over and over, with some new variations. Broadway legend Jerry Orbach was the star of *Law & Order* at that point, so I wanted to put that show and ours together in some way. Also, after seeing certain Broadway shows, I would joke that the producers or directors should be criminally charged for what they had done. That's how I came up with the title *Forbidden Broadway: Special Victims Unit*.

THEY SAY BAD ART IS NOT A CRIME

ON BROADWAY,

BUT SOME PRODUCERS SHOULD DO TIME IN JAIL.

THEY SPEND MORE MONEY THAN FORT KNOX

AND STEAL A SCORE FROM SOME JUKEBOX,

THEN END UP WITH A PALE XEROX AND FAIL . . .

. . . THEY SAY THAT CRIME HAS GONE WAY UP

ON BROADWAY,

THE PUBLIC'S GETTING RIPPED OFF EV'RY DAY.
WHEN WILL YOU PEOPLE GET ENOUGH
OF ALL THIS VAPID GLITZY FLUFF?
TAKE OUT A HANDCUFF AND GET TOUGH
AND SAY "NO WAY!"

We skewered shows like *I Am My Own Wife, Movin' Out,* and the *Fiddler on the Roof* revival that reinterpreted that beloved musical to a fault. *Bombay Dreams* was one of the last big imports from London; it wasn't especially good, but it was a new book musical, and it actually had a story. *Lennon* was one of those rare exceptions where we targeted a flop. We spoofed Yoko Ono, who turned out to be probably the most spoofable celebrity since Liza.

The economics of theatre have changed so much since our show first opened. If you have to raise so much money to do an Off-Broadway show, why not raise a little more and put it on Broadway? In the '90s, you were able to do a big Off-Broadway show for about $300,000. You can't do that now; you need at least a million. I don't know exactly why the costs zoomed so high, but they did—and it seemed like it happened almost overnight, around 2002.

Today's audiences want "The Broadway Experience." There was a time when people would seek out underground, innovative, subversive fare, but now the industry is largely tourist-driven. Younger New Yorkers are going to Starbucks or clubs, or they're at the gym or the computer. The basic New York audience that sustained Broadway and Off-Broadway shows for decades is vanishing.

There were a lot of jukebox musicals on Broadway at the turn of the century, and we felt compelled to spoof all of them. We had very funny parodies of *Doubt* and *Virginia Woolf,* shows that were made for the *Forbidden Broadway* treatment. (Some plays are actually much easier for us to spoof than musicals.) But I do wish there were more stars on Broadway. I really respect Patti LuPone and

Harvey Fierstein (Ron Bohmer) joins the cast of *Fiddler on the Roof.*

Christine Pedi (as Ethel Merman), Jason Mills (as Hugh Jackman), Jennifer Simard (as Kristin Chenoweth), and Ron Bohmer (as Billy Joel).

Bernadette Peters for dedicating their talents to the stage.

I also miss the musical play on Broadway. I think the reason why Sondheim shows go over so well in revival is because they have three-dimensional characters and each has a dramatic arc. My reaction to *Spring Awakening* was very positive, because Steven Sater and Duncan Sheik told the story so well.

In 2005, we knew we'd have to find a new home for our show, as the Douglas Fairbanks and the rest of the theatres in that complex on 42nd Street between Ninth and Tenth avenues were scheduled to be torn down. Like a gypsy, *Forbidden Broadway* was soon on the move again.

"Wicked"

OFFSTAGE CHORUS

NO AWARDS FOR WICKED!

KRISTIN

AREN'T YOU GLAD I STARRED IN *WICKED*?
I'M KRISTIN CHENOWETH, BELOVED BY YOU,
BUT I'VE BEEN CO-STARRED WITH YOU-KNOW-
　　WHO . . .

Fellow, New Yorkians, I would like to introduce to you my beloved friend and glamorous co-star: Idina Menzel.

[IDINA *enters.*]

BOTH

WE'RE BOTH SO HAPPY,
WE'RE BOTH SO HAPPY NOW,
WE'RE BOTH SO HAPPY HOW . . .

KRISTIN

. . . SHE GETS A BIG OVATION . . .

IDINA

. . . BUT SHE'S THE BIG SENSATION.

BOTH

WE BOTH DEFER THE FINAL BOW,
'CAUSE SHE'S THE BIGGER STAR RIGHT NOW!

KRISTIN

POPULAR! I'M GLAD YOU'RE SO POPULAR.
YOU'VE BEEN ON MORE TV SHOWS,
AND YOU'VE MODELED CLOTHES
SOME WOULD EVEN CALL OBSCENE.
YOU'RE IN ALL THE PR SHOTS
AND THE PROMO SPOTS;
YOU EVEN LOOK ATTRACTIVE GREEN.

IDINA

YES, I'M POPULAR!
BUT YOU'RE THE MORE POPULAR.
YOU'RE EVEN BEN BRANTLEY'S PET,
AND YOU'VE GOT A SET
OF PIPES TO RIVAL BAR'BRA COOK.
YOU'RE BLESSED WITH THOSE ROSY CHEEKS,
YOU'RE THE STAR WHO WROTE THE "I'M LOVED AND
    FAMOUS" BOOK.

KRISTIN

YOU'RE SUCH A SWEETIE THAT MY ZERO MALICE IS
PUTTING ALL MY BITCHINESS INTO PARALYSIS.

BOTH

THANK GOD YOU'VE CHOSEN ME TO BE
YOUR PAL, YOUR SISTER, AND ADVISER.
YOU'RE BIGGER NOW THAN PFIZER!
YOU'RE IN DEMAND.

KRISTIN

I LOVE THAT YOU'RE POPULAR;
IT MUST BE YOUR DESTINY
TO BE BIG AS ME.

I KNOW YOU'LL MAKE THE BIGGER STIR—STAR.
I'M GENUINELY HAPPY YOU'VE BECOME
MORE POPULER—LAR
LA-LA-LA-LA

IDINA

WHAT A LOVE FEST! LA-LA-LA-LA.

KRISTIN

SHE'S THE BEST-EST.

BOTH

I'M GLAD THAT YOU'RE SO POPULAR!

VOICE-OVER

And now the Tony Award for Best Actress in a musical!

[IDINA *and* KRISTIN *hold hands and kiss and cry and jump up and down excitedly.*]

BOTH

Ooooo!

KRISTIN

Idina, before they announce the winner, let's make a blood oath: Whatever happens, we will always love each other and be the dearest of friends.

IDINA

Yes! Always!

VOICE-OVER

And the winner is . . . Idina Menzel in *Wicked*.

IDINA

Ahh! Yes! I won! I won! I am a star! I am *the* star!!

KRISTIN

I HOPE YOU'RE HAPPY,
I HOPE YOU'RE HAPPY NOW,

I HOPE YOU'RE PROUD OF HOW
YOU STOLE FROM ME THE TONY,
YOU VULGAR, ONE-TRICK PONY.

IDINA

I AM SO HAPPY,
I AM SO HAPPY NOW,
I AM SO HAPPY HOW
I WON YOUR STUPID TONY,
YOU CUTE, OBNOXIOUS PHONY!

KRISTIN

YOU GIVE ME BACK MY FINAL BOW!

BOTH

AND NO ONE'S HAPPY RIGHT NOW!

KRISTIN

Idina, listen to me. We can still be friends. Just say you're sorry. And hand over that Tony to me.

IDINA

What?!

KRISTIN

I mean . . .

STEPHEN SCHWARTZ COULD USE THAT TONY,
FOR HE'S NEVER WON BEFORE.
YOU COULD SAVE A STARVING WRITER . . .

IDINA

I know.

KRISTIN

TRUST MY WISDOM.

IDINA

No!
I DON'T WANT TO ANYMORE!

I'LL BE THE STAR OF *WICKED*
AFTER YOU LEAVE THE SHOW,
AND ONCE THE CAST HAS CHANGED,
I'LL GRAB TOP BILLING WHEN YOU GO.

I'M GONNA TRY DEFYING CHENOWETH
SPIT IN YOUR EYE, DEFYING CHENOWETH,
AND YOU CAN'T GET ME DOWN.

KRISTIN

YOU'RE LOSING YOUR EQUILIBR'UM;
THAT GREEN PAINT SEEPED IN YOUR CERIBR'UM.
DON'T YOU DARE TRY DEFYING CHENOWETH!

BOTH

I'M/YOU'RE GONNA DIE DEFYING CHENOWETH,
I'LL WEAR THE DIVA CROWN!

[KRISTIN *is carried off by a flying monkey.*]

IDINA

SO STRAP ME IN A HARNESS
AND HOIST ME TO THE SKY!
IN ALL THE BIG SHOWS LATELY,
ALL THE LEADING LADIES HAVE TO FLY.
AND, HANGING FROM THE RAFTERS,
I'LL DANGLE LIKE A BLIMP,
PUMP UP MY VOLUME
AS I KILL MY FLYING CHIMP . . .

AND, SUDDENLY, I'M DEFYING SUBTLETY.
WITH DEATH-DEFYING LACK OF SUBTLETY,
I'LL CAPTURE WORLD RENOWN,
I'LL BLOW THE GERSHWIN UP BECAUSE
I AM THE LOUDEST WITCH IN OZ
AND NO ONE'S GONNA TURN MY VOLUME DOWN!
AHHHHHHHHH!

[*Two winged* MONKEYS *enter with a little box for* IDINA *to stand upon. When she does, the* MONKEYS *flap her cape as if she were flying.*]

DOOOOOOOOOWN!

KRISTIN and MONKEYS

WICKED! WICKED! INTERMISSION!

"Thoroughly Perky Millie"

SUTTON FOSTER AS MILLIE

Hi there! I'm *Thoroughly Modern Millie,* the worst "Best Musical" ever!

THERE ARE SHOWS, I SUPPOSE,
OVERBLOWN—HEAVEN KNOWS
BUT *MILLIE* GOES TO WRACK AND TO RUIN.
WHAT WE THINK IS SHEIK, UNIQUE, AND QUITE
    ADORABLE
IS REALLY BROAD AND ODD AND QUITE
    DEPLORABLE.
FOR EXAMPLE . . .

EVERYTHING WE DO IS THOROUGHLY PERKY
(CHEERFULLY INSIDIOUS)
EVERYTHING SO PUSHED AND THOROUGHLY
    FORCED
(AND THE SET IS HIDEOUS).
JUST LIKE AN AMATEUR,
I'LL SLAM AT YOUR BRAIN.
YOU'LL SCREAM, "GOSH DAMN IT, YOU'RE
GONNA DRIVE US ALL INSANE!"

EVERY TOE WE TAP WILL MAKE YOU FEEL SHELL-
    SHOCKED
(BATTERED AS A BOSNIAN)
EVERY SONG WE SING IS HYPER AND CUTE
(PEPPINESS AD NAUSEAM).

GOOD-BYE, SINCERITY!
IT'S THOROUGHLY THROUGH,
AND I'M SO FAKE, I'LL MAKE
YOU THOROUGHLY WANT TO KILL ME, TOO.

[*Two* CHORUS BOYS *enter with a bag of sugar for* SUTTON *and big bottles of Coke for themselves.*]

SUTTON

Come on, boys! Gimme-gimme!

[*They do a frantic dance break, run out of steam, slow down, then gulp down their Cokes as* SUTTON *sniffs her sugar. They resume their frantic dancing. When they are done, they throw the sugar and Coke offstage and sing.*]

ALL

WE ARE A FASHION MESS
OF PASSIONLESS GALL . . .

SUTTON

STRIP OFF OUR FLASHINESS
AND THERE'S NOTHING THERE AT ALL!
EVERY BIG HIT SHOW IS BASED ON A MOVIE

BOYS

(AND WE'RE GLAD TO ADD TO IT)

SUTTON

PEOPLE THINK THAT THEATRE'S FILM ON THE
    STAGE.

BOYS

(DID YOU SEE *THE GRADUATE*?)

ALL

GOOD-BYE, SMART MUSICALS!
THEY'RE DEAD IN A DITCH.
HELLO TO CORP'RATE GREED
AND THOROUGHLY MODERN BROADWAY KITSCH!

"Bombay Wet Dreams"

MAN

COME ON ALONG AND LISTEN TO
THE LULLABY OF BOMBAY

OFFSTAGE SHAKALAKA BABY

AY YI YI YI YI AYE YI YIY!

MAN

THE SIR LLOYD WEBBER BALLYHOO,
THE LULLABY OF BOMBAY

OFFSTAGE SHAKALAKA BABY

AY YI YI YI YI AYE YI YIY

MAN

THE FINGER-CYMBALS TINK-E-LING,
THE SQUEELING MATA HARIS

OFFSTAGE SHAKALAKA BABY

Aye-yi! Aye-yi! Aye-yi!

MAN

THE WATER FOUNTAIN SPRINK-E-LING
THE SOAKING SORRY SARIS . . .
WHEN A BOMBAY BABY SHAKES HER HIP
TO "SHAKALAKA BABY,"
MANHATTAN CULTURE TAKES A DIP
AND DROPS A RUNG.
GOOD-BYE, BROADWAY!
HELLO, CRASSNESS ON DISPLAY!
GOOD-BYE, GOOD JOBS!
NOW THEY'RE OUTSOURCING THE PLAY!
EVEN BROADWAY MUSICALS COME FROM BOMBAY...

[HINDU CHORUS BOY *enters with two* SHAKALAKA
BABIES.]

HINDU CHORUS BOY

HOORAY FOR BOLLYWOOD,
THAT SKANKY AND SHRI-LANKI BOLLYWOOD,
WHERE EV'RY COLOR FROM A BOX OF CRAYONS
IS SPRAYED ON RAYONS
WITH SEQUIN ON EV'RY HOOD.
DON'T COMPLAIN, THOUGH,
WHEN A RAINBOW
LANDS UPON YOUR HEAD
LIKE A BLOCK OF WOOD!

HOORAY FOR BOLLYWOOD,
WHERE CUTIES FROM CALCUTTA KNOW THEY
    COULD
GET CAST OUT FROM THEIR CASTE
WHEN CAST FOR BIG PAY
IN BOMBS FROM BOMBAY
THAT MAKE *MOOSE MURDERS* LOOK GOOD.
GO LEARN A HINDU SONG
AND WEAR A CHEAP SARONG,
YOU'LL HIT IN BOLLYWOOD!

[*He lies on the floor with two squirt bottles and creates
a magnificent fountain that showers the* SHAKALAKA
BABIES, *who writhe in exotic ecstasy.*]

ALL

SHAKALAKA BABY
HOORAY! HOORAY! HOORAY!
HOORAY FOR BOLLYWOOD!
AYE-YA!

"*Assassins* 2004"

[JOHN HINCKLEY *enters, carrying a framed portrait of
Stephen Sondheim. He strums a guitar as he sings.*]

JOHN HINCKLEY

I'M JOHN HINKLEY,
YOU ARE STEPHEN SONDHEIM ON HIGH.
STEPHEN,
TELL ME, STEPHEN, HOW I
SHOULD SING YOUR WORDS?
I WOULD DO *PASSION*,
I WOULD DO *FOLLIES*,
I WOULD PLAY *SWEENEY TODD* FOR YOU;
HE LIKED TO KILL PEOPLE, TOO.

I AM UNWORTHY OF YOUR WORDS,
STEPHEN, DARLING.
LET ME PROVE WORTHY OF YOUR WORDS!
YOU ARE A KING TO THEATRE NERDS
JUST LIKE ME,
BUT I'M AS BAFFLED
AS CAN BE.

[SQUEAKY FROMME *enters.*]

SQUEAKY

I AM SQUEAKY,
YOU ARE EV'RY LUNATIC'S GOD,
STEPHEN, DARLIN'.
CHARLIE MANSON APPLAUDS
ME AND YOUR WORDS:
WORDS LIKE "ZAPRUDER,"
WORDS LIKE "DICK NIXON."
I WILL ASSASSINATE ON CUE
IF THAT'S WHAT YOU WANT ME TO DO.

I AM UNWORTHY OF YOUR WORDS,
STEPHEN, DARLIN'.
ALL OF YOUR FANS WALK OUT IN HERDS;
LET ME BE WORTHY OF YOUR COMPLEX MELODY.

HINCKLEY

TEACH ME TO COUNT IN 5/4 TIME

SQUEAKY

PUT ME THROUGH MUSIC THEORY HELL

HINCKLEY

CUT ME WITH EV'RY PERFECT RHYME

SQUEAKY

COULDN'T YOU JUST WRITE *CAROUSEL*?

HINCKLEY

WHAT IS THAT DOTTED NOTE?

SQUEAKY

I HAVE A RAVAGED THROAT

HINCKLEY

EVEN THOUGH . . .

SQUEAKY

EVEN THOUGH . . .

HINCKLEY

I WILL ALWAYS KNOW . . .

BOTH

I AM UNWORTHY OF YOUR WORDS,
STEPHEN, DARLIN'.
I CANNOT SING YOUR MINOR THIRDS.
SINGING THIS MELODY IS KILLING ME,
I AM SO TORTURED, BUT I KNOW NOW WHAT TO DO:
I HAVE TO TURN MY GUN ON YOU,
YOUR WORDS AND YOU . . .

[*They shoot the picture of Sondheim. It flies offstage.*
SQUEAKY *takes out her knife and slices her forehead
while pouring Heinz ketchup all over the "wound."*
HINCKLEY *watches, then pulls out some McDonald's
fries and dips one in the ketchup running down her
forehead. He ponders, then eats it. Fadeout.*]

"Hugh Jackman in 'The Boy Who's Odd'"

HUGH

OH MY, BABY,
WHEN THIS SHOW IS CLOSED AND DONE
I GO TO RIO
FOR A GOOD REST.
I'M A TIRED FELLOW
'CAUSE MY SHOULDERS ACHE
FROM CARRYING THIS HEAVY, LEADEN SHOW,
AND I'LL BE FREE AT LAST
FROM THE CRITIC'S BLAST!

SOME SAY THAT OLD IS NEWER,
AND YOU CAN FIND A HIT IN THE SEWER.
IT'S TRUER NOW THAN THEN,
'CAUSE EVERYTHING OLD IS STILL OLD AGAIN!

DID YOU SEE *MAMMA MIA*?
IT'S LIKE FURNITURE FROM IKEA,
CHEAP PIECES YOU CAN MIX UP WHEN
EVERYTHING OLD IS STILL OLD AGAIN.

BROADWAY PRODUCERS IN SEARCH OF BIG SALES
RECYCLE LIZA WHEN ALL ELSE FAILS . . .

[LIZA *enters.*]

LIZA

. . . AND MOVIE STARS WHO HAVE LOST THEIR HEAD
NOW TURN UP INSIDE YOUR BED.

HUGH

DON'T THROW OLD SCRIPTS AWAY;
THEY'LL PRODUCE THEM ON OLD BROADWAY.

LIZA

WHO NEEDS NEW WRITERS WHEN . . .

BOTH

. . . EVERYTHING OLD IS STILL OLD AGAIN!

HUGH

WE WENT TO GAY-BAR LAND
AND DUG UP JUDY GARLAND!

[JUDY GARLAND *enters.*]

JUDY

I'M BACK FROM GOD KNOWS WHEN,
'CAUSE EVERYTHING OLD IS STILL OLD AGAIN!

LIZA

[*Trying to get* JUDY's *attention.*]

Mama! Mama!

JUDY

[*Pushing* LIZA *away.*]

WE THREW IN LIZA AND SEQUIN AND GLITZ

HUGH

'CAUSE OLDER SONGBOOKS ARE ALWAYS THE HITS

JUDY

AND THE MOVIE STARS YOU THOUGHT WERE LONG
    DEAD
ARE THE NEW BROADWAY STARS INSTEAD!

ALL THREE

DON'T THROW OLD STARS AWAY;
YOU CAN PLAY THEM
HUGH
IF YOU'RE NOT GAY,
AND WIN A TONY WHEN . . .

ALL THREE

EVERYTHING OLD IS STILL OLD AGAIN,

AND EVERYTHING NEW HAS MOLD AGAIN!

HUGH

[*Outdoing* LIZA *and* JUDY!]

YES!

"*Fiddler* Made a Goof"

[ALFRED MOLINA *enters.*]

ALFRED

A *Fiddler* with no Jew. Sounds crazy, no? But here in our little village of Manhattan, there is a current revival of *Fiddler on the Roof* that looks like a Branson Missouri Shtetl revue. Sitting through it isn't easy. You may ask, "Why do British directors like Sam Mendes, David Leveaux, and Trevor Nunn want to direct *Gypsy*, *Fiddler*, and *Oklahoma!*? Who knows? And how do they destroy and dismantle our masterpieces? That I can tell you in one word: Direction!

DIRECTION! DIRECTION!

[TOWNSPEOPLE *enter.*]

ALFRED and TOWNSPEOPLE

DIRECTION!
DIRECTION! DIRECTION!
DIRECTION!

ALFRED

Here in this revival of *Fiddler on the Roof,* everything is mis-directed. Golde looks like a fashion editor from *Vogue;* Tevye is played by a British Spaniard putting on a fake Midwestern accent. Even the cheery little character of Nachum the Beggar now ferociously mimes and mimics everything we do. You may ask, "Why is this simple beggar now a central character?"

I'll tell you: I don't know. But as long as a brilliant Brit is directing the show, we do exactly as he says even if nobody knows what it means.

WHO EV'RY NIGHT MUST PLAY A STUCK-UP TEVYE
LIKE HE'S DOING CHEKOV AT THE RSC,
AND WHO EV'RY NIGHT MUST UNDERPLAY
   DISDAIN
WHILE KILLING ALL THE COMEDY?
MOLINA! MOLINA!

ALL

DIRECTION!
HE'S ALFRED MOLINA!
DIRECTION!

GIRLS

AND WHO DOES DAVID TEACH TO ACT MORE UPPER
   CLASS
AND PLAY TZEITEL AND HODEL JUST LIKE AN IRISH
   LASS?
THE DAUGHTERS! FROM DUBLIN!

ALL

DIRECTION!

SALLY MURPHY

I'M SALLY!

LAURA MICHELLE KELLY

I'M KELLY!

NACHUM

I'M TRICIA!

ALL

DIRECTION!

[ALFRED *leaves.*]

KELLY

Sally, have you seen the terrible reviews we got?

SALLY

Oh, critics, critics, critics! What do they know?
These old musicals need to be turned inside out by
egomaniacal British directors.

[*They undress and then begin to sponge-bathe each
other.*]

KELLY

The only thing good about these classic shows is their
recognizable titles. They always make lots of money!

SALLY

That must be why they keep reviving *Fiddler*.

CASH-MAKER, CASH-MAKER,
MAKE ME SOME CASH,
GIVE US A JOB,
WE NEED A SMASH.
ALTHOUGH THE SCRIPT
CAN BE THROWN IN THE TRASH,
THE TITLE IS WORTH THE CASH.

KELLY

CASH-MAKER, CASH-MAKER,
I'LL LEARN THE SONG,
ALTHOUGH I'LL SING
EV'RYTHING WRONG.

SALLY

MAYBE THE AUDIENCE
WILL SING ALONG

SALLY, KELLY, and NACHUM

BEFORE THEY GIVE US THE GONG!

NACHUM

DEAR DAVID,
YOU MUST HAVE GONE MENTAL...

KELLY

...TO HAVE US
ALL TAKE A SPONGE BATH.

SALLY

REMEMBER, YOU'RE NOT
STAGING *YENTL*...

ALL THREE

YOU'LL STIR UP THE PUBLIC'S WRATH!

SALLY and KELLY

CASH-MAKER, CASH-MAKER,
FIDDLER MEANS CASH.
SYNAGOGUE GROUPS
ALL LOVE THIS SMASH!
BUT, NIGHT AFTER NIGHT,
THEY ALL SIT THERE AND THRASH...

AND YELL OUT, "OY VEY,
WHY DO WE STAY?
WHY DID WE PAY
TO SEE THIS PLAY?
AND THROW AWAY ALL OUR CASH?"

[FYEDKA *enters, looking like he just walked out of the
pages of* Instinct *magazine.*]

FYEDKA

Hello, Sally.

SALLY

[*Shyly.*]

Hello, Fyedka.

FYEDKA

I have a book for you.

SALLY

Oh.

FYEDKA

It's Madonna's new Christmas book. It's filled with eye-popping photos. Look, there's me nude sunbathing in South Beach.

[*She looks over his shoulder and reads, enthralled.*]

SALLY

I am forbidden to read such things.

FYEDKA

Then take it, hide it, and read it in your outhouse. We can discuss it over coffee at The Big Cup.

[*He goes off, but not before* ALFRED *has re-entered and seen him talking with* SALLY.]

ALFRED

Chava, what were you and that boy talking about?

SALLY

Nothing, Papa.

ALFRED

Good. Chava, you must not forget who you are and what that boy is.

SALLY

He has a name, Papa. And a hot body.

ALFRED

No, Chava! He is not one of us. He is from that other part of town: Chelsea! He is different.

SALLY

I know, Papa. But I can change him. I know I can!

ALFRED

No, Chava, no! Those boys can never change. He can never be one of us! As the "good script" says, "A straight girl may love a Chelsea boy, but where will they buy real estate together?"

SALLY

Where does the "good script" say that?!

ALFRED

I don't know, but somewhere it says something that sounds vaguely Jewish. I just can't make it sound right! It's late! It's almost Sabbath! Where's your mother? Golde! Golde!

[GOLDIE *enters.*]

GOLDIE

Here I am, but I'm Goldie now. I've Anglicized my name.

ALFRED

What are you wearing?

GOLDIE

My apron is Chanel, my babushka is Ralph Loren. It's "peasant chic."

ALFRED

Well, it's almost sundown. Quick, get the candles. Get the Manischewitz!

GOLDIE

No, this is a British interpretation of Sabbath. Get the candelabra! Get the martini glasses! Come, girls, hurry! Take those babushkas off! Put on your tiaras!

ALL

Here's cheers!

ALFRED

MAY THE QUEEN PROTECT AND DEFEND YOU

GOLDIE

MAY PRINCE PHILLIP SHIELD YOU FROM SHAME

BOTH

MAY YOU COME TO BE IN BUCKINGHAM A SHINING
    NAME

GOLDIE

MAY YOU BE LIKE FERGIE AND THATCHER

ALFRED

MAY CAMILLA SHIELD YOU FROM SIN

ALL

STRENGTHEN THEM, PRINCE CHARLES,
TO BE LIKE TONY BLAIR.
OH, HEAR OUR BRITISH PRAYER . . .

[*They try to chant like a cantor.*]

AH-AH-AH-AH-AH-AH . . .

[*They give up and switch to a very Protestant sound.*]

AH HA! HA! HA! BRITTANIA RULES THE STAGE.
A-MEN!

"Harvey Fierstein Tries Tevye"
(Added later in the run)

[*After "Cash-maker,"* HARVEY FIERSTEIN *enters,
dressed half as Tevye and half as Edna from* Hairspray.]

HARVEY

Dear God—I mean, Jerry Robbins—you cast many,
many actors in *Fiddler on the Roof.* What would be so
terrible if someone such as myself, Harvey Fierstein,
got to play Tevye?

IF I WERE A STRAIGHT MAN
AND MY CORDS WERE NOT AS RASPY
AS A PICKLED PROSTITUTE,
YOU'D BELIEVE FIVE DAUGHTERS COULD BE MINE
IF I DON'T DRESS LIKE DIVINE.

I WOULDN'T HAVE TO WEAR DRAG,
FLOUNCE AROUND IN FEATHERS
WHILE I SING "L'CHAIM" ACTING CUTE.
JERRY ROBBINS, WAY UP THERE WITH GOD,
DON'T DECREE THAT CASTING ME WAS ODD!
I'D PLAY TEVYE BUTCHER THAN ROSEANNE
IF I WERE A MACHO MAN!

Oy! My throat!

"Bernadette Peters in *Gypsy*"

OFFSTAGE VOICE

Here she is, boys! Here she is, world! Here's Bernadette.

BERNADETTE

CURTAIN UP!
LIGHT THE LIGHTS!

[*She speaks directly to the audience.*]

Hello, everybody. I'm Bernadette
Peters. Thank you. As you might
have heard, I'm currently starring
in a new revival of *Gypsy*. Would you

like to see a little more of my Tony-losing performance? Okay, here goes!

SOME PEOPLE THINK THAT I PULL IT OFF,
SOME PEOPLE THINK I JUST STAND THERE AND
    COUGH.
WELL, I'M MAMA ROSE NOW,
AND THIS MAMA'S SPREADIN' IT AROUND!
AND ETHEL MERMAN? JUST FORGET HER . . .
LET'S NOT DISCUSS ETHEL MERMAN.

MERMAN SANG IT LOUD, MERMAN DID IT FINE,
MERMAN DID IT FIRST, MERMAN DID IT BEST,
MERMAN LOOKED THE PART, MERMAN HAD A BELT,
MERMAN WASN'T MIKED, MERMAN NEVER MISSED,
MERMAN TOPPED THE LIST, MERMAN'S GOT ME
    PISSED . . .

[*She stammers.*]

M-M-M-M-Merman . . .

MERMAN HAD THE STUFF, MERMAN OWNS THE
    SHOW,
MERMAN'S GOTTA GO . . .

[*She stammers again.*]

M-M-M-Merman . . . Merman's gotta let go!

WHY DID I DO IT? WHAT DID IT GET ME?
SCRAPBOOKS FULL OF MIXED REVIEW CLIPPINGS?
STRAIN YOUR VOICE AND WHAT DOES IT GET YOU?
VAPOR RUB AND HALL'S EUCALYPTUS . . .

I HAD A DREAM
THAT I'D PLAY AN ADULT SOMEDAY
AND I'D START A CULT SOMEDAY.
BUT WAS IT TOO SOON?
SHOULD I'VE KEPT MY CROON?

AND PLAYED BABY JUNE?

WELL, SOMEONE TELL, WHY AM I MISCAST?
DON'T I GET A ROSE FOR MYSELF?
STARTIN' NOW, I'M DOIN' IT MY WAY.
GANGWAY, MERMAN, OFF OF MY HIGHWAY!
I DON'T CARE WHAT LINE I FLUB NEXT,
STARTIN' NOW I'M PLAYING THE SUBTEXT.

I'LL CRY WHERE YOU LEAST SUPPOSE,
WEEP LIKE THEY'VE TURNED ON THE HOSES,
AND SHOW ALL THOSE OLD MAMA ROSES
THIS PART'S FOR ME!

[*A sign with the names of all the famous Mama Roses— Merman, Roz, Lisa Kirk, Angela, Tyne, Bette, and Betty Buckley – is lowered from the flies. The lights on the sign flash angrily.* BERNADETTE *turns around and looks horrified.*]

FOR ME! FOR ME!

[*The lights flash faster.* BERNADETTE *runs to the sign and bangs on it.*]

FOR ME! FOR ME!

[*The lights stay on the sign, very bright. Finally,* BERNADETTE *takes out a sticker with her own name and pastes it up there. She sings with great satisfaction.*]

FOR ME!

[*She holds for thunderous applause. Then* ETHEL MERMAN *enters, singing one long, loud note and wearing a white gown that looks like it's about to devour her.* BERNADETTE *runs off, holding her ears. Merman begins the finale.*]

"Merman Finale"

MERMAN

AAAAAAH!
THERE'S NO BROADWAY LIKE MY BROADWAY
THAT'S ON BROADWAY TODAY.
EV'RYTHING ABOUT ME WAS APPEALING;
DON'T YOU WHISH I WAS ON BROADWAY NOW?
I COULD MILK APPLAUSE WITHOUT REVEALING
THAT I WAS STEALING AN EXTRA BOW!

THERE'S NO SINGERS WHO SING
ZINGERS
LIKE ME WHEN I'M AGLOW.
I DID *CALL ME MADAM* AND I NEVER
CRACKED,
TWO YEARS OF *GYPSY,* AND THAT'S
A FACT.
AS LONG AS I SHOWED UP, I DIDN'T
HAVE TO ACT!
LET'S GO ON WITH THE SHOW,
LET'S GO ON WITH THE SHOW!

IT'S ME, ETHEL MERMAN:
DE-LOVELY! DE-TOPS!
AND BROADWAY'S GREATEST STAR
WHEN IN MY PRIME.
I'M ETHEL THE MERMAN,
AND I HAD THE CHOPS
TO HIT THE BULL'S-EYE EV'RY SINGLE TIME,
BUT WHEN I SEE A MUSICAL TODAY,
I'M ABSOLUTELY CERTAIN WHEN I SAY . . .

[REX HARRISON, YUL BRYNNER, *and* MARY MARTIN
enter and join in singing.]

ALL

THERE'S NO BROADWAY LIKE OUR BROADWAY,
LIKE NO BROADWAY WE KNOW.

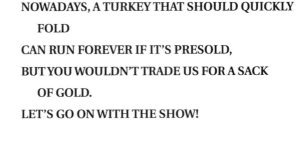

NOWADAYS, A TURKEY THAT SHOULD QUICKLY
FOLD
CAN RUN FOREVER IF IT'S PRESOLD,
BUT YOU WOULDN'T TRADE US FOR A SACK
OF GOLD.
LET'S GO ON WITH THE SHOW!

FORBIDDEN MEMORIES: **Christine Pedi**

After four years of scouring *Back Stage* and attending what seemed like hundreds of non-Equity auditions in a string of mangy, uninviting rehearsal studios, I had made the epic decision that I would never go to a "cattle call" again. I was on strike. No more wailing sixteen enthusiastic bars of "Shy" from *Once Upon a Mattress* to two or three unenthusiastic faces. No more auditions until I had an agent who would get me my own appointment time and I would be treated with the respect and civility to which I felt I was entitled. DO YOU HEAR ME?!

Great. Now what? Despite my decision, I still read *Back Stage* on the sly. The very first audition notice I saw after making this pact with myself was an open call for a non-Equity national tour of *Forbidden Broadway*. Even though I'd never done an impression in my life, I felt compelled to break my vow and go. You see, I used to sing at a Sunday afternoon, open-mike salon at Palssons on the Upper West Side when *FB* was playing there, and one week, I was given a thirty-minute solo

Christine Pedi.

slot. I had photos of me singing in front of the famous Mylar curtain and *Forbidden Broadway* logo. Maybe this audition notice was a sign? So off I went to what I swore would be my final open call—and it was.

The audition was at Theatre East, where *FB* was then playing. (I later learned that the cast called it "The Comedy Sewer," because a suspicious smell periodically seeped through the vents.) I had on a red plaid pinafore that looked like my grammar school uniform. I sang "Shy," and then I was asked by John Freedson and Gerard—whom I didn't recognize in his baseball cap—if I did any celebrity impressions. I scrunched my face up in thought and said, "Well, I do my Italian grandmother, Josephine. But, ya know, she's not really famous." They said, "Go ahead." So I did my grandmother's broken-English, Sicilian dialect, and I guess they were at least mildly amused, because they asked again if there were any celebrities I thought I might be able to do. It seemed they had more faith in my ability than I did.

I told them I had volunteered once at a Lincoln Center benefit, and Carol Channing had asked me to help her with something. Just hearing that voice say my name had blown me away. ("Chrishteeeeen, thaaaaank you so mew-uch!") I tried to re-create Channing's sound at the audition, and it seemed to go well; they sent me home with some Merman and a little Patti LuPone to work on. After the call-backs, during which everyone was terrifically supportive, they offered me my first real, professional job in the theatre.

That tour played more than forty states and sixty-seven cities in 103 days. We had only five full days off during the whole three months, and two of those were in Akron (don't ask). The tour bus had the back rows of seats removed, and our sets and costumes lived there, so we called it a "bus *in* truck" tour as opposed to the usual "bus *and* truck."

Two years later, I made my New York debut in the Equity company of *FB* at The Comedy Sewer, and I encountered the smell firsthand. (I still think Jimmy Hoffa was in that vent.) Later, the show took me all over the country and the world: L.A., London, Singapore, Australia. I even got to sing "Everything's Coming Up Merman" on the *QE2* while sailing through the muddy waters of Ho Chi Min City harbor in Vietnam. Doing various editions of the show in all those places was a crash course in comedy that could not be paralleled.

No one can ever know the amount of energy Gerard puts into writing *Forbidden*. Over the course of several years, the process of working on the show with him evolved. A shorthand developed, and it became easier to see the strong points in a piece and the stuff that could be cut away. (Gerard overwrites—God bless him for that!) Sometimes, there are major disagreements between Gerard and the actors as to whether or not a particular bit of material is funny, and sometimes you have to take one for the team and prove before a paying crowd why it just won't work. Of course, sometimes Gerard is totally right; the people love it, and you will go to your grave never understanding why. That's comedy, kids! At the end of the day, the audience is always right.

Everyone's input is welcome at *Forbidden Broadway*. Gerard often tailors the material around the actors' strengths. If you have an idea for a song or a character you'd like to try, just tell him. There's nothing more exciting than to see the seed you planted take root in his sick and fertile brain. More great numbers have been born that way.

In one edition, Bryan Batt and I were bemoaning the fact that there were no great stars on Broadway to parody any more. The Mermans and Martins were long gone.

I mentioned to Bryan that while watching *Sunset Blvd.*—in which he had covered and gone on in the role of Joe Gillis—I could not believe how annoying those body mikes were, perched practically between the eyes of the actors and, in the case of the henchmen chasing Gillis, dangling off of their fedoras like hovering bees. Bryan told me that the sound guys would shove those suckers down your throat if they could. That's when I said, "Gee, we should do some kind of number about sound and have Ethel Merman yell, 'Sing out, Louise!' at all the over-amplified actors from the back of the house." Bryan thought the opening number of *Sunset* would be the perfect song for Ethel to interrupt because it's so low and brooding.

We both ran up to Gerard and told him our idea. He listened and nodded, with a gleam in his eye that meant he was on the same page and couldn't wait to sharpen his pencils and take a stab at it. Then we broke for lunch. An hour later, he came back with one of my all-time favorite numbers, written to the tune of Irving Berlin's "You're Just in Love" from *Call Me Madam*. It was a duet between the actor playing Joe Gillis and Merman, who insisted that he learn how to project: "Ya don't need amplifyin', you'll be loud as a lion." Not one word had to be changed or tweaked. It was simply perfect. All Gerard needed was the visual we'd painted of Ethel storming the stage from the back of the house, horrified by the canned microphone sound, and his naughty genius took over and created a classic.

Doing the show is not the wacky frolic that it ultimately seems to be once it's been meticulously nipped and tucked. It all looks easy—oh, but it ain't. Routining the numbers and sketches so that Girl #1 can get offstage and change costumes in time for her next bit is like playing with a Rubik's cube. You've got to get it right, or the structure of the show topples like a house of cards. The order of the numbers changes constantly during previews, and even during the regular run. Whenever I was horribly late with a quick change, my strategy was: "If your wig is on and your genitals are covered, just get out there!"

Forbidden Broadway is rubber-chicken theatre that requires good musical comedy chops and the ability to deliver a joke. When someone comes into the company with that special "something"—the understanding that we're all in on a naughty secret—that's when it is elevated to a level of excellence. When the right material meets the right performer, *FB* creates perfect comedy karma. But the show is not for wimps. Comedy is hard work, and to some of us, it's sacred to be able to make people laugh at the world. For decades, Gerard has been reminding us how important it is *not* to take everything (and ourselves) so seriously.

As the show has touched the lives of so many, particularly young entertainers who have grown up worshipping the *FB* cast recordings, I think a mystique about Gerard has developed. I'm sure many fans expect him to be a combination of Oscar Wilde, Noël Coward, and Neil Simon: quick with a snappy comeback, full of one-liners and edgy insights. In a way, he is all of those things, but I also liken him to the Wizard of Oz.

Everyone expects the great and humorous Alessandrini to always have witty theatre parodies spewing out of him like those colored puffs of smoke the Wizard spouted at Dorothy and friends. He's a force of theatrical nature. Yet, in another way, Gerard is like the man behind the curtain. He can be shy at first meeting, a gentle fellow who successfully conjured up a fantastic creation and has lovingly tended it.

There are many levers to flip and buttons to push in sustaining the slick, sassy, satirical show that has mesmerized people for so long. If ever, oh ever a Wiz there was, the wizard Gerard is one because he has the brains to create all that magic, the courage to say what needs to be said, and most importantly, he does it all straight from his heart.

Forbidden Broadway Cleans Up Its Act. Clockwise from top left: Lori Hammel in *Ragtime*, Bryan Batt as "Rafreaky," Ed Staudenmayer as Alan Cumming, and Kristine Zbornik looking "More Miserable."

Top: *Forbidden Broadway Cleans Up Its Act.* Bottom: Our outlandishly irreverent spoof of the musical *Titanic.*

Forbidden Broadway 2001: A Spoof Odyssey. Clockwise from top left: Felicia Finley, Danny Gurwin, Tony Nation, and Christine Pedi.

Night LIFE

ENTERTAINMENT MAGAZINE

First Broadway . . .

Now

"Forbidden Hollywood"

ISSUE 639 MAY 17, 1995

Christine Pedi as Barbra and Gerry McIntyre as Satchmo.

Top: Jennifer Simard, Ron Bohmer, Christine Pedi, and Jason Mills in our wicked parody of *Wicked.* **Below: The** *Forbidden Broadway* **version of** *Rent.*

Alvin Colt's version of the *Chitty Chitty Bang Bang* car as driven by Megan Lewis.

ALVIN COLT

In 1994, I was working as a shop assistant at Grace Costumes when the "big-a-boss" of the establishment, Maria Brizzi, insisted I meet "This-a man who, you know, needs-a some-a help."

A startling six feet seven inches of Alvin Colt came lumbering through the office door. He unceremoniously dropped a huge portfolio on the desk and, in a booming voice, he exclaimed: "I am designing costumes for this little *meatball* of a revue, and let me tell you, they have *no money.* Do you know what a four-hundred-pound chicken says?" I answered, "No," and he hollered, "CHEAP!!"

I was beginning to see where this was going. The producers of the revue probably didn't have any money for an assistant, either. But Alvin Colt had designed the costumes for the original productions of *Guys and Dolls, On the Town, Li'l Abner, Destry Rides Again, Wildcat, Sugar,* and so on. I had to see what it would be like to work with him. And so my association with Alvin began.

That first project was *Forbidden Hollywood,* a send-up of movies concocted by Gerard Alessandrini as an offshoot of his successful *Forbidden Broadway* series. We went through Alvin's humorous, broadly drawn sketches, and he explained that each of the four actors would wear a basic costume to which we would add or subtract pieces and accessories. Sometimes they would change the entire costume, but those changes would have to happen *very* quickly.

Each costume had been thoroughly thought out: hats, earrings, shoes, coats. There were numbers from *Evita* (Eva Peron's evening gown with Madonna's pointy bra), *Pulp Fiction* (an Uma Thurman blow-up doll), *There's No Business Like Show Business* (Ethel Merman and that whole goofy family), and *Gone With the Wind* (a drag Hattie McDaniel). Then there was a "Falling Apart Again" costume for the actress who would play Marlene Dietrich, complete with a dangling arm. Nothing was too sacred for a laugh. The show opened in San Diego, then played Los Angeles and New York. There was even a brief tour of Japan!

Our next project was *Forbidden Broadway Strikes Back!* A huge success. There was a spoof of the egregiously overlooked *Victor/Victoria*. Alvin concocted a junk-

covered "Rafreaky" from *The Lion King* with soda cans, telephone cord, candy wrappers, chopsticks for fingernails, a canvas poncho, and a soup pan for a hat, atop which sat a bandaged Mickey Mouse. One of the wildest creations was an elephant costume with toilet plungers for the legs and feet, gray bath towels for the ears, and dryer venting for the snout! Everything was "on the cheap" but immeasurably clever and always funny.

The show's finale was an elaborate drubbing of the hit musical *Rent* that opened with "Think Punk," a parody of Kay Thompson's "Think Pink" number from *Funny Face*. Christine Pedi, one of our curvier performers, was discovered in a very tight, pink, breakaway "Chanel" suit. As she entered during the dress rehearsal, Alvin said to me in a resounding stage whisper, "Oh, Joseph. If she *farts,* the jig is up!"

For more than sixty years, Alvin Colt designed costumes for some of the most legendary shows in the history of the American theatre, yet for this "little meatball of a revue," he was quite happy to lampoon some of the very shows he had originally helped create. He worked in venues with dripping plumbing and low ceilings. He shopped the racks of clothes at all the discount department stores in search of inexpensive "finds." Our "Gentleman Giraffe" did all of this with wicked delight, enormous glee, and a wild sense of humor.

—Joe McFate

Alvin's outlandish costumes for the cast of *Forbidden Broadway Strikes Back* and for Felicia Finley and Danny Gurwin's space cadets in *Forbidden Broadway 2001: A Spoof Odyssey.*

The Lion King as spoofed by Alvin and the cast of
Forbidden Broadway Cleans Up Its Act.

Ron Bohmer as Harvey Fierstein as Tevye in *Fiddler on the Roof*, with a touch of hairspray!

Top: Jennifer Simard as Bernadette Peters taking her turn as Rose in *Gypsy*.
Bottom: "Welcome to the Tonys!" Jason Mills as Hugh Jackman and Megan
Lewis as Carol Channing, flanked by Jennifer Simard and Ron Bohmer.

The *Forbidden Broadway: Rude Awakening* cast. Clockwise from top left: Janet Dickinson, Jared Bradshaw, Erin Crosby, and James Donegan.

Clockwise from top left: Christina Bianco as The Belittled Mermaid; Ron Bohmer as The Phantom; and Jason Mills in "Bombay Wet Dreams".

Clockwise from top left: *Spamalot* meets *Sweet Charity*: Jason Mills, Megan Lewis, and Ron Bohmer; Gina Kreiezmar as one of our best Lizas; Jason Mills, Megan Lewis, and Ron Bohmer go crazy from a sugar rush in "Thoroughly Perky Millie."

Top: Christina Bianco as Maria in "Worst Side Story" confronts the cast of *In the Heights* as played by Jared Bradshaw, Michael West, and Gina Kreiezmar. Middle: Jared Bradshaw as Daniel Radcliffe strips off his Harry Potter garb to star in *Equus*. Bottom: Gina Kreiezmar as "Rafreaky."

You Gotta Get a Puppet: Jeannie Montano,
Jared Bradshaw, Michael West.

Who's Afraid of the Light in the Piazza?: 2005–06

At first, losing the Douglas Fairbanks seemed a misfortune for our show. But it turned out to be a happy accident, because we moved to the best home we ever had: the 47th Street Theatre, located at 304 West 47th St. between Eighth and Ninth avenues.

After a short break, we remounted *Forbidden Broadway: Special Victims Unit,* but we revamped it for the new space. Phill George and I added a slew of new numbers lampooning the recent Broadway hits: *Spamalot, Spelling Bee, Doubt,* etc. I wasn't sure how our show would play in the new venue, but the laughter was more rapturous than it had been for years. The theatre has great sight lines and better acoustics than any other space we've ever played in New York; the new material hit the bull's-eye there, and the older numbers seemed funnier than ever.

Because we added so much new material, we reopened *SVU* for the press, and we got some of the best reviews in our history. This was largely due to the talents of Ron Bohmer, Megan Lewis, Jason Mills, and Jeanne Montano, plus the inclusion of our outlandish parody of *The Light in the Piazza.* Also, it didn't hurt us that many of the rave reviews of *Spamalot* compared that show to ours.

A lot of spoofable things were happening on Broadway at that time. For one thing, Robert Goulet was appearing in *La Cage aux Folles.* Ron Bohmer kept suggesting that we should "do" him, and when we did, the audience went nuts.

I had some trouble figuring out how to handle *The Light in the Piazza.* Originally, I wrote a parody of the song

Laughs in the Piazza: Sarah Krulwich of the *New York Times* captured this action shot of Megan Lewis and Jason Mills.

Jason Mills, Jeanne Montano, and Ron Bohmer steal our jokes back from *Spamalot*.

"Dividing Day," called "Dividing Play," all about the fact that the critics loved the show but it may have been a bit too cerebral for the masses. Jeanne Montano performed the number brilliantly, and we were sure it was going to go over really well, but it didn't. John Freedson said, "It's thoughtful and insightful, but it's not really funny." Phill George said, "Just cut the song and spoof the flying hat." I said, "That's a terrible idea." But we tried it, and it was hilarious.

The genesis of our *Doubt/Virginia Woolf* parody was quite out of the ordinary. In 2005, John Patrick Shanley's play *Doubt*, starring Cherry Jones, was playing right across the street from a stunning revival of Edward Albee's *Who's Afraid of Virginia Woolf?* starring Kathleen Turner. During awards season, Jones and Turner were in competition for all the major honors for best actress in a play. (Cherry won the Tony.) Theatre critic Howard Kissel told me that, at a reception after one of the awards shows, Jones had offhandedly said she thought it would be funny if *Forbidden Broadway* put the two plays together. She imagined her character in *Doubt*, a severe nun, going across the street to give an intervention to Kathleen Turner as the alcoholic Martha in *Virginia Woolf*.

I explained the concept to Phill George, and this time he was the one who said, "That's a terrible idea." But I kept thinking about it and chuckling to myself, so I kept bringing it up to Phill. Eventually, I wore him down, and he said, "All right! Go ahead and write it, and I'll stage it." When he looked at my script, he grunted, "The lyrics are okay, but your dialogue is trite, and there aren't enough real lines from *Doubt* and *Virginia Woolf*." So he did an excellent rewrite, alternating actual lines from the two plays and throwing in a few barbs that he and I wrote. What we ended up with was a wonderful little one-act play written by Cherry Jones, Phill George, Gerard Alessandrini, John Patrick Shanley, and Edward Albee. Not a bad team! That sketch kept audiences doubled over in laughter for more than a year.

As it turned out, *SVU* was one of my favorite editions of the show, as well as the most successful. It was very tourist-friendly; when people saw "SVU" in the title, they immediately made the connection to *Law & Order.* That edition also had mass appeal because Alvin Colt was at the peak of his inventiveness with the costume designs— and this from a ninety-year-old man.

One of the most memorable moments in the history of *Forbidden Broadway* was the first day we rehearsed the *Chitty Chitty Bang Bang* number with Alvin's "car" costume. He turned Megan Lewis into a showgirl/automobile, with her shapely hips as

"Squeaky Todd": Jared Bradshaw as Michael Cerveris, Jeanne Montano as Patti LuPone, Michael West as Manoel Felciano.

tires, her head as a radiator, and her breasts as headlights. When she beeped her horn, her high-beams would light up. Sheer comic genius.

A number that was very difficult (all Sondheim rewrites are!) but enormous fun to put together was our take on John Doyle's revival of *Sweeney Todd,* in which the actors doubled as the orchestra. There was a lot of buzz about Patti LuPone playing the tuba as well as the role of Mrs. Lovett in the show. Was this ripe for parody or what?! Of course, we gave Patti a tuba. (Well, not exactly; we could only afford a French horn.) We also had her play the "cymbals," which were actually the lids of two cooking pots strapped inside her knees. I rechristened the show "Squeaky Todd," and the actors did their best to play off-key.

It was a blast keeping the show updated that summer. And the new location, the fabulous costumes, and the plethora of new shows on Broadway really got us excited about creating the next edition.

"Sour Charity"

CHORUS

THE MINUTE SHE WALKS ON THE STAGE,
YOU CAN TELL SHE'S JUST A WEE BIT SHAKY,
HER ANKLE'S ACHY.
CHRISTINA APPLEGATE!
AND WHEN SHE STARTS TO MOVE,
SHE'LL PROVE SHE ISN'T SO GREAT.
SHE CAN'T EVEN TURN ON A POINT;
WHEN HER ANKLE BROKE, SHE CAME BACK
MUCH TOO FAST.
HEY, CHRISTINA!
SPEND . . . A LITTLE TIME IN A CAST . . .

[CHRISTINA APPLEGATE *enters; music changes.*]

CHRISTINA

WHEN YOU COME SEE ME NOW,
YOU'LL SAY MY FOOT IS HEALED.
I WEAR AN IRON ANKLE BRACE,
BUT IT'S CONCEALED.

OKAY, I STUMBLE DOWN WHEN
MUSCLES CONTRACT,
BUT THAT DOES NOT EXPLAIN WHY
I CANNOT ACT.

TONIGHT I LANDED "POW!"
INTO OUR CARDBOARD SET.
ALL YOU WILL SAY IS "WOW,
IS SHE THE BEST WE GET
TO BE THE NEW SWEET CHARITY?"
YOU'LL NEVER BELIEVE IT
WHEN YOU SEE IT DONE BY ME!

[*Music changes.*]

THERE'S GOTTA BE SOMEONE BETTER THAN ME,

THERE'S GOTTA BE SOME STAR CURRENTLY FREE.
BUT WHEN YOU FIND HER,
TELL HER I'M NOT GETTING OUT.
I'M GONNA DO IT, GONNA GET THROUGH IT
EVEN THOUGH EV'RY ONE KNOWS THAT I BLEW IT.

CHARLOTTE DAMN-BOISE, HOW I HATE HER!
WHILE I RESTED, SHE STARRED—I WAS BESTED.
I SCREAMED AND SCHEMED AND THEN INVESTED!
    PHOOEY!

[*Music changes.*]

I'M A BRASS RING, I'M A NICKEL SLUG,
I'M A PHONY BILL!
I'M A CHEAP WINE, I'M A USELESS DRUG,
LIKE A FAKE PLACEBO PILL.
I'M AS SHRILL AS SYNTHESIZER STRINGS,
A SQUEALING FEEDBACK BLAST,
AND MY ANKLES ARE MOOSHY AS FOAM—
LIKE TOILET PAPER ON A COMB!
AND ALL KINDS STRANGE SOUNDS ARE POURING
    OUT OF ME
'CAUSE SOMEBODY HAD ME MISCAST!

"Time I Said Good-Bye"

VOICE-OVER

And now, the ex-Mrs. Andrew Lloyd Webber, Sarah
Brightman, on her "La-Luna-tic" tour.

SARAH BRIGHTMAN

TIME I SAID GOOD-BYE . . .
MY WELCOME IS WEARING THIN,
I'D BEST TURN MY UNION CARD IN.
I'VE HAD A TERRIBLE

TIME, WITH KEYS TOO HIGH.
YOU'LL SUFFER WHEN I DO TRILLS,

YOU'LL ALL GET THE WRONG TYPE OF CHILLS—
I SHOULD BE CHARGED WITH A

CRIME FOR WHAT I'VE DONE
TO OP'RA AND *PHANTOM* ONSTAGE.
TEN YEARS AGO, I WAS THE RAGE.
NOW, EV'RYBODY AGREES ,
THE PUBLIC IS DOWN ON ITS KNEES.
IT'S TIME I SAID GOOD-BYE—PLEASE!

"Ya Gotta Get a Puppet"

AVENUE Q GUY

YOU CAN OUT-ACT DE NIRO,
BE A STRASBERG HERO,
SWEEP MERYL STREEP OFF THE STAGE . . .
BUT YOU GOTTA GET A PUPPET
IF YOU WANNA BE THE RAGE.

YOU CAN WARBLE ON OR OFF KEY,
STUDY STANISLAVSKY,
BOAST YOU'RE THE TOAST OF BROADWAY . . .
BUT YOU GOTTA GET A PUPPET
IF YOU WANT A HIT TODAY!

AND ALTHOUGH WE'RE A LOW
HASTY PUDDING SHOW,
THE KIDDIES CHEER ON CUE.
FAM'LIES COME, IF THEY'RE DUMB,
BUT THEN OUT THEY GO
WHEN OUR FUZZY PEOPLE SCREW!

DON'T EXPECT THE MUPPETS:
THESE ARE HORNY PUPPETS
RATED X ON *AVENUE Q,*
BUT IF YOU GET A PUPPET
YOU CAN HAVE A HIT SHOW, TOO!

LION KING BIRD PUPPET

WHEN I SING ANYTHING DURING *LION KING,*
THE AUDIENCE IS DEAD.
BUT THEY CARE WHEN I WEAR FEATHERS IN MY
    HAIR
AND A PARROT ON MY HEAD.

ONCE I STARRED IN CHEKOV,
NOW I MAKE A WRECK OF
MY TWISTED BODY, ACHING AND BENT.
BUT IF YOU GET A PUPPET,
YOU CAN ALWAYS PAY THE RENT

PLANT FROM LITTLE SHOP OF HORRORS

SHE CAN ROAR, BUT THEY SNORE
IF THEY DON'T GET MORE
THAN SOME OLD JUNGLE CHANT.

MY ROUTINE IS OBSCENE
WHEN I DRESS IN GREEN
AS A MEAN MAN-EATING PLANT!

LITTLE SHOP OF HORRORS
WAKES UP ALL THE SNORERS;
MY TENTACLES MAKE GENTLE KIDS SCREAM.
BUT IF YOU PLAY A PUPPET,
YOU CAN MAKE THE CRITICS CREAM!

ALL

[*Singing in a round.*]

WHEN SONGS ARE ROTTEN,
WEAR SOME COLORED COTTON,
ASK FOR A MASK THAT'S BIZARRE.

[*Singing together.*]

SO NEVER GET A GIMMICK,
BE A MUPPET MIMIC—
THAT'S THE WAY TODAY TO GO FAR!

BIRD

IF YOU WANT OVATIONS, WORK FOR CORPORATIONS

PLANT

IF YOU WANNA SEND 'EM, BE A PHILODENDRUM

AVENUE Q GUY

IF YOU WANT A TONY,
FLASH A CLOTH COJONE

ALL

SO GET YOURSELF A PUPPET
AND YOU, TOO, CAN BE A STAR!

"It Sucks to Be You"

[BROOKE SHIELDS *enters.*]

BROOKE SHIELDS

Hey, *Avenue Q* Guy, where you going?

AVENUE Q GUY

Well, Look who it is! It's Brooke Shields! Hiya, Brooke!

BROOKE SHIELDS

Hi, Avenue Q, puppets!

AVENUE Q GUY

How's life on Broadway?

BROOKE SHIELDS

Disappointing.

AVENUE Q GUY

What's the matter?

BROOKE SHIELDS

My TV show went off the air, and I have to replace Donna Murphy in *Wonderful Town*. Whoever she is.

AVENUE Q GUY

Oh! I'm sorry!

BROOKE SHIELDS

Just think, I used to be a big movie star. And I always thought . . .

AVENUE Q GUY

What?

BROOKE SHIELDS

No, it sounds stupid.

AVENUE Q GUY

Awww, come on!

BROOKE SHIELDS

WHEN I WAS SEVEN, I POSED IN THE NUDE.
I THOUGHT THE PUBLIC WOULD HAVE MORE
    GRATITUDE.
BUT NOW I'M FORTY-TWO AND ONLY PURSUED
FOR DRECK . . .

AVENUE Q GUY

Yep!

BROOKE SHIELDS

OH HECK,
IT SUCKS TO BE ME!

AVENUE Q GUY

Noooo!

BROOKE SHIELDS

IT SUCKS TO BE ME!
IT SUCKS TO BE STARRING IN A MUSICAL
NO ONE WANTS TO SEE.
IT SUCKS TO BE ME!

[TOM HEWITT *enters, dressed as Dracula.*]

TOM HEWITT

Hello, guys!

BROOKE SHIELDS

Oh, look! It's Tom Hewitt, the star of *Dracula: The Musical*.

TOM HEWITT

And my show really sucks!

AVENUE Q GUY

Hi, Tom!

TOM HEWITT

I AM TOM HEWITT, AND YOU CAN CERTAINLY BET
I WILL BE BRILLIANT IN EV'RY STARRING ROLE I GET.
BUT NOW I'M DRACULA, AND IT'S THE SUCKIEST YET!

BROOKE SHIELDS

BEING STELLAR ISN'T EASY
WHEN YOUR VEHICLES ARE CHEESY

TOM HEWITT

THEY KEEP ME FLYING, THEY HOIST ME UP IN THE
    AIR.
I WAIL FRANK WILDHORN BALLLADS, BUT NOBODY
    SEEMS TO CARE.
I SHOULD BE FAMOUS, BUT A BIG BROADWAY STAR
I'M NOT— EXCEPT TO MY BOYFRIEND.
IT SUCKS TO BE ME!

BROOKE SHIELDS

ME TOO.

TOM HEWITT

IT SUCKS TO BE ME!

BROOKE SHIELDS

IT SUCKS TO BE ME!

TOM HEWITT

IT SUCKS TO BE BRILLIANT LIKE ME . . .

BROOKE SHIELDS

IT SUCKS TO BE PUSHING SIX-FOOT THREE . . .

BOTH

IT SUCKS TO BE ME!

[STEPHEN SCHWARTZ *enters.*]

STEPHEN SCHWARTZ

Hi, Brooke. Hi, Tom.

BROOKE SHIELDS

Oh, Look! It's Stephen Schwartz, the composer of *Godspell*, *Pippin*, and *Wicked*.

TOM HEWITT

Hi, Stephen!

BROOKE SHIELDS

Hey, Stephen, can you settle something for us?

TOM HEWITT

Whose life sucks more? His or mine?

STEPHEN SCHWARTZ

Mine!

MY SCORES FOR PIPPIN AND WICKED ARE ART . . .

OTHERS

Well, hardly art!

STEPHEN SCHWARTZ

THE MUSIC SOARING, THE LYRICS ARE SMART.
BUT WHEN THE TONY VOTERS VOTE WITH THEIR
    HEART,
I LOSE—AND DON'T GET A TONY.

IT SUCKS TO BE ME!

TOM HEWITT

IT SUCKS TO BE ME!

BROOKE SHEILDS

IT SUCKS TO BE ME!

STEPHEN SCHWARTZ

IT SUCKS TO BE ME,
TO BE ONE OF THE FEW
WHO WALKED OUT ON *AVENUE Q!*

ALL

IT SUCKS TO BE ME!

[JAPANESE TOURIST *enters.*]

JAPANESE TOURIST

Why you all so sad?

STEPHEN SCHWARTZ

Because our lives suck.

JAPANESE TOURIST

Ha! Did I hear you correctly? *Your* life sucks? How would you like to be a tourist like me, watching all your shows!

WE COMING TO THIS CITY FROM FAR-OFF
    OVERSEAS;
NEW YORK CITY IS A PLAYLAND FOR THE JAPANESE.
WE PAY FOR BROADWAY SHOWS WITH ENORMOUS
    FEES,
BUT EV'RY SHOW IS TACKY OR TERRIBLE—
ALTHOUGH THEY SPEND MILLIONS,
IT ALL LOOK LIKE SUMMER STOCK

WE TOURIST GO HOME MAD AND BROKE.
[*Pointing at audience.*]
IT SUCK TO BE YOU!

OTHERS

IT SUCK TO BE YOU!

JAPANESE TOURIST

YOU LOSE!
I SAY IT SUCK-A-SUCK-A SUCK-A SUCK-A-SUCK-A
    SUCK-A
SUCK-A-SUCK-A SUCK-A SUCK-A-SUCK-A SUCK-A
SUCK TO BE YOU!

[*The* JAPANESE TOURIST *and the others sing in a round,* "It sucks to be him! It sucks to be her! It sucks to be them! It sucks to be us!" *Then.*]

ALL

WE'RE SUCKING ALL TOGETHER!
MOST NEW SHOWS ARE DRECK
WHEN PUPPETS OUTDO
AND TOP THE SHOWS THAT ARE NEW
AND *AVENUE Q* WINS THE TONY, TOO!
IT REALLY SUCKS TO BE YOU,
IT REALLY SUCKS TO BE YOU,
IT REALLY SUCKS TO BE YOU!

"Can't-Can't"

PATTI LUPONE

EV'RY YEAR AT ENCORES!
THERE ARE TIMELES BORES
UNTIL PATTI LUPONE SET THEM WISE.
AND WHEN *CAN-CAN* DREW ROARS
    PLAYING AT ENCORES!
MORE AND MORE DID I REALIZE . . .

I LOVE PATTI IN *EVITA,*
I LOVE PATTI ALL ALONE,
I LOVE PATTI WHEN ON BROADWAY OR WHEN
    TOURING,

I LOVE PATTI WHEN SHE'S RIFFING AND SHE'S
SLURING.

I LOVE PATTI WHEN EMOTING!
EV'RY BALLAD MAKES ME CRY.
I LOVE PATTI—
WHY, OH WHY DO I LOVE PATTI?
SHE'S ME, MYSELF, AND I!

OFFSTAGE CHORUS

SHE LOVES PATTI AS *EVITA* . . .

PATTI

WHAT'S NEW, BUENOS AIRES?

OFFSTAGE CHORUS

SHE LOVES PATTI IN *LES MIZ* . . .

PATTI

I DREAMED I PLAYED MOST EV'RY PART . . .

OFFSTAGE CHORUS

SHE LOVES PLAYING RENO SWEENY . . .

PATTI

WHEN I SIZZLED!

OFFSTAGE CHORUS

SHE LOVES PLAYING NORMA DESMOND
WHEN SHE FIZZLED . . .

PATTI

I LOVE PATTI WHEN I'M BELTING—
BELTING ALL MY LEADING MEN.

OFFSTAGE CHORUS

WATCH OUT FOR PATTI!

PATTI

THEY HATE PATTI,

BUT BEN BRANTLEY, HE LOVES PATTI.
AND WHEN I'M LOVED,
I LOVE MYSELF AGAIN!

"Robert Goulet in *La Cage*"

GOULET

TRY TO REMEMBER . . .

I'M BOB GOULET,
AND I HAVE BEEN AROUND FOR MUCH TOO LONG.
I JUST STARRED IN *LA CAGE,*
TO EV'RYONE'S REGRET.
I LOOKED BEWILDERED WHEN I SANG . . .
OH GOD, WHAT WAS THAT SONG?
IT'S ODD WHAT I RECALL,
AND STRANGE WHAT I FORGET!

I SING LA-DA-DA-DA-DA-DA-DA
WHEN I'M DAZED AND CONFUSED.
EV'RY NIGHT I WOULD SEARCH FOR THE WORDS
I COULD BARELY REMEMBER.
LIKE THE TIME VINNIE LIFF
CAST ME IN *SOUTH PACIF-*
-IC AND I'D GET LOST A LOT,
SO I SANG LA-DA-DA-DA-DA-DA
AND THREW IN *CAMELOT.*

IF EVER I WOULD LEAVE YOU,
IT WOULDN'T BE IN SUMMER,
KNOWING YOU IN SUMMER
I KNOW I'D NEVER GO . . .

Wait! Hold on! That's not right. Okay, Johnny, here we
go . . .

IF, SOME ENCHANTED EVENING,
YOU MAY SEE A STRANGER,

YOU MAY SEE A STRANGER ACROSS A CROWDED
    ROOM,
OH NO, NOT IN SPRINGTIME, THE IMPOSSIBLE
    DREAM!
INSTEAD, I JUST GO
LA-DA-DA-DA-DA-DA,
AND THE PEOPLE ALL SAY,
"HEY! THAT'S ROBERT GOULET!"

"*Spamalot*"

TIM CURRY

IT'S TRUE! IT'S TRUE!
MIKE NICHOLS HAD A PLAN
TO SATISFY EACH MONTY PYTHON FAN . . .

A LAW WAS MADE BY FANS OF ERIC IDLE:
THEY LAUGH BEFORE THE JOKES, RIGHT ON THE
    DOT.
AND NOW THE CAST IS GETTING SUICIDAL
AT *SPAMALOT.*

OUR AUDIENCE KNOWS EVERY JOKE THAT'S
    COMING
AND PEOPLE SCREAM OUT . . .

OFFSTAGE VOICE

Wait, that's not the plot!!

TIM CURRY

It's so annoying!

SO WE TRASH *CAMELOT,*
AND MUG AND HAM A LOT,
AND MONTY PYTHON FANS GET HOT
WHEN THEY SEE *SPAMALOT*!

"This Is the Song They Stole from Us"

SIR CHRISTOPHER SIEBER

ONCE IN EVERY SHOW, THERE COMES A SONG LIKE
    THIS.
IT STARTS OUT SOFT AND LOW AND ENDS UP WITH
    A KISS.
OH, WHERE IS THE SONG THAT GOES LIKE THIS?
WHERE IS IT? WHERE? WHERE?

SARA RAMIREZ OF THE LAKE

A SENTIMENTAL SONG
THAT CASTS A MAGIC SPELL;
THEY ALL WILL HUM ALONG,
AND WE'LL OVERACT LIKE HELL!
OH, THIS IS THE SONG THAT GOES LIKE THIS.

BOTH

YES IT IS! YES IT IS!

SIR CHRISTOPHER SIEBER

NOW WE CAN GO STRAIGHT INTO THE MIDDLE
    EIGHT,
A BRIDGE THAT IS TOO FAR FOR ME . . .

SARA RAMIREZ OF THE LAKE

I'LL SING IT IN YOUR FACE WHILE WE BOTH
    EMBRACE . . .

[*Key change, upward modulation.*]

BOTH

. . . AND THEN WE CHANGE THE KEY . . .

SIR CHRISTOPHER SIEBER

BUT WAIT, THERE'S SOMETHING STRANGE . . .

SARA RAMIREZ OF THE LAKE

THE LYRICS DIDN'T CHANGE . . .

SIR CHRISTOPHER SIEBER

WE'RE *FORBIDDEN BROADWAY* HERE . . .

SARA RAMIREZ OF THE LAKE

THE WORDS ARE REAL AND CLEAR . . .

BOTH

WE STOLE "THE SONG THAT GOES LIKE THIS!"

SARA RAMIREZ OF THE LAKE

NOW ERIC IDLE'S PISSED.

SIR CHRISTOPHER SIEBER

BUT ONE SONG WON'T BE MISSED.

SARA RAMIREZ OF THE LAKE

WHY SHOULD HE MAKE A FUSS?

SIR CHRISTOPHER SIEBER

HE STOLE THIS JOKE FROM US.

BOTH

SO WE'LL STEAL IT BACK FROM THAT WUSS!

[*Another upward modulation.*]

SARA RAMIREZ OF THE LAKE

A JOKE ON CHANGING KEYS?

SIR CHRISTOPHER SIEBER

WE ALWAYS DO THAT. PLEEEASE!!!

SARA RAMIREZ OF THE LAKE

AND RHYMING "DAMN REFRAIN"
WITH "WE WILL GO INSANE" . . .

BOTH

SO WE'LL SING THEIR SONG AND MAKE THEM CUSS,
FOR THIS IS THE SONG THEY STOLE FROM US!

"Imagine Yoko Ono"

CURLY FROM OKLAHOMA!

THERE'S A BRIGHT GOLDEN JUKEBOX ON
    BROADWAY,
THERE'S A BRIGHT GOLDEN JUKEBOX ON
    BROADWAY.
IT'S NOT RICHARD RODGERS, THAT GENIUS OF
    LATE,
'CAUSE THE SONGS ALL CAME OUT OF JOHN
    LENNON'S ESTATE!

OH, WHAT A TERRIBLE GENRE!
OH, WHAT A TERRIBLE BLIGHT!
BEACH BOYS AND BEATLES ON BROADWAY,
TORMENTING FOLKS EVERY NIGHT.

[YOKO ONO *enters and begins churning butter.*]

Hi, Aunt Eller!

YOKO

Scare me to death! What are you doing 'round here?
No Rodgers and Hammerstein on Broadway now. Only
jukebox.

CURLY

Hey, wait a second! Aunt Eller is from Oklahoma, not
Yokohama. Who the heck are you?

YOKO

Silly cowboy, I'm Yoko Ono.

CURLY

Yoko Ono? What the Sam Hill are you doing on
Broadway?

YOKO

Collecting royalties. You see, every 1960s rock and roller had a wife, and every wife now holds the music rights.

CURLY

Oh, I get it!

YOOOOO-KO ONO!
IS THE NEW BIG BROADWAY BOSS IN TOWN.

YOKO

IT'S JOHN LENNON'S LIFE, BUT I'M THE WIFE,
SO I TOOK A KNIFE AND CUT IT DOWN!

CURLY

YOOOOO-KO ONO
HAS GONE LO-O-O-O-CO, YOU KNOW.

YOKO

YOU'LL SCREAM, "WHAT DID YOU DO?"
YOKO ONO!

BOTH

YOKO ONO! OH NO!

CURLY and CHORUS

YO-KO OH-NO, YO-KO OH-NO, ETC.

YOKO

IMAGINE FIVE JOHN LENNONS
WHEN A SEAT YOU BUY.
NO GROSS BELOW US;
ABOVE, TOMATOES FLY.
IMAGINE ALL THE CRITICS
SHRIVEL UP AND DIE!
YEAH-HE HE HE!

IMAGINE WE'VE A STORY,
ALTHOUGH IT'S HARD TO DO.
IMAGINE WE'VE GOOD WRITERS

AND OUR DIRECTOR HAD A CLUE.
IMAGINE ALL SUBSIDIARIES
GIVE ME 6.25 PERCENT OF WEEKLY NET
YEAH-EEE-EEE.

YOU MAY SAY I'M CONTROLLING,
BUT I HELPED JOHN ALONG,
SAVED HIM FROM THE BEATLES
AND THEIR INSIPID SONG.

People remember me as the woman who broke up the Beatles, but I don't want to be remembered for that. I want to be remembered as the woman who destroyed Broadway.

YOU MAY SAY THAT I'M A DREAMER,
BUT MORE JUKEBOX SHOWS TO COME.
ALL SHOOK UP IS PRETTY SHAKY,
GOOD VIBRATIONS DUMB, DUMB, DUMB.

Don't give peace a chance. Give me a piece.

[*She makes a gentle "peace" sign.*]

Two percent.

"Chitty Chitty Bomb Bomb"

OFFSTAGE VOICES

CHIITTY BANG BANG
CHITTY CHITTY BANG BANG
CHITTY BANG BANG
CHITTY CHITTY BANG BANG
CHITTY BANG BANG
PRETTY SHITTY BANG BANG

TRULY SCRUMPTIOUS

WHAT DO YOU SEE, YOU PEOPLE GAZING AT ME?
YOU SEE A NEW BROADWAY MUSICAL

THAT'S . . .

TRULY NAUSEOUS,
WE'RE TRULY, TRULY NAUSEOUS;
CANDY-COLORED SETS AND DOGGIE CAST.
TRULY NAUSEOUS,
PRODUCERS ARE SO CAUTIOUS;
NOW THEY JUST REGURGITATE THE PAST.
THE CHILDREN ARE ANNOYING,
AND ALL THE SONGS SO CLOYING.
YOU'LL LEAVE TRULY AGHAST.

POTTS

DON'T WASTE YOUR MONEY
ON SOMETHING THAT'S FUNNY,
AND DON'T SEE A DRAMA SUPREME.

TRULY

IF YOU SEEK PERFECTION,
THIS SHOW'S A CONFECTION

BOTH

BUT SO SUGAR-COATED YOU'LL SCREAM!

TOO SWEET, TOO SWEET,
THE PLOT IS TOO STICKY,
THE BOOK HAS NO MEAT . . .
TOO SWEET, TOO SWEET,
THE PRESCHOOL MUSH,
SUGAR-RUSH TREAT!

TRULY

WE'LL SOON HAVE MORE DROP-INS
WHEN OLD MARY POPPINS
MOVES IN FOR A THIRTY-YEAR RUN.

POTTS

YOUR EARS WILL BE RINGING
WHEN TARZAN STARTS SWINGING,
AND WHEN *DOCTOR DOLITTLE*'S DONE.

BOTH

A KIDDIE ROUTINE
THAT'S SO SQUEAKY CLEAN
YOU'LL WANT TO DO
SOMETHING OBSCENE!

[CHITTY *enters, with her horn blowing.*]

ALL

OH, YOU CHITTY CHITTY BANG BANG,
CHITTY CHITTY BANG BANG, WE HATE YOU!
YOU'RE A KIDDIE KIDDIE CLAP TRAP;
TRAPPING LITTLE KIDS IS WHAT YOU DO.
BIG SET, AUTOMATED CAR,
BUT STORY SO BIZARRE
THEY FROWN.

CHITTY

BANG BANG PRETTY KIDDIE CLAP TRAP . . .

POTTS and TRULY

WE'D LIKE TO SHOOT YOU DOWN . . .

CHITTY

BANG BANG PRETTY KIDDIE CLAP TRAP . . .

POTTS and TRULY

MOST WITLESS SHOW IN TOWN!

CHITTY

SO SWEET AND ADORABLE,
WE'RE NEARLY DEPLORABLE.
ACT ONE IS A SNORABLE DELIGHT!
ALTHOUGH WE'RE SPECTACULAR,
TO US, THE VENACULAR

ALL

WE'RE VULGAR, WE'RE VAPID,
WE'RE TRITE!

HEY, KIDDIE, GO, KIDDIE,

BUT YOU BETTER KNOW, KIDDIE,

DADDY'S SPENDING MONEY LIKE A PUTZ.

YOUR TICKET, HIS TICKET,

MOM'S TICKET, FRIEND'S TICKET—

HE WILL WANNA STICK IT UP YOUR BUTTS.

YES, CHITTY, YOU'RE PRETTY,

AND THE FLYING CAR

WILL BE THE BIG STAR IN THE END.

BUT, ON BROADWAY, YOU'RE A CLAP TRAP,

DESIGNED TO CONDESCEND!

ALL

BANG BANG KIDDIE KIDDIE CLAP TRAP,

WE DO NOT RECOMMEND.

POTTS

BANG BANG CHITTY,

CHITTY CHITTY BOMB!

"Squeaky Todd"

[TOBY *is discovered in a strait-jacket.*]

TOBY

ATTEND THE TALE OF SQUEAKY TODD,

THE NEW REVIVAL THAT'S VERY ODD.

THEY SHAVED THE ORCHESTRA DOWN TO TEN;

WE'LL NEVER HERE FULL ORCHESTRATIONS AGAIN.

WE PLOD ALONG WHERE FEW HAVE PLOD

AT SQUEAKY TODD,

THE NEWEST *SWEENEY* THAT'S SQUEAKY

MICHAEL CERVERIS

I'M MICHAEL CERVERIS. I'M INTENSE.

I SQUINT AND GLARE AT THE AUDIENCE.

TO LEARN AN INSTRUMENT TOOK ME WEEKS,

AND AFTER A YEAR NOW, MY PLAYING STILL REEKS.

PIRELLI

I LEARNED THE SCORE FROM MY I-POD

AT *SQUEAKY TODD...*

ALL

THE NEWEST SWEENEY THAT'S SQUEAKY

[PATTI LUPONE *enters playing a tuba.*]

SWING YOUR TUBA HIGH, PATTI!

TRY TO HARMONIZE.

MUTE IT, MUM,

WITH COTTON FROM

YOUR PADDED THIGHS!

PATTI

THE WHOLE PRODUCTION'S AVANT-GARDE;

TO PLAY AND SING IS EXTREMELY HARD.

THE SHOW'S SO DARK, I AM GOING BLIND!

WHOEVER DESIGNED IT IS OUT OF THEIR MIND.

MICHAEL CERVERIS

AND PATTI'S MINI-SKIRT IS MOD

AT *SQUEAKY TODD...*

ALL

THE CHEAPER SWEENEY THAT'S SCARY.

ALWAYS DIFFICULT, STEPHEN IS,

HE'S THE METER-UNEVEN WIZ.

IS IT FIVE-FOUR? IS IT TWELVE-EIGHT?

YOU COUNT AND YOU COUNT, BUT YOU STILL COME

  IN LATE.

SINGING SONDHEIM IS HARD ENOUGH;

PLAYING CELLO, HE'S EXTRA TOUGH.

STEPHEN IS SLICK, STEPHEN IS SUBTLE,

STEPHEN WILL WRITE AND ACTORS SCUTTLE...

[*They repeat the above section in a round.*]

HERE'S STEPHEN, STEPHEN, STEPHEN. STEPHEN,
  STEEEEEE—PHEN!

[STEPHEN SONDHEIM *enters, carrying a little white
coffin. All take a birthday cake and hat out of it.*]

SONDHEIM

ATTEND MY SHOW CALLED *SQUEAKY TODD*.
I'M STEPHEN SONDHEIM, THE BROADWAY GOD.
MY BIRTHDAY PRESENT IS THIS NEW HIT,
BUT JONATHAN TUNICK IS HAVING A FIT.
IT'S SQUEAKY. IT'S *SQUEAKY TODD* --
THE NEWEST SWEENEY THAT'S OFF-KEY!

PATTI

Blow out your candles, Stephen!

[*They play their instruments badly once more.*
SONDHEIM *shakes his head and blows out his candles.*
Blackout.]

FORBIDDEN MEMORIES: Daniel Reichard

I am honored to have been a part of the twentieth-anniversary edition of *Forbidden Broadway* with the incredible Kristine Zbornik, Michael West, and Donna English. They were all seasoned veterans of the show, and I was coming in as the newbie.

Forbidden was my first paying gig in New York City, so I really wanted to do a great job. Nervously, I went into rehearsal under the direction of Gerard and the marvelous Phill George and Bill Selby. The masters of *Forbidden Broadway* were teaching me the Cameron Mackintosh number, and Mandy Patinkin, and the *Les Miz* medley. It was surreal, because I had listened to this stuff in high school and college with my theatre friends and now I was onstage in New York, doing it.

We rehearsed and rehearsed, until one day—like a bat out of hell, like a ball out of a cannon, like, umm, a fiddler on the roof—I was thrown onstage into my first performance. I had had one single rehearsal with all the costume, wig, and facial hair changes the day before, and it hadn't gone very well. But in our first performance, everyone kept me on track, and the audience roared with laughter and cheered heartily during our curtain call. The show was beautifully reviewed and we were featured in the *New York Times, Entertainment Weekly,* the *New York Post,* and others. Not bad for my first time on a New York stage, huh?

When it came time for me to move on from the production, I was auditioning for the lead role in a new musical, *Radiant Baby,* at The Public Theatre, under the direction of George C. Wolfe. Gerard was the only

Daniel Reichard with Kristine Zbornik.

person George could call to ask about my work. I hear that he said some nice stuff, and I got the part. Truly, *Forbidden Broadway* began my life as a New York City actor, and it taught me lessons about performing that still help me in my work. Thank you, Gerard!

My favorite character to play in *Forbidden* was Mandy Patinkin; I really got what Gerard and Phill were making fun of in the lyrics and the staging. It was a total blast to do every night, and my Mandy was always reviewed as my best impression. I also loved playing Rex Harrison, even though my colleague and friend Michael West would joke to me that it was the *worst* impression he had ever heard.

Once, during a sparsely attended matinee, I was over-enthusiastically singing "It's Too High" in the legendary *Les Miz* spoof. At the end of the number, I was supposed to lift my arms above my head and then quickly bring by hands down to my throat as if I was choking to death. Well, I somehow hit the microphone out of the stand and into the audience. There was no one in the first, second, or third rows, and probably only a dozen or so people in the crowd. Imagine me jumping off the stage, crawling on my hands and knees through the first couple of rows, trying to find that damn microphone. All the while, the stage was empty, music was vamping, and one single audience member was laughing hysterically *at* me (not *with* me). I found the mike, jumped back onstage, hopped on the imaginary turntable, went around in a circle, put the mike back on the stand, and then imaginary-turntabled myself off that stage!

Any actor who was in *Forbidden Broadway* secretly (or not secretly) loves it if he is later portrayed by someone else in the show. When *Jersey Boys* became a worldwide hit, I knew it wasn't going to be long before we were targeted. I was delighted to hear that Michael West was playing me in the sketch. The essence of me, according to Michael? Just talk in a really high-pitched voice. How rude! I'll never speak to him again.

Rude Awakening: 2007

In October 2007, *Forbidden Broadway* had a very rude awakening—not the sobering kind, but a new edition called *Rude Awakening,* named after the musical *Spring Awakening.* There may have been lots of teenage angst and depression in that show, but in ours we were having a fine time celebrating our twenty-fifth anniversary.

To keep a show running twenty-five years takes a lot of gall and clever finagling. Two of the people who come instantly to mind for their hard work are Harriet Yellin, our brilliant co-producer, and Glenna Freedman, our press agent since the mid-'80s. Glenna has certainly done a phenomenal job of cajoling the press; her expertise and devotion have kept the image of *Forbidden Broadway* shining. Harriet has been a den mother to us all, and her presence and love have given the show that "warm, fuzzy feeling" actors often refer to when describing their experience with *Forbidden.*

When the big day of our anniversary finally arrived, we had the honor of having 47th Street between Eighth and Ninth avenues renamed "Forbidden Broadway." It was a great ceremony. There was a mayoral proclamation, and the best part was that Chita Rivera presented it. After the festivities, it was back to business.

The post–9/11 years on Broadway were interesting in that the era of the blockbuster seemed to be waning and there were many different types of shows on the boards. Now, there was room for *Spring Awakening* and *Grey Gardens* as well as *Jersey Boys.* Somebody figured out that family musicals could be tremendously profitable. I think that started with Disney, but it crossed over to shows like *Chitty Chitty Bang Bang.*

If you go back fifty years, a lot of Broadway shows were very sophisticated and adult, so much so that you couldn't make them into movies without editing some of the dialogue and the lyrics. (Just ask Cole Porter.) In the early 2000s, all these family shows like *Wicked* and the Disney musicals were playing, and I think *Grey Gardens* and *Spring Awakening* were a reaction to that. Broadway sort of split into two camps: "Are we going to see something dark, like *Grey Gardens,* or are we going to see something pink, like *Legally Blonde*?"

Left: Jared Bradshaw, Janet Dickinson, James Donegan, and Erin Crosby get "Totally Bleeped" in our version of *Spring Awakening*. Right: Janet Dickinson as Christine Ebersole as Edie Beale in our *Grey Gardens* parody.

It's possible to make a great deal of money on Broadway, and this has led to producers trying to second-guess what the public wants. That's how you get something like *Cry-Baby*, which was more or less modeled after *Hairspray*. Though *Mamma Mia!* was a huge success, it was followed by several other jukebox musicals that were mega-flops: *Good Vibrations, Lennon, The Times They Are a Changin'*. These shows might have killed the genre—but then came *Jersey Boys*.

There was another obnoxious trend at the time: People were taking movie musicals, rewriting them (not always for the better), and putting them on Broadway. I always wanted to do a number where Noël Coward would come on and sing, "Don't put that movie on the stage, Mr. Mackintosh, don't put that movie on the stage!"

Again, some original musicals did open in the mid-2000s, but they were exceptions. I was impressed when I saw *Spring Awakening*, because I didn't know the original Frank Wedekind play at all but I had no trouble being drawn into the story. I thought it took a lot of integrity for the creators of the musical to write the show they wanted to write. Although the show had a decent run and gained a lot of loyal fans, it never reached a mass audience, perhaps because of the explicit lyrics.

West Side Story and *A Chorus Line* were considered edgy and groundbreaking in their day, but they eventually became mainstream hits. Because this never happened with *Spring Awakening,* our audiences never responded fully to our elaborate spoof of that show. Conversely, many of our other numbers seemed light and silly because there were so many light and silly shows playing on Broadway. This dichotomy affected the balance of *Forbidden Broadway*; to me, some of it felt a little repetitive and whiny.

A definite bright spot of our twenty-fifth anniversary edition was our take on the latest revival of *Company.* Since that groundbreaking Sondheim/Furth musical has substance to it, as well as wit, it was challenging but ultimately a lot of fun to spoof it. On top of that, it featured major performances by Raúl Esparza, a new Broadway star, and Barbara Walsh, who had appeared in our show. On top of *that,* the fact that John Doyle again had the actors doubling as the orchestra was a real gift to us from the gods of comedy.

"Unaccompanied"

[*Moody lights come up on an intense young man as he enters and then stands center stage. We hear three voices singing a fugue.*]

WOMEN'S VOICES OFFSTAGE

RA-ÚL, RA-ÚL, RA-ÚL ESPARZA PLAYING BOBBY.
RA-ÚL, RA-ÚL, RA-RA
RA-ÚL PLAYING BOBBY
WEIRDLY!

[*Music changes. Various company cast members enter.*]

WOMAN 1	MALE	WOMAN 2
RAÚL.	RAÚL.	
		RAÚL, DARLING.
	RAÚL, FELLA.	
RAÚL.		RAÚL, DARLING.
	RAÚL, RAÚL.	RAÚL, DARLING
RAÚL, DID YOU SEE MY NEW CELLO?	RAÚL, FELLA. RAÚL.	ANGEL, I'LL BE PLAYING THE
RAÚL.	RAÚL, BOY.	OBOE.

RAÚL, HONEY.

I'LL BE PLAYING PATTI'S OLE TUBA SWEETIE.	HOW ABOUT A SING-ALONG SUNDAY	WHY DON'T WE ALL HAVE A RECITAL, DARLING?
RAÚL, MARTA LOST HER VIOLIN PART STAGE RIGHT.	RAÚL, RAÚL RAÚL, FELLA. RAÚL, RAÚL RAÚL, FELLA.	DO YOU LIKE MY BONGOS? RAÚL, RAÚL, RAÚL, HONEY. RAÚL, DARLING. RAÚL, FELLA. RAÚL, HONEY.
SAXOPHONES ARE PHALLIC.	APRIL LEFT HER CLARINET CHART HOME TONIGHT.	

ALL

RAÚL, WE'LL PLAY MUSIC AT DINNER,
WE'LL PLAY SOME SONDHEIM FOR YOU,
EVEN THOUGH THE SOUND WILL BE THINNER.
JUST BE THE THREE OF US
SUBBING THE ORCHESTRA—
YOU'LL LOOOOATHE US!

RAÚL

NO STRINGS, NO DRUMS, UNACCOMPANIED.
HE SINGS, SHE HUMS, UNACCOMPANIED.
ONE FLUTE GOES TOOT, I EXCLAIM;
THEY SQUEAK, I SHRIEK, CLIMBING A WALL.
PARTS SHARED, CHORDS BARED, WHAT A SHAME!
ORCHESTRATIONS HAVE TO BE SMALL,
SO SMALL

ALL

AND ALL PLAYED BY THE CAST.
YOU'LL BAWL, HEARING US BLAST
A SCORE THAT YOU LOVE
BY ALL

RAÚL

THOSE POOR EXPLOITED ACTORS, MY FRIENDS!
THOSE POOR EXPLOITED ACTORS, MY
    OVERWORKED FRIENDS!

ALL

BUT THAT'S WHAT IT'S ALL ABOUT, ISN'T IT?
CUTTING THE BUDGET FAT OUT, ISN'T IT?
CUTTING THE ORCHESTRA OUT—
BARGAIN BIN *COMPANY*!
WE'RE A COMPANY!
UNACCOMPANIED!
THIS NEW *COMPANY*'S
UNACCOMPANIED!
COMPANY!

[RAÚL *stops them with a scream.*]

RAÚL

STOOOOOOOOOOOOOOOOOOOOOOOOOOOOOP!!!

SOMEBODY NOTICE I'M HURT,
SOMEBODY NOTICE I'M DEEP,
SOMEBODY NOTICE MY FROWN
AND HELP ME GET SLEEP

AND FIN'LY COME DOWN
FROM BEING INTENSE,
BEING INTENSE . . .

IN *TICK, TICK . . . BOOM!* I WENT BANG,
CABARET PUT YOU THROUGH HELL,
IN *NORMAL HEART* I THREW FOOD
AND TANTRUMS AS WELL.
IT'S FUN BEING RUDE
AND ODDLY INTENSE.
I LIKE INTENSE.
I AM INTENSE!

I AM CONFUSED,
MOCKING EACH PHRASE.
YOU'LL FEEL ABUSED,
HOLDING BACK PRAISE.
BUT INSANE IS INSANE,
NOT INTENSE . . .

IN *CHITTY BANG BANG* I CRIED;
KIDDIES WERE ALL TERRIFIED.
GEORGE FURTH SAID, "GIVE HIM THE HOOK"
AND SHOUTED, "YOU SHNOOK,
YOU REWROTE MY BOOK
AS HITCHCOCK SUSPENSE.
IT DOESN'T MAKE SENSE!"
BEING INTENSE!
BEING INTENSE!

"Slow People"

DAVID HYDE PIERCE

I'M A SPECIAL KIND OF BROADWAY STAR FOR
SLOW PEOPLE,
I'M DAVID HYDE PIERCE FROM TV
THEY KNOW MY FACE FROM *FRAZIER*
AS THAT STUCK-UP CHAP;
I STEP ON THE STAGE,

THEY STAND UP AND CLAP.

I AM DROLLER THAN YOUR DENTIST, BUT TO
SLOW PEOPLE,
I'M FLASHY AS A CHARISMATIC STAR,
AND TO THE UNINFORMED STRAIGHT,
IF YOU'RE FAMOUS, YOU'RE GREAT—
AND I RATE RIGHT UP THERE SO FAR!

YOU WOULD THINK I WAS OLIVIER TO
SLOW PEOPLE.
JUST ASK THE NEXT TOURIST YOU SEE!
IF I DO SHAW OR SHAKESPEARE,
THE PUBLIC ATTENDS;
THEY THINK I'M THE GUY
FROM *SEINFELD* OR *FRIENDS*.

MEDIOCRITY IS MECCA TO A
SLOW PERSON.
THEY WANT TO SEE A TONY-WINNING STAR,
AND THEY'LL GROVEL AND FAWN
IF YOU STAND THERE AND YAWN,
AND GO ON HOW BRILLIANT YOU ARE!

[*Big pullback and key change.*]

IT'S AN HONOR TO BE SO BELOVED BY
SLOW PEOPLE!
THE GEN'RAL PUBLIC FEEDS A BROADWAY SHOW.
IT GOES OVER THEIR HEAD,
BUT WITHOUT THEM, WE'RE DEAD,
SO INSTEAD, THE SHOW MUST BE SLOW . . .

OFFSTAGE CHORUS

NO SUBTEXT FOR SLOW PEOPLE!

DAVID HYDE PIERCE

. . . AND LOW.

OFFSTAGE CHORUS

LET'S PANDER TO SLOW PEOPLE

DAVID HYDE PIERCE

YOU KNOW!

OFFSTAGE CHORUS

THE ARMIES OF SLOW PEOPLE

ALL

WILL GO!

"Greyer Gardens"

CHRISTINE EBERSOLE

Oh, hi! Thank heaven you're here at Grey Gardens!
Even though I won the Tony Award for Best Actress
in a musical, business has been very slow—in fact,
nonexistent. We're gone! Mary-Louise Wilson, who
plays my mother, warned me about doing obscure and
intellectual musicals like *Grey Gardens*. She wanted me
to revive *Mame*. We had quite a fight. I told her . . .

I'VE LIVED THROUGH IT ALL, AND AS I RECALL,
THE ART OF WRITING WAS IN FREE-FALL.
I WANTED A PART THAT TUGGED AT THE HEART,
BUT SOMETHING WITH A TWIST.
BUT ALL WRITERS ARE NOW DOORMATS
AND CORPORATION FLOOR-MATS.
BUT, THANK GOD, I FOUND THAT CERTAIN SOUND
THAT MADE THE GENIUS LIST,
AND STILL THE AUDIENCE . . . LOOKS PISSED.

AND THAT'S THE EVOLUTION OF THE MUSICAL
    TODAY!
IT STARTED WITH FRANZ LEHAR AND ENDS WITH
    MICHAEL MAYER.
AND THAT'S THE EVOLUTION THAT DESTROYED THE
    SINGING PLAY:

THEY'RE POLARIZED AND THEY'RE SO EXTREME,
ONE'S BRECHTIAN, LIKE A HORRID DREAM.
THE OTHER POP-POLLUTION MAINSTREAM!
DA-DA-DA-DA-DUM . . .

What a lovely tune! But that's all you are going to get of it. Just listen to this: "*Grey Gardens* has successfully moved to Broadway. Christine Ebersole, a former Broadway soubrette once known as 'Broadway Belter Ebersole . . .'" They called me "Broadway Belter Ebersole." It's true. That was my, whaddayacallit, my sobriquet. Anyway, "Miss Ebersole gives the performance of her generation in a musical that is half great: You choose which half." Why, that's the most disgusting, atrocious review ever written in America.

CLOSED!
ALL OF THE GOOD SHOWS END UP CLOSED.
C-L-O-S-E-D!
GOOD THEATRE FIGHTS FOR SURVIVAL
WHILE THE BIG BUCKS FLOW
WHEN THE FACISTS GO
TO SEE A *GREASE* REVIVAL.
DA-DA-DA-DUM . . .
PEOPLE ARE SO DUMB.

Honestly, Broadway is starting to look more like Branson, Missouri. They can close you down for singing a lovely introspective ballad and replace you with *Staples: The Musical!*

AND THAT'S THE EVOLUTION OF THE MUSICAL
    TODAY:
YOU GET A FRESH IDEA, THEY STILL WANT *MAMA
    MIA!*
ARMIES OF CONFORMITY ARE MARCHING ON
    BROADWAY.
THE META-MUSICAL NEED NOT BE THE END OF
    MUSICAL HISTORY
PICK UP AMERICAN FLAGS AND FLAUNT,

BUT USE BINOCULARS IF YOU WANT TO SEE.
RE-ROUTE THE EVOLUTION!
COME START A REVOLUTION WITH ME!
DA-DA-DA-DA-DUM!

"The Belittled Mermaid"

ARIEL

LOOK AT MY TAIL. ISN'T IT NEAT?
NOTICE THEY BOUND UP MY LEGS AND MY FEET.
WOULDN'T YOU THINK I'D BE GLAD
SO GLAD I'M A BROADWAY STAR?

THEY'VE GOT GADGETS AND GIZMOS APLENTY,
THEY'VE GOT MILLIONS OF TIE-INS GALORE.
YOU WANT SOUVENIR DOLLS?
WE'VE GOT TWENTY!
BUT I FEEL I'M NOT REAL,
I WANT MORE . . .

I THOUGHT I'D BE WHERE THE ACTORS ARE,
I THOUGHT I'D WORK AS A FOSSE DANCER,
I THOUGHT I'D WEAR PRETTY HIGH HEEL SHOES
    ON MY . . .

What do you call 'em? Oh . . . feet!

FLIPPIN' MY FINS I DON'T GET TOO FAR,
LEGS ARE REQUIRED TO BE A DANCER;
HAVING A TAIL, YOU CAN NEVER FEEL QUITE
    COMPLETE.

WANTED TO SING, WANTED TO DANCE,
NOW I'M A STAR AND I GET MY CHANCE—
BUT WHEN I BOW, BROADWAY IS NOW
PART DISNEY WORLD.

DRESSED LIKE A WORM, I HAVE TO SQUIRM LIKE I'M
    AN OTTER.

DISNEY SHOULD PAY DOUBLE EACH DAY WHEN I
    CRASH-LAND!
BETCHA I'M PANNED SPITTING OUT SAND,
OR END UP TUNA-CANNED IN WATER.
TEENAGE WOMEN LOVE MY SWIMMIN'
BUT I CAN'T STAND!

I'M READY TO GO FROM THIS SOGGY SHOW.
OUT-OF-TOWN CRITICS FILLETED AND FRIED ME,
AND THEIR REVIEWS MAKE ME ANGRY
AND—WHAT'S THE WORD—BURN!
NOW IS MY TURN, I GOT MY WISH,
BUT I'M A DIVA PLAYING A FISH!
IT'S SUCH A SHAME, BROADWAY BECAME
PART DISNEY WORLD.

[*A lobster comes in on a pole . . . she kisses him.*]

It's my leading man!

"Wickeder" (Idina Solo Version)

IDINA

I AM THE STAR OF WICKED,
AND MY REPLACEMENTS KNOW
I AM THE GREAT IDINA,
AND I'LL FOREVER OWN THIS SHOW!

I MADE MY MARK DEFYING SUBTLETY—
OUT OF THE PARK, DEFYING SUBTLETY
AND YOU CAN'T BRING ME DOWN.

SO STRAP ME IN A HARNESS
AND HOIST ME UP TO THE SKY!
IN ALL THE BIG SHOWS LATELY,
ALL THE LEADING LADIES HAVE TO FLY.

AND, HANGING FROM THE RAFTERS,
I'LL DANGLE LIKE A BLIMP,

PUMP UP MY VOLUME
AS I KILL MY FLYING CHIMP . . .

AND SUDDENLY I'M DEFYING SUBTLETY.
WITH DEATH-DEFYING LACK OF SUBTLETY,
I'LL TEAR THIS THEATRE DOWN,
I'LL BLOW THE GERSHWIN UP BECAUSE
I AM THE LOUDEST WITHIN OZ,
AND NO ONE'S GONNA TURN MY VOLUME DOWN!
AAHHHHHHHHHHHH!

MONKEYS

WICKED! WICKED! WICKED!

"Don't Monkey With Broadway"

TWO FLYING MONKEYS

WE'RE THE *WICKED* FLYING MONKEYS.
OUT OF COSTUME, WE ARE CUTE MANHATTAN
    HUNKIES
WHO CRUISE
HELL'S KITCHEN
WALKING IN TWOS
EV'RYWHERE WE LOOK, CONSTRUCTION
THREATENS BROADWAY WITH DESTRUCTION.
OUR INSTRUCTION IS GO
UP TO MAYOR BLOOMBERG AND SAY
WHOA!

FIRST MONKEY

GIVE THE RICH THE CITY DUMP . . .

SECOND MONKEY

THE WEST SIDE TO DONALD TRUMP . . .

BOTH

BUT PLEASE, DON'T MONKEY WITH BROADWAY!

FIRST MONKEY

OUTLAW EV'RY CIGARETTE . . .

SECOND MONKEY

PUT A STARBUCKS AT THE MET . . .

BOTH

BUT PLEASE, DON'T MONKEY WITH BROADWAY

FIRST MONKEY

BROADWAY'S TAWDRY AND TIGHT,
AND IT'S CRAMPED EV'RY NIGHT,
BUT IT'S STILL FRIGHT'NING

SECOND MONKEY

IN A BAFFLING WAY.

FIRST MONKEY

SO RE-TILE EV'RY SUBWAY STOP,
CLOSE UP SHOP ON MOM AND POP

BOTH

BUT PLEASE, PLEASE,
I BEG ON MY KNEES,
DON'T MONKEY WITH OL' BROADWAY!

FIRST MONKEY

THROW OUT SHAKESPEARE FROM THE PARK,
MAKE DUANE READE A NEW LANDMARK,
BUT PLEASE . . .

BOTH

DON'T MONKEY WITH BROADWAY!

SECOND MONKEY

BUILD IN MIDTOWN SOMETHING DUMB

FIRST MONKEY

LIKE A YANKEE STADIUM

BOTH

BUT PLEASE, DON'T MONKEY WITH BROADWAY!
THINK WHAT STARS SING AND DANCE
ON THIS ROAD OF ROMANCE:

FIRST MONKEY

BERNADETTE

SECOND MONKEY

AND LUPONE

IRST MONKEY

AND EVEN ORFEH.

SECOND MONKEY

ORFEH?

FIRST MONKEY

NO WAY!

BOTH

OY VEY!
SO BREAK THE PHILHARMONIC'S LEASE,
MOVE ASTORIA TO GREECE,
BUT PLEASE, PLEASE,
I BEG ON MY KNEES,
DON'T MONKEY WITH OL' BROADWAY!

"Rude Awakening"

WENDLA

MAMA, WHO BORE ME
IN *SPRING AWAK'NING,*
I RUB MY BOOBIES
EVERY TIME I SING.
PLEASE DON'T ABHOR ME
IN *SPRING AWAK'NING;*
PUBESCENT ANGST
IS A RUDE AWKENING.

[MELCHIOR *enters.*]

MELCHIOR

Don't worry, Wendla. I'll tutor your sex education. I've been reading Goethe's *Debbie Does Deutschland.*

WENDLA

Melchior Gabor! What are you doing here?

MELCHIOR

I come here to think. This is my secret hiding place.

WENDLA

Two chairs are your hiding place?

MELCHIOR

They're from Ikea; the best Swedish pine. What are you doing here?

WENDLA

I'm picking flowers for my mother and for my funeral in act two.

MELCHIOR

How symbolic—and exciting. Something has been released in me—in my lederhosen, to be exact. Let's have intimate relations!

WENDLA

What's "intimate relations"?

MELCHIOR

Well, you attach four ropes to a platform, pull it up into the air, then we both climb on, I pull down my suspenders, a little horizontal choreography, and then we turn off all the lights, and the audience goes to the toilet.

WENDLA

All right!

[*They climb onto the piano.*]

CHORUS

I BELIEVE, I BELIEVE,
OH, I BELIEVE ALL WILL BE FORGIVEN.

[*When they are finished,* WENDLA *is hugely pregnant.*]

WENDLA

Oh, no!

MELCHIOR

What's wrong?

WENDLA

Anemia again!

[MOTHER *enters suddenly.*]

MOTHER

Oh, God! What have you done?

WENDLA and MELCHIOR

Mother!

[*To each other.*] That's my mother, not yours. Stop doing that!

[*To* MOTHER.]

Mother!

MOTHER

Actually, I am both of your mothers.

WENDLA and MELCHIOR

Both? But that would mean . . . eeew!

MOTHER

Let me explain. In some scenes, I am Melchior's mother, and in others, I am Wendla's. I also play a piano teacher, and when I wear this hat, I'm Frau Knuppledick. Four different characters, all wearing the same dress.

WENDLA and MELCHIOR

That's confusing.

[*To each other.*]

Cut that out!

MOTHER

The hat helps.

WENDLA

Ouch!

MOTHER

What is it, dear?

WENDLA

My anemia. It kicked!

[MOTHER *takes from her pocket a bottle with a skull and crossbones symbol on it.*]

MOTHER

Oh, dear! Vitamin time! Open wide.

[*She pops a pill into* WENDLA*'s mouth.*]

Good girl. Now, Wendla, go have a tasteful offstage death.

[WENDLA *gags her way toward the wings.*]

Offstage, dear, offstage!

[MOTHER *now changes to* FRAU KNUPPLEDICK.]

FRAU KNUPPLEDICK

Melchior Gabor, I have something most distasteful to discuss with you: I found a *Spring Awakening* script in your dressing room. Did you write this?

MELCHIOR

No, Frank Wedekind wrote it in 1891 . . .

FRAU KNUPPLEDICK

Silence! You must answer only the precisely stated questions with a swift and decisive "Yes" or "No." Do you expect this show to play in Denver?

MELCHIOR

Well, perhaps if it stars Donny and Marie Osmond . . .

FRAU KNUPPLEDICK

Zip it! Donny and Marie wouldn't touch this script. And look at these filthy lyrics! Barbra Streisand will never record these songs.

MELCHIOR

Oh, I don't know. She might identify with "The Bitch of Living" . . .

[FRAU KNUPPLEDICK *begins to beat Melchior with a stick.*]

FRAU KNUPPLEDICK

Quiet!

MELCHIOR

Ow. Ow. Ow. Dammit!

FRAU KNUPPLEDICK

Do you really think this show can play Louisville? Tulsa? Beantown?

[MELCHIOR *unzips his fly, pulls a microphone out, and sings.*]

MELCHIOR

THERE'S A MOMENT YOU KNOW . . . YOU'RE
    SCREWED,
'CAUSE THE LYRICS YOU SING ARE WAY TOO LEWD.
WE COULD TOUR RIGHT NOW THE BLUE HAIR
    ZONE,
BUT WE'RE NOT *THE DROWSEY CHAPERONE.*

[MORITZ *and* WENDLA *enter.*]

MORITZ

AND IF SEX AND SWEARING MAKES THEM JUMP,
JUST IMAGINE WHEN YOU BARE YOUR RUMP!
YOU CAN ASK YOURSELF, HEY, WHAT HAVE YOU
    DONE?
UNDID YOUR FLY, AND THE PALM BEACH CROWD
    BEGAN TO RUN.

WENDLA

WE'D BE PACKED IF WE'D JUST CLEAN UP,
BUT SQUEAKY CLEAN IS FAR WORSE STILL.

MELCHIOR

AND WE'RE DULL IF WE SPEAK OUR LINES

ALL THREE

AND YOU KNOW—UH-HUH—WE WILL!
SO THEY'LL CENSOR US AND THEY'LL MAKE A FUSS
WHEN WE TAKE THIS SHOW OUT ON A BUS.
TOTALLY BLEEPED! 'CAUSE IN SEX WE'RE STEEPED.
NO FOUR-LETTER WORDS FOR US! TOTALLY
    BLEEPED!

FRAU KNUPPLEDICK

CAN'T YOU GIVE US SOMETHING NICE?
SOUND OF MUSIC SET ON ICE?
CATS? *TARZAN*? *HIGH SCHOOL MUSICAL*?

MELCHIOR

"DISAPPEAR," YOU SAY—BUT IF WE DIE,

YOUR REPLACEMENT PLAY MIGHT BE SOME BIG-
    ASS LIE.
SO WE'RE HERE TO STAY; WE'LL NEVER QUIT,
'CAUSE OUR BARE-ASS SHOW IS A BIG-ASS HIT!

FRAU KNUPPLEDICK

Mechior Gabor, answer me!

MELCHIOR, MORITZ, and WENDLA

WE'LL BE BLEEPED, ALL RIGHT, AND EV'RY NIGHT,
ALL THE YOUNG ADULTS WILL WONDER WHY.
TOTALLY BLEEPED! BUT WE STILL GET HIGH,
SO COME ON, GIVE US A TRY!

YEAH, WE SWEAR ALL RIGHT, BUT NOT FOR SPITE,
BECAUSE RAUNCHY THEATRE GETS KIDS HIGH.
TOTALLY BLEEPED!

MORITZ and WENDLA

ELECTRONIC DICKS . . .

MELCHIOR

WILL POP OUT MY FLY!

MELCHIOR, MORITZ, and WENDLA

DON'T FORGET THE BROADWAY CLASSICS,
SHOCKING IN THEIR DAY:
RENT, LA CAGE, AND *HAIR* AND *EQUUS*
NOW DON'T SEEM RISQUÉ.
CABARET AND *WEST SIDE STORY*
SHOOK UP EVERYTHING;
MAYBE THE NEW *CHORUS LINE*
IS *SPRING AWAKENING*?

WE'LL BE BLEEPED, ALL RIGHT, AND EV'RY NIGHT,
ALL THE YOUNG ADULTS WILL WONDER WHY.
TOTALLY BLEEPED! BUT WE STILL GET HIGH,
SO COME ON, GIVE US A TRY!
TOTALLY BLEEPED!

FORBIDDEN MEMORIES: Denice Dawn

I performed in several editions of *Forbidden Broadway* in Boston and New York, and I'll never forget how a pie plate helped me get through the 1990 edition at Theatre East.

I had just moved from Boston to take the position of understudy, and Marilyn Pasekoff got sick during the week when the critic from the *New York Times* was coming.

I hadn't had a chance to begin rehearsals for the "Teeny Todd" number, and I may have seen it performed once. I had no idea how I would remember the lyrics. Then a little light went off in my brain and I said, "Quick, get me a pie plate!" I wrote the lyrics on the inside of the plate, which instantly became my most valuable prop ever.

My biggest concern was to angle the plate so that no one in the audience would see the lyrics. I was never so pie-plate focused in my entire life, and the experience left me with a great respect for kitchen items. To this day, I cannot see an aluminum pie plate without remembering the one that saved my career.

The story was leaked that I performed the number without a single rehearsal, and we ended up getting a great write-up from the *Times*. How much fun for us all! (There's still a copy of that review somewhere in my mother's house in Boston.)

One of my favorite onstage mishaps happened during a tango number, when one of

Denice Dawn.

my four-inch-heel black stiletto shoes went flying off into the audience. (Fortunately, it didn't impale anyone.) After the number, I went crawling on my hands and knees to the edge of the stage and said to the audience, "Does anyone have my shoe?" Someone seated at one of the front tables handed it to me, and I slunk offstage in the nick of time as the lights came up for the next number.

Performing with the *FB* family was one of the happiest times in my life (tears now falling down my face).

Now and Forever: 2008–Infinity

By the spring of 2008, things were looking up, due in large part to the return of some big stars to Broadway. With Patti LuPone headlining a revival of *Gypsy,* we were off and running. I also felt reinvigorated by the excellent revivals of *South Pacific* and *Sunday in the Park with George;* I'd never really spoofed those shows before and was more than happy to do so. What greater challenge can a parodist ask for than to rewrite "Some Enchanted Evening" and "Putting It Together?"

The new edition of the show was titled *Forbidden Broadway Goes to Rehab,* and the more we worked on it, the more jazzed we became. We put in new spoofs of Liza, Bernadette, and Kristin (Chenoweth). Add to this Mel Brooks handing out twofers for *Young Frankenstein,* plus Daniel Radcliffe strutting naked in *Equus,* and our own special version of the Pulitzer Prize–winning play *August: Osage County.*

We've spoofed relatively few plays over the years; musicals are much better targets because they're so big. Generally speaking, we only tackle plays if they're marketed like musicals of if they have well-known stars: *Amadeus, Speed-the-Plow, Master Class, August: Osage County.* With plays, it always helped if we could make them into musicals. As I've noted about through-composed shows, one good thing about them is that they avoid the drop in energy that happens when the characters stop singing and start talking. We've had to be careful of that in our show. For example, we initially had a problem with our *Spring Awakening* spoof because there was too much dialogue and not enough singing in it.

Kristen Mengelkoch and Jared Bradshaw in *Forbidden Broadway Goes to Rehab.*

But I love spoofing plays. They're easier to do because when you're writing dialogue, you obviously don't have to set a certain number of syllables to a certain section of music, and you don't have to rhyme anything. What a relief! Still, we've avoided having lengthy dialogue sequences in *Forbidden Broadway* because of that drop in energy.

Of course, the focal point of any new edition of *FB* is the Tony Award–winning Best Musical of that season. Spoofing *In the Heights* wasn't easy because I had to learn to write Latino hip-hop. Needless to say, this was a daunting task for a guy who's devoted most of his career to rewriting the lyrics of Cole Porter and Jerry Herman. After spending two weeks deciphering the rhyme scheme, scansion, and vocabulary of the show's title song, I felt like I had decoded the Rosetta stone.

"Some Endangered Species": Christina Bianco and Jared Bradshaw spoof *South Pacific*.

I was ecstatic that eventually I was able to write a successful spoof in the vocabulary of Lin-Manuel Miranda, and I was very excited to show it to the cast. To my surprise when I brought it in to them, they looked confused, and Phill said: "This number isn't very good. Maybe you should do a rewrite." But Michael West, who was slated to play Lin-Manuel, said, "I like it! Let's give it a try." David Caldwell, who had been our excellent musical director for five years at that point, meticulously lined up the music and the parody lyrics.

After several days of working on the number, we put it all together. It sounded great and it was also quite different from anything else we had ever done in *Forbidden*. It helped that Phill and the cast came up with some terrific comic bits, such as having Maria from *West Side Story* burst onto the scene. Bill Selby, our longtime assistant director and standby, added the cherry on top when he suggested I change the last line of the song to "It's *West Side Story* light."

"In the Heights" with Jared Bradshaw, Michael West, and Gina Kreiezmar.

A last-minute addition to *Forbidden Broadway Goes to Rehab* was the "All That Chat" number. This was an example of where the difficulty of routing the show comes into play. The running order had been set near the end of previews, but one very old number remained: "Glossy Fosse," our spoof of *Chicago*. We needed something new, and *In the Heights* had to come after it to make the show seem fresh and super-topical. So my assignment was to create a new number that would only require very simple, black costumes into which the actors could quickly change from the tuxes and cocktail dresses they wore in the title number, and it had to be two and a half minutes in length to give Michael just enough time to change into Lin-Manuel. But, as the second number in the show, it couldn't be filler; it had to hit one out of the park. And it had to be a very well-known song, so the audience would immediately be in on the joke of the rewritten lyrics.

I thought "All That Jazz" from *Chicago* would be good source material, but what could the parody be about? During a rehearsal break one day, I was racking my brain and poring over my notes while the actors annoyed me by talking excitedly about the delightfully nasty things they had read on "All That Chat," a theatre message board on the Web site TalkinBroadway.com. I was about to sweetly and politely scream at them to shut up when I thought: "All That Jazz . . . All That Chat." There it was, right in front of me!

Of course, I did not come up with the phrase "All That Chat." It belongs to the site's creator(s). But I had a great time turning the "All That Jazz" lyrics inside out and making fun of people like Bruce Memblatt partaking in endless online arguments over whether Michael John LaChiusa's *The Wild Party* is better than Andrew Lippa's.

As hard work as *Forbidden Broadway* has always been, there's an aspect of it that makes you feel like you're living in an old MGM musical. Everything's in Technicolor, the world sings, and we laugh and laugh as we put the show together. Just like in those classic musicals, there's enough drama to keep the story going—but nothing too serious. In the end, it all comes together and everyone is cheering. The music soars and a mixed chorus sings "oohs" and "aahs," albeit a chorus of only four overworked actors.

In 2009, *Forbidden Broadway* concluded its run at the 47th Street Theatre—but, of course, there is always the possibility of a continuation. In fact, I've already been considering titles for the next edition. How about: *Forbidden Broadway: Grand Theft Show Tune?*

Gina Kreiezmar, Christina Bianco, and Jared Bradshaw as the "chatterati" of All That Chat.

In the meantime, we had other worlds to conquer. In the spring of 2009, we had several upscale productions on the West Coast, including a run at The Opera House At Santa Barbara—a long way from Palsson's Supper Club. And in July 2009, *Forbidden Broadway* returned to London for the third time. This time it was presented at The Menier Chocolate Factory, a small but prestigious hot spot for exciting new productions. Created and run by the ingenious young producer David Babani, their productions include recent award-winning revivals of *Sunday in the Park with George*, *La Cage aux Folles*, and *A Little Night Music*.

David's commitment to produce this new version seemed divinely appropriate, since *Forbidden* was one of the first shows he produced in London when he was only nineteen! At the time, it was his first transfer to the West End, when the show moved to The Albery Theatre from the Jermyn Street Theatre. By 2009, David's reputation and expertise had developed impressively. Phill George again directed, while I was kept busy writing eight new numbers especially for the London en-

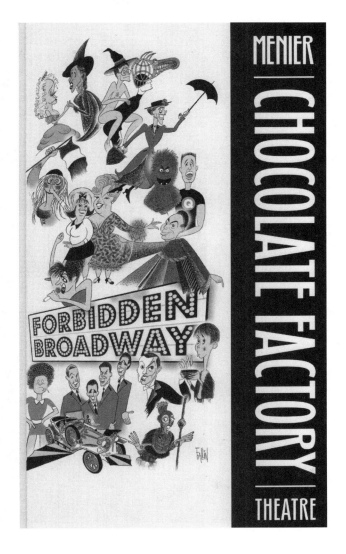

gagement, which included spoofs of David's aforementioned revivals. I didn't go easy on them, despite the conflict of interest, but David has a marvelous sense of humor and laughed as loud as anybody.

I also included an *Oliver!* parody that I had written in 1984 when that show was revived on Broadway with Patti LuPone and Ron Moody. The revival closed before I could try the number in *Forbidden Broadway*, but I kept it safely tucked in the drawer for over twenty-five years. Since another revival of *Oliver!* was playing in London at the same time as our new production of *Forbidden Broadway*, it fit right in the routine. It brought the house down and proved that my instincts to never throw anything away were correct.

People often ask me if I have written other shows besides *Forbidden Broadway*. The answer is yes, of course! I have a whole trunk full of unproduced musicals for which I have written the lyrics, the books, and sometimes the music. I think the main reason why they have never been done is that *FB* has been such an overpowering force

Gerard Alessandrini in 2008.

in my career. Usually, producers want to do *Forbidden Broadway* before they'll even look at anything else I've written—because the title is so recognizable, and also because it's a small show with big entertainment value. As Christine Pedi often says, "*Forbidden Broadway* is a lot of bang for your buck."

But I still continue to work on "real" musicals. I think I've learned a lot from observing, studying, and parodying so many Broadway shows, and I hope to utilize that expertise and someday be part of the creative team of a musical play.

As for the future of Broadway, that's impossible to predict, because it all goes in cycles and everything changes so fast. There are so many trends, and what may be true for three years straight may not be true for the next three years. Broadway is completely subject to the whims of public taste; I've seen many flop shows that I thought might have been hits a season or two earlier, and vice versa. The theatre has been christened "The Fabulous Invalid," and so it is. It often seems on the verge of death, but then it rises from the ashes in full glory. And, I suspect, so will *Forbidden Broadway.*

Stephen Sondheim, who had been to see our show many times, was kind enough to attend *Forbidden Broadway Goes to Rehab* right after we announced that it would be our last edition for a while. He greeted me by looking straight into my eyes and asking, "Are you sorry/grateful?" I suppose I should have laughed at his wit and insight, but I could only think to respond with a truthful answer: "I'm grateful."

"All That Chat"

BEBE NEUWIRTH

Hello, suckers. Did you pay good money to see a Broadway show, when you could've just stayed home and read what's online? Well, this isn't 1996 anymore. It's 2008. Get with it!

COME ON, BABE, GET ON THE INTERNET
AND ALL THAT CHAT!
I HEAR THAT DATALOUNE IS EVEN MEANER YET
THAN ALL THAT CHAT.

FRANK LANGELLA'S HOGGIN' WHOOPI'S SPOT,
BUT AS THOMAS MORE, SHE SAID HE'S NOT SO HOT!
CHECK OUT THE RUMOR MILL AND GOSSIP MADE
    TO KILL
ON ALL THAT CHAT . . .

[MALE *and* FEMALE *CHICAGO* DANCERS *enter and begin typing on laptop computers.*]

MALE CHICAGO DANCER

OH! WHAT HAPPENS OFFSTAGE
IS MORE FUN THAN ON . . .

BEBE

ON ALL THAT CHAT!

MALE CHICAGO DANCER

Send!

FEMALE CHICAGO DANCER

OH! I READ THAT BROADWAY
IS A BABYLON

BEBE

ON ALL THAT CHAT!

FEMALE CHICAGO DANCER

Send!

MALE CHICAGO DANCER

RA-U-U-U-U-L ESPARAZA SLEPT WITH CHITA.

FEMALE CHICAGO DANCER

CH-I-I-I-I-I-TA FIN'LLY SLEPT WITH RITA.

ALL

AND I HEAR TOM WOPAT'S QUEER

FOR ALL (send!) THAT (send!) CHAT!

[*CHICAGO* DANCERS *repeat in counterpoint while* BEBE *sings.*]

BEBE

I JUST READ THAT *BRIGADOON* IS DEAD
ON ALL THAT CHAT;
THE WORKSHOP DIDN'T WORK,
AND SO THE BAD NEWS SPREAD
ON ALL THAT CHAT.

HOLD ON, HON, I'M HOOKIN' UP TO LINKS
WHERE THERE'S AN *EQUUS* CLIP WHERE DANNY
    RADCLIFFE STINKS.
IT HASN'T OPENED YET, BUT HE'S A BLOGGER'S PET
ON ALL . . . THAT . . . CHAAAT.

MALE CHICAGO DANCER

So, Checky, that's final, huh? You prefer Andrew Lippa's *Wild Party* to Michael John LaChiusa's? Send!

FEMALE CHICAGO DANCER

Yeah. I'm afraid so, Bruce Memblatt. I hate Michael John LaChiusa. Send!

MALE CHICAGO DANCER

Oh, Checky? Send!

FEMALE CHICAGO DANCER

Yeah? Send!

MALE CHICAGO DANCER

Nobody trashes Michael John LaChiusa's *Wild Party* on my Facebook. Send! Control! Alt! Delete!

[*The* FEMALE *CHICAGO* DANCER *gets it and dies; both* DANCERS *exit.*]

BEBE

WHO NEEDS THEATRE TIX WHEN
YOU CAN GET YOUR KICKS
ON A-A-A-A-LL
TH-A-A-A-T
CH-A-A-A-T!
THAT CHAT!

"Forbidden *In the Heights*"

LIN-MANUEL MIRANDA

LIFE BITES IN WASHINGTON HEIGHTS,
I WANNA BREAK AWAY
AND TAKE A ROLE IN
BOEING-BOEING OR SOME OTHER PLAY.
RAP IS GRATING, TRICKY, AND DAUNTING;
WE USE WORDS LIKE "AWNING"
TO MIS-RYHME "GOOD MAWNING."

[PIRAGUA GUY *enters with cart selling ices and souvenirs from* In the Heights.]

PIRAGUA GUY

Ice-cold piragua! Or souvenirs from *In the Heights*!
CDs! Bodega mugs! Stuffed barrio rats!

LIN-MANUEL MIRANDA

Yo, piragero, como estas?

PIRAGUA GUY

Como siempre. But you better not speak Spanish anymore. We just won the Tony, and now our audience is 90 percent bridge-and-tunnel Jewish.

LIN-MANUEL MIRANDA

Si, senor mensch. I won't be a *meshugena*!

PIRAGUA GUY

Oy! What a *goyim*!

LIN-MANUEL

I AM MIRANDA
AND YOU BETTER MEMORIZE MY NAME!
MY REASON FOR FAME
IS GREATLY EXAGGERATED,
EXACERBATED BY THE FACT
I CANNOT ACT.
WHEN THINGS GET COMPLICATED,
I'VE INCORPORATED
TOO MUCH EXPOSITION
IN RAPPER DEPOSITION.
YOU'RE WISHIN' I WOULD SHUT UP?
WELL, SHOVE IT!
I WROTE THIS RAP AN' LOVE IT.
DID YA GET THAT?
GOOD, YA GOT IT, LET'S MOVE ON.
HERE IS THE WHOLE CAST:
AWW, DAMN, THEY'RE COMIN' ON TOO FAST!

THE COMMUNITY

IN THE HEIGHTS,
ALL OF THE WHITES JUST RUN AWAY.

PIRAGUA GUY

SOCIALITES
CRY OUT WITH FRIGHT,
"WHAT DID THEY SAY?"

THE COMMUNITY

IN THE HEIGHTS

LIN-MANUEL MIRANDA

WILL IT SURVIVE
A MATINEE?

ABUELA

HE RECITES RAP
WHERE THERE OUGHT TO BE A PLAY!

LIN-MANUEL MIRANDA

HERE'S THE PLOT,
IT'S MOVING LIKE AN ESCALATOR—
WRITE IT DOWN NOW,
I'M GONNA TEST YOU LATER—
WE'RE A CONTEMPORARY *WEST SIDE STORY*,
FULL OF LATINOS, BUT NOT AS GOOD OR GORY.

[MARIA *from* West Side Story *enters, brandishing a gun.*]

MARIA

Don't you touch him! How many bullets in this gun,
Chino? Enough for you? And you? And still have one
left for Stew??

THE COMMUNITY

Who?

CHRISTINA

You know, Stew. From *Passing Strange*.

THE COMMUNITY

IN THE HEIGHTS,
WE DON'T KNOW STEW
FROM *PASSING STRANGE*.
IN THE HEIGHTS,
WE'RE URBANITES
WITH NOT MUCH RANGE!
IN WASHINGTON . . .

[*Blackout. Random Spanish until* ABUELA *says "Ai, Con Ed!"*]

IN THE HEIGHTS
BROADWAY IGNITES,
BUT WILL IT STAY?
OR WILL TOURISTS FROM JAPAN
STAY FAR AWAY?

IN THE HEIGHTS—
TOO MULTI-CULTURAL YOU SAY?

[*Lights up.*]

IT DELIGHTS,
BUT, YEAH, WILL IT PAY?

LIN-MANUEL MIRANDA

BUT AS FOR THE CITY, IT'S A PITY
IT'S GETTING TOO PRETTY.

[*He sings the next section in counterpoint to* THE COMMUNITY *singing "In the Heights."*]

YOU'LL MISS THE LATE NIGHTS,
YOU'LL MISS THE BEANS AND RICE,
THE SYRUP AND SHAVED ICE,
THE PORNO AND THE VICE.

THE COMMUNTITY

IN THE HEIGHTS, IN THE HEIGHTS, IN THE HEIGHTS!

LIN-MANUEL MIRANDA

SO TURN UP THE HOUSE LIGHTS:
THE PUBLIC UNITES TO MAKE SHOWS
ABOUT LATINOS FOR WHITES!

LIN-MANUEL AND ABUELA

NO FIGHT, NO BITE—
IT'S *WEST SIDE STORY* LITE
IN THE HEIGHTS . . .

ALL

TONIGHT!

Forbidden *South Pacific*"

KELLI O'HARA

WHEN MY HAIR IS A BRIGHT CANARY YELLOW,
I CAN TURN CHRISTINE EBERSOLE TO GREEN.
SO SHE CALLS ME A COCKEYED INGENUE
'CUZ I'M NEVER DISDAINFULL OR MEAN.

I HAVE HEARD SUTTON FOSTER RANT AND BELLOW,
"WE'VE PROGRESSED AND THE GOODY GIRL IS
    DEAD!"
BUT I'M ONLY A COCKEYED INGENUE,
AND PEROXIDE HAS SEEPED IN MY HEAD.

WHEN KRISTIN CHENOWETH
SAYS ROMANCE IS A MYTH,
TOO CUTESY-CUTE, SHE MUST RESIGN.
BUT I'LL MAKE YOU BELIEVE
MY HEART IS ON MY SLEEVE
AND THIS IS NINETEEN-FORTY-NINE.

SO MY BRA BOUNCES LIKE A BOWL OF JELLO,
AND I PUT PATTI'S PATIENCE TO THE TEST,
BUT I'M STUCK WITH NO CHOICE
AND MY HIGH-PITCHED VOICE,
AND I CAN'T GET INTO MY CHEST!
NOT THIS CHEST.

[*To* PAULO.]

Now, tell me about you. You share equal billing with me, but I've never heard of you.

PAULO

Alright, Kelli, I'll tell you.

[*Very dramatically.*]

I keeled a man.

KELLI

Keeling? Is that some sort of Polynesian sport with coconuts and balls?

PAULO

No, I *keeled* a man. Don't you understand-a me?

KELLI

That's a very poor French accent.

PAULO

I use the same one for Spanish and Italian. Do you approve?

KELLI

You've just told me you use one all-purpose accent, and yet I know it's all right. You even keeled a man and I could care even less.

[*They laugh.*]

PAULO

Kelli, one waits so long for a good revival of classic musical, and when at last it comes, one cannot risk losing the Tony.

KELLI

Yes.

PAULO

Work comes for people likes us only once every sixty years. You might say we are raiders of the lost art.

SOME ENDANGERED SPECIES,
LIKE THE SINGING DRAMA,
MIGHT GIVE YOU A TRAUMA
INSIDE A CROWED ROOM.
BUT PEOPLE STILL GO,
THEY GO EVEN WHEN
THEY'VE HEARD THESE OLD STANDARDS AGAIN
   AND AGAIN.

KELLI

WHO CAN EXPLAIN WHY
OSCAR WAS SO WISE?

PAULO

FOOLS IMITATE HIM
WHILE *CRY-BABY* DIES!

SOME ENDANGERED SPECIES,
BARITONES AND TENORS,
MEZZOS AND SOPRANOS
CAN PACK A CROWDED ROOM.
SO HELP THEM SURVIVE
AND DO SOMETHING NEW
OR, ALL THROUGH YOUR LIFE,
THEY'LL REVIVE *XANADU*.

ONCE YOU HAVE BEEN TO *SPAMALOT*, YOU'LL KNOW—
AT INTERMISSION,
YOU'LL GET UP AND GO!

"Feed the Burbs"

MARY POPPINS

EARLY EACH DAY, DOWN AT TKTS,
THE CROWDS FROM CONNECTICUT COME.

THEY PREFER A SMART PLAY, BUT THEY ALL
   ACQUIESCE,
AND INSTEAD THEY ATTEND SOMETHING DUMB.
DISNEY AND CAMERON KNOW WHAT THEY WANT,
NOTHING TOO EDGY OR BLUE.
THEY SELL THEM A BRAND NAME WITH BIG BALLY-
   HOO
CAM'RON KNOWS WHAT EXACTLY TO DO-OO:

FEED THE BURBS, TEPID A SHOW,
TEPID, VAPID, TITLES THEY KNOW.
FEED THE BURBS, HUMONGOUS SIZE,
WHILE OVERHEAD A SCARED ACTRESS FLIES.

ALL AROUND NEW YORK CITY, IN JERSEY,
   AND GLEN COVE,
THE BUYERS ARE UNAWARE.
THEY KNOW MARY POPPINS, AND THINK THEY'LL
   LEAVE SMILING—
INSTEAD, THEY JUST SIT THERE AND STARE.

THOUGH OLD FILMS ARE NO RISK TO DO,
LISTEN, CAREFUL, THEY'RE SWIND-E-LING YOU!
FEED THE BURBS, THAT'S WHAT THEY SAY
TEPID, VAPID MUSICALS PAY.

"Let Me Enter Naked"

BURLESQUE MALE ANNOUNCER VOICE

Wichita's one and only burlesque theatre presents Miss Daniel Rose Radcliffe!

[*Lights up on* DANIELLE RADCLIFFE *in a Harry Potter warlock robe.*]

DANIEL RADCLIFFE

LET ME ENTER NAKED,
LET ME MAKE YOU DROOL.
I'M AN ADOLESCENT,

FOREVER PREPUBESCENT . . .

OFFSTAGE VOICE

Give 'em a scarf!

DANIEL RADCLIFFE

. . . I'M BARELY OUT OF SCHOOL!
I NEED SOME HYPE FAST,
BECAUSE I'M TYPECAST
AS HARRY POTTER REFINED.

OFFSTAGE VOICE

Dip!

DANIEL RADCLIFFE

SO LET ME ENTER NAKED
AND SHOW YOU MY CUTE BEHIND, YES SIR!
YOU'LL LOVE BIG BEHIND . . .

Hello, everybody! My name's Daniel, what's yours?
I used to be in Gryffindor, but recently I've been
Slytherin! Hello, (sir/madam). Yes, you in the third row.
Don't be shy! Are you a Quidditch fan? Did you come to
see my Golden Snitch?

LET ME ENTER NAKED,
LET ME STRUT UNCUT.
GIRLS DON'T ASK THEIR MAMA
TO SEE A CLASSIC DRAMA—
THEY COME TO SEE MY BUTT!
SOME OL' REDNECK WUSS
ATTENDING *EQUUS*
WOULD THINK HE WASTED HIS TIME,
BUT HARRY POTTER NAKED
MAKES THIS OL' CREAKY PLAY SEEM SUBLIME,
AND YOU'LL HAVE A REAL GOOD TIME!

Expeliamus!

"Patti LuPone in *Gypsy*"

OFFSTAGE VOICE

And now, this year's annual revival of *Gypsy,* starring
Patti LuPone.

PATTI

Anybody who misses my performance is dead! If I die,
it won't be from quittin', it'll be from killing myself to
get better parts!

SOME PEOPLE THINK I'M THE BEST,
AND, IT'S TRUE, I ECLIPSE THE REST:
BETTE MIDLER AND ROZ RUSSELL,
LA MERM, TYNE,
ALL PLAYED HER TOO BENIGN.
THEIR MAMA ROSE WAS ROT . . .

[*Interjection.*]

Ibegtodifferwithyou, Arthur!

BUT NOT MINE!

[BOYD GAINES *enters.*]

BOYD

It's great to see you again, Patti.

PATTI

Again? I'm sorry, but do we know each other?

BOYD

Well, sure. It's me, Boyd Gaines. We do eight shows a
week together.

PATTI

Oh, you're that funny little man they brought in to say
those other words that happen when I'm not speaking.

BOYD

That's right.

PATTI

I'm sorry I didn't recognize you. You used to be someone called Mandy Patinkin.

BOYD

Well, I sure recognize you! I saw you in *Evita*.

PATTI

[*Correcting him.*]

As Evita. How was I?

BOYD

Who remembers? I was just a little boy at the time. I can't believe I'm all grown up and sharing billing with such a big Broadway star.

PATTI

Sharing? Funny.

BOYD

What?

PATTI

FUNNY, YOU'RE AN ACTOR WHO'S TASTED
CRITICAL PRAISE SO FAR;
FUNNY, HERE IN *GYPSY*, YOU'RE WASTED.
SMALL PART, ISN'T IT?

FUNNY, THOUGH YOU'RE HANDSOME AND MANNISH,
NO ONE KNOWS WHO YOU ARE.
FUNNY, NEXT TO ME YOU JUST VANISH.
SMALL PART, ISN'T IT?

WE HAVE NOTHING IN COMMON.
I'M THE PHENOMENON!
I'LL TAME CRITICAL FORCES,

YOU CAN TRAIN HORSES FROM NOW ON.

FUNNY, YOU'R A MAN WHO'S BECOMING
MY UNIMPORTANT PAWN.
LUCKY I'M CONTROLLING AND NUMBING,
SMALL PART, ISN'T IT?
USELESS, AREN'T YOU?
SMALL, AND USELESS, AND GONE.

BOYD

Patti, I've got to give you some sobering news: Dainty June ran away! She took a part in *Spiderman: The Musical*.

PATTI

What!?!

[LAURA *runs onto the stage.*]

LAURA

Mamma Patti, I just heard the news. It's time to let go, Mama Patti. We all got our Tonys. Let's call it quits.

BOYD

I can make fifty-two dollars a week at the Roundabout, doing obscure revivals.

LAURA

You can stay mostly at home on your Connecticut farm and sometimes do cute little supporting parts in shows like *Noises Off*.

PATTI

Never! I'm never giving up this part. Do you think I am going to let Sutton Foster play Mama Rose in the next annual revival? I ain't quittin'! Ever!

I HAVE A DREAM
I'LL STAR IN A NEW *GYPSY*.
I'LL PROVE I'M A TRUE GYPSY,

BUT WHEN I GET THROUGH WITH *GYPSY* . . .

I'LL BE SWELL! I'LL BE GREAT!
I'LL SERVE BERNADETTE'S HEAD ON A PLATE.
I'LL ERASE MAMA ROSE
BECAUSE EV'RY THING'S COMING OUT PATTI!

I'LL PLOW THROUGH AND SUCCEED,
LIKE A BULLDOZER PICKING UP SPEED.
EV'RY NERVE I'LL EXPOSE—
HONEY, EV'RYTHING'S COMING OUT PATTI!

I CAN DO IT,
AND I'LL MAKE PEOPLE STAND.
I'LL GET THROUGH IT,
AND TAKE THE SCEN'RY AND CHEW IT!

CURTAIN DOWN! DIM THE LIGHTS!
ARTHUR LAURENTS AND I HAD BIG FIGHTS.
YOU CAN TELL IT WAS HELL:
HEADS WOULD SWELL, HE WOULD YELL,
"THAT BITCHY STAR THEY TALK ABOUT IS YOU!"
BECAUSE EV'RY SONG I SING SOUNDS LIKE RENO
    SWEENY TODD,
EVERY DRESS I WEAR LOOKS LUMPY AS SANTA
    CLAUS,
EV'RY SCENE I PLAY IS SUCKY AS LOLLIPOPS,
EV'RYTHING'S COMING OUT PATTI FOR ME AND
    FOR . . . ME!

"Glitter and Be Glib"

[*Lights up on* KRISTIN CHENOWETH, *wearing a dazzling "Glinda the Good Witch" gown and holding a magic wand.*]

KRISTIN

POPULAR! I'M EVER SO PUPULAR.
THE FANS THAT I'M COZY WITH

TELL ME, "CHENOWITH,
YOU'RE MY FAV'RITE
SINGING STER . . . STAR."
I'M GENUINELY HAPPY
I'VE BECOME SO POP-U-LER . . . LAR

And yet sometimes, when I'm reflective—which is hardly ever—I say to myself, "Kristin Chenoweth, do you miss the glamour of Broadway? Or do you want to sell out to the tawdry world of Hollywood?" So here I am, on television, my heart breaking. Forced to glitter, forced to be glib . . .

GLITTER AND BE GLIB,
THAT'S WHAT I AD-LIB
WHEN THERE'S NO ARTISTIC CHANCE.
FORCED TO BE SO CUTE,
I'M AS RIPE AS FRUIT,
SO DEMURE AND CHARMING,
CRTICS DROP THEIR PANTS.

AND YET, IN HOLLYWOOD, I LOVE TO REVEL,
AH-HA!
I HAVE NO STRONG OBJECTION TO THE FAME,
AH-HA!
IT'S TRUE I SOLD OUT TO A NETWORK DEVIL,
HA-HA!
IF YOU WERE ME, I BET YOU'D DO THE SAME!

IT'S NOT SO TOUGH
TO BE BENIGNLY CHEERFUL;
I'LL SHOW I'VE HAD ENOUGH
OF BEING TV FEARFUL!
I HAVE A HIT—
I DON'T MIND A BIT.

POP-POP-POPULAR SMASH!
I'VE A POPULAR SMASH.
TRUE, IT'S POPULAR TRASH,
BUT IT'S PROMINENT CASH.

POP-POP-POPULAR ME,

WICKED IS HISTORY.

NO MORE THEATRE FOR ME:

I LOVE TV!

WICKED NO MORE;

IDINA I ABHOR.

BROADWAY? NO WAY!

POP CULTURE'S HERE TO STAY.

OBSERVE HOW PERKY I CAN FEEL

ABOUT SELLING OUT TO A MOVIE DEAL!

I'M POPULAR AND TOP THE LIST,

I'M POPULAR AND POP-U-LIST.

POP-POPULAR

Oh yeah! That's what you think! Why are you telling *me*? No! I can't stand it!

GLITTER AND BE GLIB!

And that's my new philosophy!

"Considerably Over Priced"

[OLIVER *and the* ARTFUL DODGER *enter through the audience. They ad lib friendly lines to the patrons while picking their pockets. After they have fleeced the audience, they go on stage showing their goods to each other.*]

DODGER

How much have you made?

OLIVER

I've got these! Enough to see a show.

DODGER

Oh no, Oliver, you have to pick a lot more pockets to afford to see a show!

OLIVER & THE ARTFUL DODGER

CONSIDERABLY HIGH PRICED

CONSIDERABLY NOT FOR THE FAMILY

AT SEVENTY POUNDS A SEAT

AND TWICE THAT AFTER YOU PARK AND EAT

DODGER

CONSIDERABLY TOO HIGH

CONSIDERABLY DUBIOUS QUALITY

OLIVER

I'VE EVEN SEEN SHOWS FOR FREE

WHERE I WOULD RATHER HAVE WATCHED T.V.

DODGER

BACK IN THE OLDEN DAYS OF 1991 OR SO

TWENTY QUID A SHOW WAS HIGH

NOW AT THE HALF PRICE BOOTH

SIXTY POUNDS A SINGLE SEAT

IS CONSIDERED QUITE A BUY!

OLIVER

CONSIDERED TO SEE A SHOW

BUT STAYING AT HOME SUFFICED

'CAUSE ONCE I SAW THE PRICE

MY BANK ACCOUNT SAID "WHOA!"

BOTH

CONSIDERABLY OVER PRICED!

DODGER

NOW WE GOT *SISTER ACT*, *JERSEY BOYS* AND *OLIVER!*

ROWAN ATKINSON'S A STITCH

OLIVER

THEATRE IS LOTS OF FUN IF YOU ARE A KID TODAY

AND YOUR FATHER'S FILTHY RICH

BOTH

CONSIDER THE ADS OF LATE
HOW CLEVER'LY THEY ENTICED
AND AFTER SOME CONSIDERATION YOU WILL STATE
CONSIDERABLY OVER PRICED!

"Nancy's Song"

DODGER

Oh look Oliver! There's Nancy, your substitute
prostitute mother!

[NANCY *enters on a crutch and bandaged up*]

OLIVER

Nancy, what happened to you?

NANCY

Oliver! What? Oh this. Nothing at all. I was just
snogging with Bill Sykes.

DODGER

I'll show him!

NANCY

No Dodger! No Oliver! It's just his way of tellin' me he
loves me. You wouldn't undrestand. It's a Dickens thing.

[*The boys shrug and leave.* NANCY *sings*]

AS LONG AS HE BEATS ME
OH YES, HE DOES BEAT ME
IN SPITE OF EQUITY
I'M GLAD THAT HE BEATS ME

I'VE GOT TO PLAY NON-STOP
THE SUBTEXT ON THE TOP

SO GET THE RIDING CROP
BE SURE THAT HE BEATS ME

WHEN THE LIBRETTO IS GETTING THIN
THE SEX AND VIOLENCE
BRINGS FAMILIES IN…

[BILL *steps out on stage and slaps her down. While on
the floor, she spits out teeth, then blissfully continues.*]

I'LL SUFFER CAM'RON'S SCORN
I'LL LIMP FOR MATTHEW BOURNE
AND DO THIS WORN SOFT PORN
AS LONG AS HE BEATS ME!

"You Can't Stop the Camp"

MARISSA

YOU CAN'T STOP THE TRENDY TRENDS
POP CULTURE BRINGS TODAY,
AND IN *HAIRSPRAY,* NO ONE HERE PRETENDS
WE HAVE SOMETHING DEEP TO SAY.

SO DON'T TRY TO STOP OUR DANCIN' FEET
AND OUR RACIAL EXPOSÉ.
AND OUR SETS SPIN ROUND AND ROUND AND
    ROUND,
AND THE VOLUME IS PUMPED TO A BLARING SOUND
BUT *HAIRSPRAY* WILL ASTOUND
AS THE GOOD-TIME CHAMP,
AND YOU CAN'T STOP THE CAMP,
YOU CAN'T STOP THE CAMP!

To prove my point, let me introduce the greatest Diva
of the new century!

HARVEY

I AM HARVEY FIERSTEIN,
AND I LIKE THE WAY I AM.

WHEN I DID *TORCH SONG TRILOGY*,
THEY DIDN'T GIVE A DAMN!
AND SO I GAVE THEM BACK MY PULITZER
BECAUSE NOW I AM A HAM.

I DID SERIOUS DRAMA
AND IT WASN'T MUCH FUN
AND IT DIDN'T PAY,
(SO) I DESCENDED TO DRAG
AND NOW I PLAY A VAMP
AND YOU CAN'T STOP THE CAMP!

BILLY ELLIOT

I AM BILLY ELLIOT,
I'M A BROADWAY LEADING MAN,
AND IN ELTON JOHN'S NEW NELLIE HIT,
I FLY LIKE PETER PAN!

AND ON THE WEST END I WAS QUITE UNIQUE,
BUT IN NEW YORK, I'M AN ALSO RAN
BECAUSE EV'RY NEW SHOW IS A CHILD MACHINE:
SPRING AWAKENING, EQUUS, AND NOW *THIRTEEN.*
ANY ACTOR WHO'S PAST SIXTEEN
IS NOW CALLED "GRAMP,"
AND YOU CAN'T STOP THE

ALL

TACKY, SILLY, WACKY SHOWS
FROM PLAYIN' BROADWAY,
AND IT'S TRAUMA DOIN' DRAMA
OR A SERIOUS PLAY,
AND BURSTING INTO SONG IS

UNACCEPTABLE AND SO GAY!

NOW YOU CAN'T STOP THE
MIGHTY META-MUSICAL
FROM HITTING THE SCREEN,
AND EVEN JOHN TRAVOLTA
IS A BIG OL' QUEEN.

WE'RE SICK OF VAPID MUSICALS
BUT KITSCHY CLICHÉ IS CHAMP,
AND YOU CAN'T STOP THE CAMP:
Spamalot!
YOU CAN'T STOP THE CAMP:
Young Frankenstein!
YOU CAN'T STOP THE CAMP:
9 to 5!
YOU CAN'T STOP THE CAMP:
Kevin Spacey!
YOU CAN'T STOP THE CAMP!

"Putting Up Revivals"

SONDHEIM

I'M STEPHEN SONDEIM, AND I'M VERY HEP.
CELEBRITIES LOVE SONDHEIM—INCLUDING
    JOHNNY DEPP.
THE PEOPLE ALL KNOW WHAT THEY LIKE,
AND THEY LIKE WHAT THEY KNOW.
AND SO MY CLASSIC MUSICALS ARE S.R.O.
WHEN THEY COME BACK TO LIFE . . .

HIT BY HIT, PUTTING UP REVIVALS!
SHOW BY SHOW, *SUNDAY IN THE PARK* IS ALWAYS
    SMART.
COMPANY AND *FOLLIES* A SALVATION,
EVEN THOUGH IT'S RISKY DOING ART;
SWEENEY TODD A GRAND GUIGNOL SENSATION,
FORUM IS A COMIC REVELATION.
EV'RY YEAR ANOTHER SONDHEIM CLASSIC,

EVEN THOUGH THEY'RE PRACTIC'LY JURASSIC,
BUT EV'RY SHOW HAS HEART.

I'M PUTTING UP REVIVALS, ONE BY ONE.
SOON THEY'LL DO *MERRILY* AND *PASSION*,
I'LL GET THROUGH, TAKING ALKA SELTZER AND
    SOME TUMS.
TINY ORCHESTRATIONS ARE THE FASHION,
SO THEY USE PIANO, BASS, AND DRUMS,
OTHERWISE MY BRILLIANT COMPOSITION
ISN'T GOING TO GET MUCH EXHIBITION.

ART IS EXPENSIVE!
EV'RY MINOR DETAIL IS A MAJOR INVESTMENT,
SO THEY SHRINK DOWN THE SCALE WHILE THE
    CRITICS AND PRESS VENT,
"I ENJOYED IT MORE WHEN THEY FIRST DID IT.
NOW THEY SHRUNK THE ORCHESTRA AND HID IT."
IN THE EIGHTIES, ALL THE CRITICS PANNED IT;
NOW THEY ALL REVERE AND UNDERSTAND IT.

SHOT BY SHOT, PUTTING UP WITH RIVALS.
NOW WHAT'S HOT HAS TO BE A KIDDIE SHOW TO
    PAY,
OR THEY DO A SIR LLOYD WEBBER FREAK SHOW—
EVERYTHING IS CARDBOARD OR CLICHÉ,
EV'RYTHING A HAPPY OR A BLEAK SHOW,
EITHER THAT OR MOUNT A MORE ANTIQUE SHOW.
NOW I AM A TREND FOR EXPLOITATION
AND ANOTHER SONDHEIM CELEBRATION . . .

ART IS CONFUSING!
FIRST YOU GET AN AWARD FOR YOUR LIFETIME
    ACHIEVEMENT,
BUT IT CUTS LIKE A SWORD, FOR IT FEELS LIKE
    BEREAVEMENT.
SO YOU DISAPPEAR LIKE A MAGICIAN,
TRYING TO AVOID THE ADULATION
WHILE THEY REARRANGE YOUR COMPOSITION,
GIVING IT A MODERN CONNOTATION.

TRYING TO BE KIND, YOU GIVE PERMISSION
WHILE THE RIGHTS ARE IN NEGOTIATION,
EVEN THOUGH YOU DO HAVE THE SUSPICION
ALL PRODUCERS WANT IS ADMIRATION
AND DON'T LIKE MAKING ART
OR PUTTING UP REVIVALS . . .

HIT BY HIT, NOTE BY NOTE,
AD BY AD, QUOTE BY QUOTE,
FAD BY FAD—
AND THAT IS THE STATE OF MY ART!

[BERNADETTE *enters.*]

BERNADETTE

HELLO, STEVE.
WHERE'D YOU GO, STEVE?
GOT A NEW SHOW, STEVE?

SONDHEIM

It's good to see you, Bernadette.

BERNADETTE

I never forgot you, Steve. You gave me so much.

SONDHEIM

What did I ever give you?

BERNADETTE

Many things: *Sunday in the Park. Into the Woods.* Vocal damage. But enough about me. Are you working on something new?

SONDHEIM

No, I'm not.

BERNADETTE

That's not like you, Steve.

SONDHEIM

I'VE NOTHING TO SAY.

WELL, NOTHING THAT'S NOT BEEN SAID.

BERNADETTE

SAID BY YOU, THOUGH, STEVE.

DON'T WORRY IF YOU FEEL WHOREY, MOVE ON.

THE FRESHNESS OF *WEST SIDE STORY* IS GONE;

JUST KEEP MOVING ON.

LET'S FINALLY PUT UP *ROAD SHOW* OR *BOUNCE*.

DON'T WORRY IF MICHAEL RIEDEL

WILL NEEDLE OR POUNCE,

JUST KEEP MOVING ON.

[RED RIDING HOOD *and* SWEENEY TODD *enter.*]

RED RIDING HOOD

ANYTHING YOU DO,

LET IT COME FROM YOU.

SWEENEY TODD

SWEENEY TODD, PART TWO

BERNADETTE

WRITE A SHOW FOR ME

[*All start asking him to write a show for them, their voices overlapping and rising.*]

SONDHEIM

Order!

ALL

SONDHEIM

IN THE NEW CORP'RATE ORDER OF BROADWAY

IS NOW SEEN AS A GENIUS OF CLASS,

BUT ALAS . . .

DRECK LIKE *SHREK* POPS UP LIKE TREES,

SONDHEIM'S DOWN UPON HIS KNEES,

BROADWAY'S DAMAGING HIS LIVER.

BUT BE THANKFUL WE HAVE

SONDHEIM!

SONDHEIM!

SONDHEIM!

SONDHEIM

Broadway. A blank stage or season. My favorite. So many possibilities!

[*Fadeout. The End.*]

"Ta-Ta"

FULL COMPANY

WELL, TA-TA, FOLKS,

GLAD YOU GOT THE JOKES

AND BELOW-THE-BELT REPARTÉE.

IT'S BEEN LOT'S OF FUN,

BUT WE'VE GOT TO RUN—

OR SHOULD WE SAY "RUN AWAY"?

BUT WE'RE SURE TO MEET

ON THAT ZANY STREET:

FORBIDDEN BROADWAY!

FORBIDDEN MEMORIES: **Ron Bohmer**

I was lucky enough to appear in *Forbidden Broadway* twice in my career: at the very beginning, when I'd only had my Equity card for a few months, and again years later after I'd had a few successes. (I won't say at the *end* of my career . . .)

In 1986, I was the definition of a struggling actor. I went to auditions during the day and drove a carriage in Central Park at night to pay the bills. My agent called one day with an audition for *FB*, and they sent over the George Hearn parody "I Ham What I Ham" for me to learn. I thought I was far too young for the show, which I had never seen, and I didn't think I was particularly funny. Luckily, Gerard is funny enough for all of us, and I was just so damned committed to the audition that he took pity on me and hired me.

I became a member of the fifth-anniversary cast, 1986-87, with Barbara Walsh, Craig Wells, and Roxie Lucas. At the piano was Mark Mitchell, or sometimes Phil Fortenberry. I was green as the day is long, but over the passing months, my awesome cast-mates taught me a lot about funny.

Ron Bohmer and friends.

I was shocked at how little money we made, but I soon learned that there are many forms of coin in showbiz. Aside from the sheer joy of doing this hysterical show each night, the big coin here was that *everybody* in the industry came to see us. Casting directors, producers, you name it. The big deal that year was the arrival of *Les Miz* on Broadway. The entire creative staff of that show was in love with *FB* and came repeatedly: Trevor Nunn, John Caird, the works. We all ended up with auditions for *Les Miz*, a job I did not get (then).

My favorite brush with greatness was having Sondheim in the audience while I performed the role of, well, Sondheim. *Sunday in the Park with George* was running—I saw it from standing room at least twelve times—so Barbara Walsh and I came on as George and Dot and sang "Sondheim Tonight!" At the end, I would take off my painter's smock and remove my Seurat beard to reveal another beard—and I was Sondheim. Then I would sing "Send in the Crowds," the great man's lament that his shows played to half houses even though they were loved by the critics. He was delighted. What a thrill!

I got to rejoin the show years later for *Forbidden Broadway: SVU,* and I'm most grateful to Gerard for writing a Robert Goulet number especially for me. I pestered him incessantly about it after Goulet joined the cast *of La Cage aux Folles,* and when we moved the show from the Fairbanks on 42nd Street to our new home on 47th, we added Goulet. I'll never do anything onstage more satisfying than walk on with a mustache and slicked hair, martini and cigarette in hand, and belt out, "TRRRYYY TO REE-MEM-BER . . . uuhh . . ."

But Will It Play in Sheboygan?

By the summer of 1989, *Forbidden Broadway* had been running in New York for seven years. Other productions had been limited to a few large cities with sophisticated theatre audiences: Philadelphia, Chicago, D.C., L.A., and Boston. The general perception was that the show wouldn't work elsewhere, because who would get all the inside jokes? Such was the (supposed) curse of *Forbidden Broadway*.

I had been part of the cast of the Boston production, which was then in its fifth smash year at the Terrace Room Theatre. Now, Boston had a theatre-loving audience for sure; it was still one of the big Broadway tryout towns. But that didn't necessarily mean there were enough of those people to keep *FB* running in a 250-seat house for five years. University students were also coming. So were the whale-watching, leaf-loving tourists who stayed in the mammoth Boston Park Plaza, where the Terrace Room Theatre was located. And they all adored the show.

When I was onstage, I could see which numbers in particular made people laugh so hard that they fall out of their chairs. So when a bold producer from Kansas City named Mark Edelman called in the summer of 1989 and asked if we felt the show could play a long run there, I told Gerard that I thought it would work if we picked the numbers that always went over in Boston: Evita, Annie, Merman and Martin, "Screamgirls," Liza, and a few others. Those numbers would play anywhere—we hoped.

I went to Kansas City to direct the production, convinced that we would have to cast ringers from New York to make the show as brilliant as it should be. To my surprise

Forbidden Broadway **producer John Freedson.**

and delight, I found that Kansas City had talent to spare; Lori Blalock, Deanna Hurst, Don Richard, K. C. Helmeid, and Susan Kingwill gave the New York and Boston companies a run for their money.

The show was an enormous hit in Kansas City, playing for more than a year. Night after night, audiences laughed at Patti's musical berating of Barbra, Lauren Bacall's mannishness, Jennifer Holliday's histrionics, the misery of *Les Miz,* Annie's advanced age, and Liza's one note. It was all there in the writing. Gerard had always told me that he wrote each joke with his mother in Needham, Massachusetts, in mind. Would she get everything? Would his aunt Erminie and cousin Madeline? If a joke passed the Alessandrini test, it could be certified to hit the laugh-o-meter for any audience, anywhere.

John Freedson and Gerard Alessandrini in London.

Hot off our success in K.C.—where we played return engagements in 1990, 1993, 1996, and 2003—we decided to really test the limits of the show's appeal. Big League Theatricals approached us and asked if we would like to put together a non-Equity tour to play one-night stands and split weeks in towns like Sheboygan, Wisconsin; Klamath Falls, Idaho; Seguin, Texas; and Pella, Iowa. I was engaged to direct the tour, and I was concerned about whether non-Equity performers would have the chops to handle the material. Well, one of the people who attended that non-union call was a young woman named Christine Pedi, who told us that she didn't know if she could do impressions and then blew us away with her channeling of Channing, Merman, and Liza.

Gerard and I fought over Christine; he wanted to put her immediately into the New York show, but ultimately he relented and let me have her for the tour. We both realized that if anyone could sell the humor of *Forbidden Broadway* to an audience in Sheboygan, it was Christine. By the way, that non-Equity call also brought us Lori Hammel, who went on to star in *Forbidden Broadway Cleans Up Its Act* in 1998 and still does an occasional road date of the show more than twenty years later.

One of the great things about touring *Forbidden Broadway* is that it has a unit set consisting entirely of a Mylar curtain and a decorative portal to scale down the prosceniums of some of the huge vaudeville-era houses we played: the 2,700-seat Proctors Theatre in Schenectady, New York; The Corn Palace (that's not a joke!) in Mitchell,

South Dakota; the mammoth Garden State Arts Center in Holmdel, New Jersey, where Judy Garland once fell asleep onstage; and so on. Twenty-two feet of playing width, sixteen feet of height, a grand piano, Alvin Colt's fabulous costumes, and a cast full of outsize personalities were all we needed to make magic.

Over the years, the show has wowed audiences in small towns all over the country. We often get letters from presenters in which they express surprise that their audiences had such a great time at the show, but it's no longer a surprise to us. As we've learned over the years, the jokes in *Forbidden Broadway* are so well set up that even if you don't understand the specific references to Tommy Tune and Twiggy or whomever, you laugh at the brilliant delivery, the wit of the lyrics, the pratfalls of the staging.

You might be surprised at which numbers have played well in Peoria. Sometimes it's a spoof of a really popular show, like *Jersey Boys*. Sarah Brightman's "Time I Said Goodbye" always slays 'em. But what about *Aspects of Love*? Who in Middle America ever heard of that Andrew Lloyd Webber flop? Yet, for many years, that number was a staple of every regional and touring production of the show. Three half-naked people standing behind a sheet and singing "I Sleep with Everyone" is just funny.

In Japan, where we have done four productions of the show (with supertitles), the audiences laughed so uncontrollably every time "Julie Andrews" modulated down another half step in "I Couldn't Hit the Note" that we wondered whether the supertitles actually said, "Laugh here so as not to offend the American guests." In fact, the people just got the musical in-joke. In Singapore, the cast was treated like rock stars, swarmed by fans for autographs outside the theatre. In London, after a sold-out run at the tiny Jermyn Street Theatre, we transferred for the summer to the West End's Albery. At this writing, a new production is running at the Menier Chocolate Factory.

A special thrill for me is presenting *Forbidden Broadway* in concert with symphony orchestras around the world. The show incorporates some of the greatest songs of Richard Rodgers, Jule Styne, Frederick Loewe, and Stephen Sondheim; hearing that music performed by massed strings, trumpets, and timpani is pure heaven. I sit in the back and cry.

Yet after all this, when presenters from all over the country converge on New York in January to scope out shows and when they see *Forbidden Broadway*, many of them still say to me: "I had a great time at your show, but my audience in Akron will never get it." After I finish banging my head against a wall, I calmly tell them that we've had twenty years of success in small towns throughout the U.S., and I explain the secret of *Forbidden Broadway:* The show somehow makes everyone feel like a showbiz insider. They nod, and some of them believe me and book the show for their upcoming season. They're never sorry that they did.

—John Freedson

Forbidden Spin-Offs!

With almost any showbiz success, thoughts of a sequel come up at some point. Even while creating various editions of *Forbidden Broadway*, I was haunted by the idea of related *Forbidden* shows. I had always wanted to do *Forbidden Opera*, because I had studied opera and I'm a big fan of the genre, but the commercial potential for that seemed low. So I turned to the movies for inspiration. I love Hollywood films, both classic and contemporary, and I thought *Forbidden Hollywood* might be a fun and exciting project.

On the one hand, this spin-off would be easier to create than *Forbidden Broadway* because so many more films exist as compared to stage shows, and also because movies have far greater recognition among the masses. The downside was the topical nature of the medium; one year, everybody could be talking about a movie or a star, and the next year, they could be almost forgotten. So I decided that if we were going to tackle the movies, we had to cover the history as well as the contemporary. In a sense, I was inspired by *That's Entertainment*, the terrific (as Liza would put it) compilation of sequences from great MGM musicals. The chance to rewrite the lyrics of songs from classic films like *Singin' in the Rain* was enticing.

John Freedson and Harriet Yellin headed the team that mounted the first production of *Forbidden Hollywood* in Los Angeles in 1995. We tried the show out in San Diego and experimented with dozens of numbers. I drove the talented cast crazy as we

Whitney Allen and Mark David Kaplan as Gwyneth Paltrow and Roberto Benigni in *Forbidden Hollywood*.

worked on "That's the Bible!"—a spoof of *The Ten Commandments* and *Ben Hur*. The number was long, rather leaden, and more than a little sacrilegious. To the great relief of the cast, I finally dropped it. But other numbers that we worked and worked, such as Bette Midler singing "Who's Gay in Hollywood?" and a Woody Allen sketch, eventually paid off.

The cover of *That's Insufferable,* a mockumentary by Gerard and the *Forbidden Hollywood* cast.

While the show was a great success in L.A., it didn't fare nearly as well in New York and Chicago, where presumably people don't care as much about film and its history. This spin-off also had the handicap of not spoofing a medium through its own medium, as *Forbidden Broadway* does. In fact, late at night after performances of *Forbidden Hollywood* in L.A., the cast and I had a raucous time making a video that spoofed movies. I christened it *That's Insufferable!* The actors played stars like Liza and Dietrich introducing clips from questionable movie musicals.

Not surprisingly, the numbers that worked best in *Forbidden Hollywood* were somehow related to Broadway. "Hits and Bombs" spoofed *Guys and Dolls* and other ridiculous stage-to-screen transfers, like *Hello, Dolly!* My personal favorite sequence was all about the bizarre overuse of color filters in the film version of *South Pacific;* changing "Bali H'ai" to "Blurry Hues" hit the bull's-eye. Likewise Audrey Hepburn in *My Fair Lady* singing "Dub Me" (to the tune of "Show Me"), with the assistance of Marni Nixon. An ancient Marlene Dietrich (the magnificent Susanne Blakeslee) sang one of my nastiest parodies, "Falling Apart Again." And Liza (Christine Pedi), in Weimar Republic–era hot pants and a Fosse bowler hat, bemoaned the loss of her Hollywood star power in "Bye-Bye, Mein Film Career."

Even though *Forbidden Hollywood* wasn't embraced by the public as *Forbidden Broadway* had been, I loved writing and directing it with the enthusiastic help of Phill George. Alvin Colt had a field day creating the fabulous, witty costumes. The original cast of *Forbidden Hollywood* also included Jason Graae—"the brilliant actor with too many vowels in his last name," as Phill would say—and Mr. Super Personality, Gerry McIntyre. Brad Ellis was the original musical director. I had worked with him for years, and we spoke the same creative language. It was a dream to collaborate with all these mega-talented people.

Left: Jason Graae, Christine Pedi, Gerry McIntyre, and Susanne Blakeslee relocate to Vermont for the ultimate movie sequel, *The Sound of Music: Part II,* **in** *Forbidden Hollywood.* **Right: Michael McGrath (as Pavarotti), Susanne Blakeslee (as Barbra Streisand circa 1966), Mary Denise Bentley (as Eydie Gorme), and Herndon Lackey (as Elvis circa 1976) in** *Forbidden Christmas.*

Another spin-off I loved writing was *Forbidden Christmas.* In the 1980s, while *Forbidden Broadway* was playing in Boston and we were using that production to try out new numbers, I very much wanted to attempt a Christmas show. It seemed logical, because so many musicals had Christmas references or songs, and also because so many people attend the theatre at holiday time.

Changing "We Need a Little Christmas" (from *Mame*) to "We Need a Broadway Christmas" and mixing the holiday festivities with parodies of stage celebrities was a blast. We also spoofed recording stars such as Frank Sinatra, Barbra Streisand, and Elvis Presley inappropriately performing Christmas carols. (We had Elvis sing "White Christmas," and he would rub his nose after the word "white." The audience howled at the cocaine reference, but after a few performances, someone from the Berlin estate called me and said, "You take that bit out of the show *immediately*!")

The Christmas show even took a little dip into the opera world when we had Luciano Pavarotti sing "O Holy Note." It was a bit sacrilegious, but also hysterically funny—especially when Luciano hit his high C and shattered the eyeglasses of the altar boys in attendance. We have continued to present the Christmas version of the show on and off for years.

Left: Susanne Blakeslee as Marlene Dietrich in *Forbidden Hollywood*. Right: The company of *Forbidden Vegas*: Eric Lee Johnson, Valerie Fagan, Michael West, and Carter Calvert.

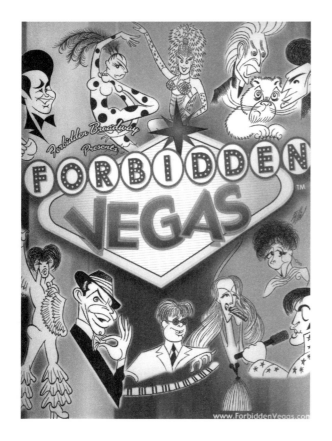

Our third and final spin-off was *Forbidden Vegas*, which premiered in that world-famous tourist mecca at the Weston Casarina Hotel off "the strip." As Pete Blue, who worked on the show, pointed out, the venue seemed like a tornado had picked up a Weston hotel in Idaho and dropped it in the middle of Vegas; the place had a definite Midwestern feel about it. We targeted the obvious subjects—Celine Dion, Elton John, Steve and Eydie, and the Blue Man Group—along with classic Vegas acts like Frank Sinatra and Wayne Newton.

The *Forbidden Broadway* sequels met with varying degrees of success in various cities. We still occasionally do new editions of the Hollywood and Christmas shows. And, who knows, I may get around to *Forbidden Opera* someday—that is, if I don't have a problem with the Puccini estate. Maybe Andrew Lloyd Webber can help us get the music rights?

How to Write Your Own
Forbidden Broadway–Style Parody

It's very simple to create your own parody lyric. You too can be a plagiarist alongside many of the greats! Just follow these simple instructions. This formula doesn't date, so you can use it for any show or any star at any time. Start by selecting a well-known, catchy show tune, then choose and insert names and words as follows:

[INSERT NAME OF STAR OR FAMOUS BROADWAY CHARACTER]

[*Sings blissfully.*]

I'M [insert name of star]

YOU PROBABLY KNOW ME AS [insert star's most famous theatrical, film, or TV role]

I [write something dishy about someone with whom the star has worked]

WE [rhyme with a clever word]

I AM [choose one]
   (a) too old
   (b) too fat
   (c) too dead

THAT'S WHY I ALWAYS WANTED TO [insert a vicious crime or nasty thought]

LIGHT THE LIGHTS...

BROADWAY ISN'T WHAT IT USED TO BE; I LONG FOR THE DAYS WHEN ACTORS [choose one]

(a) sang better

(b) projected clearer

(c) had decent scripts

AND DANCED LIKE [choose one]

(a) Bob Fosse

(b) Michael Bennett

(c) Jerome Robbins

BUT I LOVE BROADWAY ANYWAY, 'CAUSE THERE'S

(a) no tune like a show tune

(b) no business like show business

(c) no way I'm gonna get a job anywhere else

[*End by raising your hands above your head for the last, big high note, or drop dead on the musical button. Blackout.*]

Music Rights and Recordings

When we first did *Forbidden Broadway* at Palsson's Supper Club, I went to BMI for advice, and someone there said, "First of all, you can't just use other people's music in your show!" I said, "But we're already doing that." He said, "But you won't be able to open." I said, "We're already open, and we're playing to packed houses every night." He said, "But you can't *do* that." Lehman Engel came into the office and said, "You idiot, haven't you read the rave review in the *New York Times*? The show is a hit! Sign him up and get him the rights!"

Lehman and Maurice Levine helped us a lot with the music rights, but I think even more important was the fact that people like Stephen Sondheim, Comden and Green, Kander and Ebb, Jerry Herman, and Sheldon Harnick saw the show early on. They enjoyed it, they knew exactly what we were doing, and they certainly didn't want to stop the show. So Lehman and Maurice advised us to basically go to the publishers and lease each of the original songs for use in our show, which is what we ended up doing. I'm very grateful for their assistance; if it hadn't been for them, *Forbidden Broadway* might not have continued.

A rumor arose that Andrew Lloyd Webber denied us use of his songs for our parodies, forcing us to rewrite the melodies, but that's

Ken Fallin's art for the back cover of our original Off-Broadway cast album.

not accurate. When the show moved to Theatre East, Jonathan Scharer, our producer there, wanted to get contracts for every song in the show, and we just couldn't get the contracts for the Lloyd Webber material signed in time for the opening. So, for a while, we used a homemade pastiche tune for the *Phantom* sequence. But we did eventually get the rights squared away, and from then on we were able to use the original melodies. Actually, Lloyd Webber has been one of our show's biggest fans from the beginning. In fact, in 1982, the cast went and performed our *Cats* and *Evita* numbers for him at his birthday party.

For our first recording, I believe Hugh Fordin worked for about a year and got individual clearances to record each song as a parody. Some of the rights were denied, like the Kander and Ebb number for Lauren Bacall and some of the Rodgers and Hammerstein material. Later, Hugh realized he could secure the rights much more easily by paying the usual fees for each song as if we were going to record them in full without changing the lyrics. Luckily for us, the rules for song parodies are much looser than they used to be, thanks to people like "Weird Al" Yankovic.

By the time we finally got all the clearances to record our first album, it was the spring of 1984. We didn't record all of the numbers in the show—partly because we didn't have all the clearances, and partly because it was still the vinyl era and we could only fit forty-five minutes worth of material onto an LP. Twenty-seven years later, Nora, Fred, and I went back into the studio and recorded nearly all of the missing material for inclusion on a remastered version of the original album.

My *Forbidden Broadway*

BY JERRY JAMES

I served as stage manager for more than 3,000 performances of *Forbidden Broadway*, from 1983 to 1993, at Palsson's and Theatre East. Most of the shows went off without a single hitch, but there were always times when something went wrong, either in rehearsal or in performance. I remember:

- The color wheel used for the "Blurry Hues" number falling into the dinner plate of the ambassador from Iceland the night he was hosted by Sella Palsson.

- An actor needing to break down a door one night in order to make his entrance in *Cats*.

- The actress who was all set to enter as Lauren Bacall—except that she was supposed to be Carol Channing.

- An actor entering as Kevin Kline—a number early.

- An actress fleeing a rehearsal in tears under the mistaken impression that Gerard had written a number proclaiming Andrew Lloyd Webber to be more important than Jesus.

- The snowfall effect for the last moment of the Christmas show on the stage of Theatre East—where I, a short man, could stand on tiptoes and touch the ceiling—producing an "Awwww!" from the audience at every performance. Except for the one where the snow pipe came loose from its moorings and hit an actor on the head. (Fortunately, the pipe was made of PVC.)

- The Saturday afternoon when an emergency replacement from the Boston cast was flown in after a frantic morning of phone calls resulted in her being located in Washington. With no time for a complete run-through before curtain, no one realized she didn't know the pastiche tune Gerard had written for the Mary Martin–Ethel Merman duet. (At the time, he had permission to use "Old-Fashioned Ballad" in the Boston show but not in New York; after Irving Berlin died, the distinguished composer became much easier to deal with.) When the two actresses began singing two different melodies, the result was the most avant-garde performance of the duet in history. For the second show that night, we cut the number.

My daughter Rachel grew up with *Forbidden Broadway,* first attending rehearsals in her stroller. This could cause the occasional problem; her second-grade teacher didn't seem to be amused when Rachel sang "I Sleep with Everyone," Gerard's parody of "Love Changes Everything" from *Aspects of Love.* Still, it was a joy for a child to grow up in that world of imagination.

Both Palsson's and Theatre East are gone now. But it was a good time. And except for doing eight shows a week at Palsson's for the munificent sum of $175, I would do it all again.

Honors and Awards

Over the years, *Forbidden Broadway* has received numerous honors. Here is a partial list of the major awards:

2009 Drama Desk award to *Forbidden Broadway*'s creators, casts, and designers, who made the show an unparalleled New York institution

2009 New York Drama Critics Special Citation to Gerard Alessandrini for *Forbidden Broadway*

2008 Drama Desk Award for Outstanding Revue to *Forbidden Broadway: Rude Awakening*

2006 Tony Honor to *Forbidden Broadway*/Gerard Alessandrini for Excellence in the Theatre

2005 Drama Desk Award for Outstanding Revue to *Forbidden Broadway: Special Victims Unit*

2002 Drama Desk Award for Outstanding Revue to *Forbidden Broadway 2001: A Spoof Odyssey*

1998 Drama Desk Award to Gerard Alessandrini for Best Lyrics, *Forbidden Broadway Cleans Up Its Act*

Gerard and his mom with Angela Lansbury, who presented Gerard with a 2006 Tony Honor for Excellence in the Theatre.

1997 Drama Desk Award to Gerard Alessandrini for Best Lyrics, *Forbidden Broadway Strikes Back!*

1997 Drama League Award to Gerard Alessandrini for Lifetime Achievement

1997 Lucille Lortel Award to Gerard Alessandrini for Outstanding Body of Work

1993 Lucille Lortel Award for Outstanding Musical to *Forbidden Broadway 1993*

1991–1992 Obie Award in Recognition of Outstanding Achievement in Off-Broadway Theatre

1991 Elliot Norton Award to Gerard Alessandrini for Lifetime Achievement

1991 Joseph Jefferson Award to Gerard Alessandrini for Best Director, *Forbidden Broadway 1990*

1986 New England Theatre Conference Special Recognition Award to Gerard Alessandrini, creator of *Forbidden Broadway*

1985 Drama Desk Special Award to Gerard Alessandrini and *Forbidden Broadway*

1985 Outer Critics Circle Award to Gerard Alessandrini

Gerard and his family devour his Tony Honor. Left: Cousins Linda Pirro and Madeleine Minotti. Right: Gerard with his parents, Aldo and Florinda.

Favorite Celebrity Visitors
to *Forbidden Broadway*

Mary Martin, George Burns, and Carol Channing with Gerard.

Top: Michael Berresse and his [title of show] guys with our [title of show] guys.
Middle: Elaine Paige and 2008 cast. Bottom: Shirley MacLaine was a frequent
visitor to *Forbidden Broadway*.

Clockwise from top: Mayor Ed Koch with the 1985 cast. Carol Channing and Imogene Coca with Gerard. Ann Miller sings "That's Entertainment!" with Gerard, Fred, and Nora.

Top: Gerard and Whoopi Goldberg.
Bottom: Rosie O'Donnell and 1996
cast.

Top: Ethel Merman signs the *Annie Get Your Gun* cast album for Nora. Bottom: Joan Rivers and the *FB* company.

Top: Christine Ebersole and the cast of *Forbidden Broadway: Rude Awakening*. Middle: Mary Tyler Moore visits with the 1985 cast. Bottom: Cheyenne Jackson sandwiched by our Xanadudes.

Top: Carol Burnett and our company.
Bottom: Gerard with two great ladies of
musical theater: Carol Channing and
Chita Rivera.

Top: Stephen Sondheim surrounded by the cast of *Forbidden Broadway Goes to Rehab*. Middle: Lin-Manuel Miranda with Michael West as his *FB* incarnation. Bottom: Elaine Stritch with Roxie Lucas as Elaine.

CONTRIBUTORS

Gerard Alessandrini is best known for creating, writing, and directing all the editions of *Forbidden Broadway* and *Forbidden Hollywood* in New York, Los Angeles, London, and all around the world. He was also a member of the original cast of *Forbidden Broadway*. Alessandrini hails from Needham, Massachusetts, and the Boston area, where he graduated from the Boston Conservatory of Music. In 1982, he created and wrote *Forbidden Broadway*, which has spawned twenty editions and ten cast albums (DRG Records). His television credits include writing comedy specials for Bob Hope and Angela Lansbury (NBC) and Carol Burnett (CBS); he also wrote "Masterpiece To-night" (PBS), a satirical revue saluting Masterpiece Theatre's twentieth anniversary. He has written articles for the *New York Times* and many other notable publications, and he contributed reviews to *The TheaterMania Guide to Musical Theatre Recordings*. As a performer, he has had featured singing roles in Disney's animated film classics *Aladdin* and *Pocahontas*; he can also be heard on four of the nine *Forbidden Broadway* cast albums. Alessandrini's directing credits include many industrials for ABC-TV, Canada Dry, Mobil, and American Express, as well as a regional production of Maury Yeston's musical *In the Beginning*, the Equity Library Theatre revival of Lerner and Loewe's *Gigi*, and the Brooklyn Opera Company production of Mozart's *Abduction from the Seraglio*. In the summer of 2001, he co-directed a production of Irving Berlin's last musical, *Mr. President*, which he also updated and "politically corrected." Among his many other credits are an evening of his original theatrical songs (music and lyrics) entitled *Tonight We Sing*. He is the recipient of an Obie Award, an Outer Critics Circle Award, two Lucille Lortel Awards, and multiple Drama Desk Awards (Best Lyrics) for *Forbidden Broadway;* a lifetime achievement award from the Drama League; and a 2006 special Tony Honor for Excellence in Theatre.

Michael Portantiere has been a theatre journalist for more than thirty years, having worked as an editor and/or writer for such media as *In Theatre* magazine, *Back Stage*,

TheaterMania.com, Playbill, and Stagebill. He edited and contributed reviews to *The TheaterMania Guide to Musical Theatre Recordings*, published in 2004 by Back Stage Books. Michael also wrote the liner notes for recordings of *Little Me* (Varèse Sarabande), *The Most Happy Fella* (JAY Records), and *Sweeney Todd* (the New York Philharmonic recording, starring George Hearn and Patti LuPone). In his career as a journalist, he has interviewed scores of theatre notables, including Julie Andrews, Angela Lansbury, Jerry Herman, Kristin Chenoweth, and Raúl Esparza. Currently, Portantiere is an adjunct theatre professor at Wagner College, a regular columnist for BroadwayStars.com, a frequent contributor to AfterElton.com, and a professional photographer whose photos have appeared in the *New York Times*, the *Daily News*, and many other media outlets. (His work may be sampled at FollowSpotPhoto.com.) He holds an M.A. in Theatre Education from New York University.

Carol Rosegg is a very lucky person. She lives in New York City with her family and gets to photograph theatre, dance, and opera all over the country. What could be better!

Henry Grossman wanted to be an actor. He studied photography at a vocational high school in order to support himself between acting jobs, and won a theatre scholarship to Brandeis University. He began taking pictures for *Time, Life*, and *Newsweek*, and contributed to *People* magazine while acting on Broadway in *Grand Hotel*. Grossman also sang at the Met for two years as a principal artist (tenor). He is currently completing his second photo book on the Beatles. His subjects have included Richard Burton and Elizabeth Taylor, Gielgud, Kirk Douglas, JFK, LBJ, Nelson Mandela, Luciano Pavarotti, Maria Callas, and *Forbidden Broadway*.

Ken Fallin was still wet behind the ears in 1983 when *Forbidden Broadway* creator Gerard Alessandrini discovered him singing, dancing, and drawing caricatures in Shubert Alley. At that fateful moment, it was decided that Fallin would always and forever create the caricature images that became the graphic symbol of *Forbidden Broadway* all over the universe. More than twenty-five years later, his involvement continues with the current London revival of the show proudly displaying the newest Fallin drawings to promote that production. Luck, wit, and a razor-sharp pen have enabled Fallin to land exciting commissions, illustrating for such major venues as the *Boston Herald*, the *Chicago Tribune, Ladies' Home Journal, InStyle*, Showtime, American Express, BMG records, Disney, Belvedere Vodka, and CNBC. Some Broadway names who possess their own Fallin caricatures are Carol Channing, Frank Langella, Patti LuPone, Brian Dennehy, Lypsinka, Cameron Mackintosh, Barbara Cook, Bette Midler, Charles Busch, and Bernadette Peters. Since 1994, the *Wall Street Journal* has regularly featured Fallin's witty and stylish caricatures of world leaders and artistic icons on the Editorial and Arts and Leisure pages. To see more of his work, please visit www.kenfallin.com.

INDEX